LLC (Limited Liability Company) Mastery Handbook

A 9 Step Beginners System on How to Start, Run, and Grow a Small Business

Master Branding, Accounting, Tax Advantages, Expansion Strategies and More

David Whitehead

Silk Publishing

Disclaimer

The information contained in this book is for general informational purposes only. The information is provided and while we endeavor to keep the information up to date and correct, we make no representations or warranties of any kind, express or implied, about the completeness, accuracy, reliability, suitability or availability with respect to the book or the information, products, services, or related graphics contained in the book for any purpose. Any reliance you place on such information is therefore strictly at your own risk.

In no event will we be liable for any loss or damage including without limitation, indirect or consequential loss or damage, or any loss or damage whatsoever arising from loss of data or profits arising out of, or in connection with, the use of this book.

Through this book, you may be able to link to other websites which are not under the control of [Your Name]. We have no control over the nature, content, and availability of those sites. The inclusion of any links does not necessarily imply a recommendation or endorse the views expressed within them.

Every effort is made to keep the book up and running smoothly. However, David Whitehead takes no responsibility for, and will not be liable for, the book being temporarily unavailable due to technical issues beyond our control.

Contents

The Simple 9 Step Guide to Launching Your LLC

Introduction

Success depends upon previous preparation, and without such preparation, there is sure to be failure.

— Confucius

This book is designed to be your definitive guide to starting and managing a Limited Liability Company (LLC). Whether you are an aspiring entrepreneur with a groundbreaking idea or an experienced business owner looking to expand your ventures, this guide will provide you with the knowledge and tools needed to make informed decisions and build a successful LLC.

Choosing the right business structure is one of the most critical decisions you will make when starting a new business. The structure you select will affect various aspects of your business, including legal liability, taxation, and management. The LLC is a popular choice among entrepreneurs because it offers flexibility, limited liability protection, and favorable tax treatment. However, it is essential to understand the intricacies of this business structure to maximize its benefits.

This book is structured to take you through the entire process of forming and managing an LLC, step by step. From understanding what an LLC is and its advantages and disadvantages, to navigating legal requirements, financial management, branding, and expansion strategies, you will find comprehensive and practical guidance in each chapter.

About the Author

I am passionate about helping entrepreneurs achieve their dreams. With years of experience in business consulting and entrepreneurship, I have seen firsthand the challenges and rewards of starting and managing an LLC. My goal is to share my knowledge and insights to help you avoid common pitfalls and make informed decisions that will set your business on a path to success.

Importance of Choosing the Right Business Structure

When starting a business, the choice of business structure is crucial. The right structure can provide you with the necessary legal protections and tax benefits while allowing for growth and flexibility. An LLC offers a unique combination of limited liability protection and pass-through taxation, making it an attractive option for many entrepreneurs.

Limited liability protection means that as an owner, your personal assets are generally protected from business debts and liabilities. This is a significant advantage over sole proprietorships and partnerships, where personal liability is unlimited. Pass-through taxation allows the LLC's profits to be taxed only once at the individual level, avoiding the double taxation faced by C-corporations.

However, LLCs also have certain disadvantages. For instance, they can be more complex and costly to establish and maintain compared to sole proprietorships. Additionally, the rules governing LLCs can vary significantly from state to state, adding another layer of complexity.

Preview of Book Content

Here is a brief overview of what you can expect in each chapter of this book:

1. **Understanding the LLC Landscape**: This chapter will introduce you to the concept of an LLC, its benefits, and its drawbacks. You will also learn how an LLC compares to other business structures and what the future holds for this type of business entity.
2. **Industry-Specific Considerations**: Learn how to tailor your LLC to fit your specific industry. This chapter includes case studies and success stories to illustrate challenges and opportunities in various sectors.
3. **Legal and Regulatory Requirements**: Discover the legal basics of forming an LLC, including registering your business and ensuring compliance with state and federal regulations. This chapter will also cover intellectual property protection.
4. **Tax Implications and Financial Management**: Understand the tax advantages and obligations of an LLC. Get tips on financial planning, setting up accounting systems, and hiring financial advisors to help you manage your business effectively.
5. **Building Your Brand and Marketing Your LLC**: Learn how to define your brand identity, create a marketing strategy, and leverage digital tools and platforms to promote your business. This chapter will also cover how to measure the effectiveness of your marketing efforts.
6. **Technology and Digital Transformation**: Explore the digital tools available for LLC formation and management. This chapter will cover online legal services, cybersecurity considerations, and how to use technology to drive growth and innovation.
7. **Social Responsibility and Sustainability**: Incorporate sustainable practices and corporate social responsibility

initiatives into your LLC. Learn how to engage with local communities and build a purpose-driven brand.

8. **Personal Development and Entrepreneurial Mindset**: Develop the mindset needed to succeed as an entrepreneur. This chapter will cover goal setting, time management, overcoming challenges, and maintaining work-life balance.

9. **Global Perspectives and Expansion Strategies**: Learn how to expand your LLC internationally, navigate global business regulations, and manage cross-cultural communication. This chapter includes case studies of successful international expansions.

10. **Future Trends and Innovations**: Stay ahead of emerging technologies and regulatory developments. Anticipate future challenges and position your LLC for long-term success.

11. **The Simple Step Guide to Launching Your LLC**: This chapter provides a straightforward, step-by-step guide to starting your LLC, from researching your business idea to reviewing and adapting your strategies for success.

Conclusion

By the end of this book, you will have a clear understanding of what it takes to launch and manage an LLC successfully. You will be equipped with practical knowledge and actionable steps to turn your business concept into a thriving company. Your journey to entrepreneurial success starts here. Let's get started!

Chapter 1
Understanding the LLC Landscape

What is an LLC?

A Limited Liability Company (LLC) is a type of business entity that combines the characteristics of both a corporation and a partnership or sole proprietorship. It offers the flexibility and simplicity of a partnership while providing the limited liability protection typically associated with corporations. This structure is designed to meet the needs of business owners who want to protect their personal assets while maintaining operational flexibility.

As an LLC owner, often referred to as a member, you enjoy protection from personal liability for business debts and claims. This means that creditors cannot pursue your personal assets, such as your home or personal bank accounts, to satisfy business debts. This is a significant advantage, especially for small business owners who might otherwise risk their personal savings and assets.

Basic Features of an LLC

To fully understand why an LLC might be the right choice for your business, let's break down its key features:

1

1. **Limited Liability Protection**
2. **Flexible Management Structure**
3. **Pass-Through Taxation**

Limited Liability Protection

One of the primary benefits of an LLC is its limited liability protection. As mentioned, this means that the personal assets of the members are generally protected from the business's liabilities. If your LLC faces a lawsuit or incurs debt, your personal assets are usually not at risk. This protection is similar to that offered by a corporation but comes with fewer formalities and complexities.

However, it's important to note that limited liability protection is not absolute. There are circumstances, such as fraud or personally guaranteeing a loan, where you could be held personally liable. Understanding these exceptions is crucial for maintaining the protective barrier that an LLC offers.

Flexible Management Structure

An LLC provides a great deal of flexibility in how it can be managed. Unlike corporations, which are required to have a board of directors and corporate officers, an LLC can be managed directly by its members or by appointed managers. This flexibility allows you to choose a management structure that best suits your business needs.

There are two primary management structures for LLCs:

1. Member-Managed LLC:

In this structure, the members (owners) are directly involved in the day-to-day operations of the business. This is common in smaller LLCs where the owners want to have hands-on control over business activities.

2. Manager-Managed LLC:

In this setup, the members appoint one or more managers to handle the daily operations. The managers can be members or external individuals hired for their expertise. This structure is often preferred by larger LLCs or those where some members prefer a more passive role in management.

The flexibility in management also extends to decision-making processes. Members can decide how to distribute profits, allocate voting rights, and make significant business decisions based on their operating agreement, which is a key document that outlines the rules and structure of the LLC.

Pass-Through Taxation

Another significant feature of an LLC is pass-through taxation. This means that the LLC itself does not pay federal income taxes. Instead, the profits and losses "pass through" to the members, who report them on their personal tax returns. This avoids the double taxation issue faced by C-corporations, where the corporation pays taxes on its profits, and the shareholders also pay taxes on the dividends they receive.

Pass-through taxation provides several advantages:

Tax Savings:

By avoiding double taxation, you can save a substantial amount on taxes. This is particularly beneficial for small businesses where profit margins can be thin.

Simplicity:

Tax filing is generally simpler for an LLC compared to a corporation. You report your share of the profits and losses on your personal tax return, reducing the complexity of separate corporate tax filings.

However, it's essential to understand that LLCs can choose how they want to be taxed. By default, a single-member LLC is taxed as a sole proprietorship, and a multi-member LLC is taxed as a partnership. But

LLCs can also elect to be taxed as an S-corporation or a C-corporation, which may provide tax benefits in certain situations. Consulting with a tax professional can help you determine the best tax classification for your LLC.

Other Important Features

In addition to the core features mentioned above, there are other aspects of LLCs that you should be aware of:

Formation and Compliance Requirements

Forming an LLC involves filing Articles of Organization with the state in which you plan to operate. This document includes basic information about your business, such as its name, address, and the names of its members. Each state has its own requirements and filing fees, so it's important to check with your state's business registration office for specific details.

Once your LLC is formed, you will need to comply with ongoing requirements, such as filing annual reports and paying any associated fees. These requirements vary by state, so maintaining compliance is crucial to keeping your LLC in good standing.

Operating Agreement

Although not required in all states, having an operating agreement is highly recommended. This internal document outlines the ownership and management structure of your LLC, as well as the rights and responsibilities of the members. It serves as a roadmap for how the business will be run and helps prevent misunderstandings and disputes among members.

Lifespan and Continuity

An LLC can have a perpetual existence, meaning it continues to exist until it is formally dissolved. This provides stability and continuity for the business. However, an LLC can also be set up with a predefined duration or be dissolved upon the occurrence of certain events, such as the departure of a member, if specified in the operating agreement.

Capital Raising

While LLCs can raise capital by bringing in new members or obtaining loans, they cannot issue stock like corporations. This might limit your options for raising funds compared to a corporation. However, the ability to bring in investors without giving up control can be a significant advantage for some businesses.

Transferability of Ownership

Transferring ownership interests in an LLC can be more complex than in a corporation. The operating agreement typically outlines the process for transferring ownership, and members usually need to approve the transfer. This ensures that new members are compatible with the existing ones and share the same vision for the business.

Understanding what an LLC is and its fundamental features is the first step in deciding whether this business structure is right for you. An LLC offers a combination of limited liability protection, flexible management, and favorable tax treatment, making it an attractive option for many entrepreneurs. By providing a solid foundation of what an LLC entails, you are now better equipped to consider how this structure aligns with your business goals and needs.

Advantages and Disadvantages of LLCs

When considering the formation of an LLC, it's important to understand the benefits and drawbacks associated with this business structure. Knowing the advantages and disadvantages will help you make an informed decision that aligns with your business goals and personal circumstances.

Advantages of LLCs

1. **Limited Liability Protection**
2. **Tax Flexibility**
3. **Ease of Formation and Maintenance**
4. **Flexible Management Structure**
5. **Enhanced Credibility**
6. **No Ownership Restrictions**
7. **Profit Distribution Flexibility**

Limited Liability Protection

One of the most significant advantages of forming an LLC is the limited liability protection it offers. As a member of an LLC, you are generally not personally liable for the business's debts and obligations. This means that if your LLC is sued or incurs debt, your personal assets, such as your home, car, and personal bank accounts, are usually protected. This protection is a major reason why many entrepreneurs choose to form an LLC instead of operating as a sole proprietor or a partnership.

It's important to note that limited liability protection is not absolute. Personal liability may still arise if you personally guarantee a business loan, commit fraud, or fail to maintain the separation between your personal and business finances. Ensuring that you follow legal and financial best practices can help maintain this protection.

Tax Flexibility

LLCs offer a high degree of tax flexibility, which can result in significant tax savings. By default, a single-member LLC is treated as a disregarded entity for tax purposes, meaning the business's income is reported on your personal tax return, similar to a sole proprietorship. Multi-member LLCs are treated as partnerships, with income and expenses passing through to the members' personal tax returns. This avoids the double taxation issue faced by C-corporations, where income is taxed at both the corporate level and again when distributed to shareholders as dividends.

Additionally, LLCs can elect to be taxed as an S-corporation or a C-corporation. This flexibility allows you to choose the tax treatment that best suits your financial situation. For example, electing S-corporation status can potentially reduce self-employment taxes, while C-corporation status might be beneficial if you plan to reinvest profits back into the business.

Ease of Formation and Maintenance

Forming an LLC is relatively straightforward and less complex compared to other business structures like corporations. The process typically involves filing Articles of Organization with the state, paying a filing fee, and creating an operating agreement. The operating agreement outlines the management structure and operating procedures of the LLC, providing clarity and preventing future disputes among members.

Once formed, maintaining an LLC is generally easier than maintaining a corporation. There are fewer formalities, such as mandatory annual meetings and extensive record-keeping requirements. Most states require LLCs to file an annual or biennial report and pay a fee, but these requirements are usually less burdensome compared to those for corporations.

Flexible Management Structure

LLCs offer a flexible management structure that can be tailored to fit your business needs. Unlike corporations, which are required to have a board of directors and officers, LLCs can be managed directly by their members (member-managed) or by appointed managers (manager-

7

managed). This flexibility allows you to choose a management structure that aligns with your business size, complexity, and the level of involvement you and other members wish to have in daily operations.

In a member-managed LLC, all members participate in the decision-making process and day-to-day operations. This is common in smaller businesses where owners want hands-on control. In a manager-managed LLC, the members designate one or more managers to handle the business's daily operations, which can include members or external hires. This structure is often preferred by larger businesses or those with passive investors.

Enhanced Credibility

Forming an LLC can enhance your business's credibility. Customers, suppliers, and potential investors often perceive an LLC as a more established and professional entity compared to a sole proprietorship or partnership. This perception can be particularly beneficial when seeking financing, entering into contracts, or establishing business relationships.

Having "LLC" in your business name signifies that you are serious about your business and committed to its formal structure. This can instill greater confidence in your business from external parties, helping you to grow and expand your operations more effectively.

No Ownership Restrictions

LLCs do not have restrictions on the number or type of owners, known as members. This means that you can have as many members as you want, including individuals, corporations, other LLCs, and even foreign entities. This flexibility can be advantageous if you plan to raise capital, bring in partners with diverse expertise, or expand your business internationally.

Additionally, LLCs allow for various classes of membership interests, each with different rights and responsibilities. This feature provides further flexibility in structuring ownership and profit distribution to meet the needs of your business and its members.

Profit Distribution Flexibility

Unlike corporations, which must distribute profits based on the percentage of shares held by each shareholder, LLCs offer flexibility in how profits and losses are distributed among members. The members can agree to distribute profits and losses in any manner they see fit, regardless of ownership percentage, as outlined in the operating agreement.

This flexibility allows you to reward members based on their contributions to the business, whether in terms of capital, time, or expertise. It also provides a mechanism to align the financial interests of the members with the business's goals and performance.

Disadvantages of LLCs

1. **Self-Employment Taxes**
2. **Varying State Regulations**
3. **Limited Life Span**
4. **Complexity in Raising Capital**
5. **Administrative Requirements**
6. **Potential for Member Disputes**
7. **Costs**

Self-Employment Taxes

One of the drawbacks of an LLC is that members may be subject to self-employment taxes on their share of the profits. Unlike corporate shareholders who may receive dividends, which are taxed at a lower rate, LLC members typically must pay self-employment tax on their earnings. This tax includes both the employer and employee portions of Social Security and Medicare taxes, which can be a significant financial burden.

However, you can mitigate this by electing S-corporation status for your LLC. As an S-corporation, you can pay yourself a reasonable salary, which is subject to payroll taxes, and then take additional profits as distributions, which are not subject to self-employment taxes. It's advisable to consult with a tax professional to determine if this election is beneficial for your specific situation.

Varying State Regulations

The rules and regulations governing LLCs vary significantly from state to state. This can create complexity, especially if you plan to operate in multiple states. Each state has its own requirements for forming and maintaining an LLC, including filing fees, annual report requirements, and taxes.

For example, some states impose franchise taxes or annual fees on LLCs, which can add to your costs. Additionally, the definitions of limited liability and the legal protections available to members can differ, affecting the degree of personal asset protection. Understanding and complying with the regulations in each state where you operate is crucial to avoid penalties and maintain your LLC's good standing.

Limited Life Span

In some states, the default rule is that an LLC has a limited life span and may dissolve upon the death or withdrawal of a member, unless otherwise specified in the operating agreement. This can pose challenges for business continuity and succession planning.

However, you can address this potential drawback by including provisions in your operating agreement that allow the LLC to continue operating in the event of a member's departure. Establishing clear guidelines for transferring ownership interests and admitting new members can help ensure the long-term stability of your business.

Complexity in Raising Capital

While LLCs offer flexibility in ownership and profit distribution, they may face challenges when raising capital compared to corporations. LLCs cannot issue stock, which is a common method for corporations to attract investors. Instead, LLCs must rely on bringing in new members or obtaining loans to raise funds.

Attracting investors can be more complex because investors may prefer the familiarity and perceived stability of corporate structures. Additionally, venture capitalists and other institutional investors may have specific requirements or preferences that align more closely with corporate governance and equity structures.

Administrative Requirements

Although LLCs have fewer formalities than corporations, there are still administrative requirements that you must adhere to. These include maintaining accurate records, holding and documenting meetings (if required by your operating agreement), and filing annual or biennial reports with the state.

Failure to comply with these requirements can result in penalties, fines, or even the dissolution of your LLC. It's important to establish a system for managing these administrative tasks to ensure ongoing compliance and to keep your business in good standing.

Potential for Member Disputes

The flexibility in management and profit distribution can sometimes lead to disputes among members, especially if there are no clear guidelines or if expectations are not aligned. Disagreements over the direction of the business, allocation of profits, or management responsibilities can disrupt operations and harm the business.

Having a comprehensive operating agreement is essential to mitigate this risk. The operating agreement should outline the rights and responsibilities of each member, decision-making processes, dispute resolution mechanisms, and procedures for adding or removing members. Clear communication and regular meetings can also help prevent misunderstandings and conflicts.

Costs

Forming and maintaining an LLC involves costs that you need to consider. These costs include filing fees for Articles of Organization, annual or biennial report fees, franchise taxes, and fees for legal and accounting services. While these costs are generally lower than those associated with forming a corporation, they can still add up, particularly if you operate in multiple states or if your business requires specialized legal or financial advice.

Additionally, if you elect to be taxed as an S-corporation, there may be additional costs associated with payroll services and compliance with S-corporation requirements. It's important to budget for these expenses and assess whether the benefits of forming an LLC outweigh the costs for your specific business situation.

Conclusion

Understanding the advantages and disadvantages of forming an LLC is crucial in determining if this business structure is the right fit for you. The limited liability protection, tax flexibility, ease of formation, and flexible management structure make LLCs an attractive option for many entrepreneurs. However, the potential drawbacks, such as self-employment taxes, varying state regulations, and challenges in raising capital, must also be considered.

By carefully weighing these factors and consulting with legal and financial professionals, you can make an informed decision that best supports your business goals and personal circumstances. With the right approach and planning, an LLC can provide a solid foundation for your business, offering the protection, flexibility, and credibility needed to succeed in today's competitive market.

Comparison With Other Business Structures

When deciding on the best business structure for your company, it's essential to compare the key features, benefits, and drawbacks of various options. The main business structures to consider are sole proprietorships, partnerships, S-corporations, and C-corporations. Each structure has unique characteristics that may make it more or less suitable for your specific needs. Here, we'll explore how LLCs compare to these other structures and highlight scenarios where an LLC might be the preferable choice.

LLCs vs. Sole Proprietorships

Sole Proprietorships

A sole proprietorship is the simplest and most common form of business structure. It is owned and operated by a single individual, and there is no legal distinction between the owner and the business. This means that the owner is personally liable for all business debts and obligations.

Advantages of Sole Proprietorships:

- **Simplicity**: Easy to establish and operate with minimal legal and administrative requirements.
- **Control**: The owner has complete control over all business decisions.
- **Tax Benefits**: Business income is reported on the owner's personal tax return, avoiding double taxation.

Disadvantages of Sole Proprietorships:

- **Unlimited Liability**: The owner is personally liable for all business debts and legal actions.
- **Difficulty Raising Capital**: Limited ability to attract investors or secure loans compared to other structures.

- **Limited Lifespan**: The business typically dissolves upon the owner's death or decision to stop operations.

LLCs

Compared to sole proprietorships, LLCs offer significant advantages in terms of liability protection and flexibility. While both structures provide simplicity and pass-through taxation, an LLC protects your personal assets from business liabilities, which is not the case with a sole proprietorship.

When an LLC Might Be Preferable:

- **Liability Protection**: If you want to protect your personal assets from business liabilities.
- **Growth Potential**: If you plan to bring in partners or investors in the future.
- **Professional Image**: If you want to enhance your business's credibility with a formal structure.

LLCs vs. Partnerships

Partnerships

Partnerships involve two or more people sharing ownership of a business. There are two main types of partnerships: general partnerships (GPs) and limited partnerships (LPs). In a general partnership, all partners manage the business and share equal responsibility for debts. In a limited partnership, there are both general and limited partners, with the latter having limited liability and no management authority.

Advantages of Partnerships:

- **Ease of Formation**: Simple to establish with minimal legal requirements.
- **Combined Resources and Expertise**: Partners can pool their skills, knowledge, and resources.

- **Pass-Through Taxation**: Profits and losses pass through to partners' personal tax returns, avoiding double taxation.

Disadvantages of Partnerships:

- **Unlimited Liability (GPs)**: General partners are personally liable for business debts and obligations.
- **Potential for Conflicts**: Disagreements among partners can disrupt business operations.
- **Limited Lifespan**: The partnership may dissolve if a partner leaves or dies unless otherwise specified in a partnership agreement.

LLCs

An LLC offers the liability protection of a limited partnership while allowing all members to participate in management. Unlike a general partnership, where all partners have unlimited liability, an LLC shields its members from personal liability. Additionally, LLCs can be more appealing for raising capital, as they provide a more structured and professional business entity.

When an LLC Might Be Preferable:

- **Liability Protection**: If you want to protect all members from personal liability.
- **Management Flexibility**: If you want a flexible management structure without the restrictions of a limited partnership.
- **Business Continuity**: If you want to ensure the business can continue despite changes in membership.

LLCs vs. S-Corporations

S-Corporations

An S-corporation is a special type of corporation that allows profits, and some losses, to be passed directly to the owners' personal income without being subject to corporate tax rates. To qualify as an S-corporation, your business must meet specific IRS requirements, including having no more than 100 shareholders, all of whom must be U.S. citizens or residents.

Advantages of S-Corporations:

- **Pass-Through Taxation**: Income passes through to shareholders' personal tax returns, avoiding double taxation.
- **Limited Liability**: Shareholders have limited liability protection.
- **Self-Employment Tax Savings**: Only salaries (not distributions) are subject to self-employment taxes.

Disadvantages of S-Corporations:

- **Strict Requirements**: There are stringent eligibility criteria and operational requirements.
- **Limited Flexibility**: S-corporations have less flexibility in profit distribution compared to LLCs.
- **Increased Scrutiny**: The IRS closely monitors S-corporations for compliance, especially regarding reasonable compensation for shareholder-employees.

Comparison With LLCs:

- **Flexibility in Ownership**: LLCs can have unlimited members and various types of owners, while S-corporations are limited to 100 shareholders and specific ownership types.

- **Fewer Restrictions**: LLCs have fewer operational and eligibility restrictions, providing greater flexibility.
- **Tax Options**: LLCs can choose to be taxed as S-corporations if desired, offering the best of both worlds.

Scenarios Favoring LLCs:

- You have more than 100 owners or non-U.S. owners.
- You seek flexibility in profit distribution.
- You want fewer operational restrictions and compliance requirements.

LLCs vs. C-Corporations

C-Corporations

A C-corporation is a separate legal entity from its owners, providing limited liability protection. C-corporations can have an unlimited number of shareholders and are subject to corporate income taxes. Profits are taxed at the corporate level and again when distributed as dividends to shareholders.

Advantages of C-Corporations:

- **Limited Liability**: Shareholders are not personally liable for the corporation's debts and obligations.
- **Unlimited Shareholders**: C-corporations can have an unlimited number of shareholders, including foreign and institutional investors.
- **Capital Raising**: Issuing shares makes it easier to raise capital from investors.

Disadvantages of C-Corporations:

- **Double Taxation**: Profits are taxed at both the corporate and shareholder levels.

- **Complexity and Cost**: Forming and maintaining a C-corporation involves more complexity, higher costs, and extensive regulatory requirements.
- **Formalities**: C-corporations must adhere to strict corporate formalities, including holding annual meetings and maintaining detailed records.

Comparison With LLCs:

- **Taxation**: LLCs avoid double taxation through pass-through taxation, providing potential tax savings.
- **Simplicity**: LLCs are easier to form and maintain, with fewer regulatory requirements and formalities.
- **Ownership Flexibility**: While C-corporations can have an unlimited number of shareholders, LLCs offer flexibility in profit distribution and management structures.

Scenarios Favoring LLCs:

- You want to avoid double taxation.
- You seek a simpler and less costly structure.
- You prefer flexibility in management and profit distribution.

Scenarios Where an LLC Might Be the Preferable Choice

Personal Liability Protection

If you want to protect your personal assets from business liabilities, an LLC is often the preferable choice over sole proprietorships and general partnerships, which do not offer this protection.

Tax Flexibility

LLCs provide significant tax flexibility. If you are looking for a structure that allows you to choose how your business is taxed—whether as a sole proprietorship, partnership, S-corporation, or C-corporation—an LLC offers this versatility.

Simpler Formation and Maintenance

Compared to C-corporations and even S-corporations, LLCs are easier to form and maintain. If you want to minimize the complexity and cost of compliance, an LLC is a practical option.

Flexible Management

LLCs allow for flexible management structures, which can be tailored to your business's needs. If you prefer a management setup that gives you direct control or allows you to appoint managers, an LLC provides this flexibility.

Profit Distribution

If you want the ability to distribute profits in a way that is not strictly tied to ownership percentages, an LLC allows for customized profit-sharing arrangements as outlined in your operating agreement.

Enhanced Credibility

Forming an LLC can enhance your business's credibility with customers, suppliers, and potential investors. If you are looking to establish a more professional image and attract business partners, an LLC can be beneficial.

Growth and Investment

LLCs can attract investors who may prefer the limited liability protection and flexible management structures. If you plan to grow your business and bring in additional members or investors, an LLC provides an accommodating structure.

Operating in Multiple States

If you plan to operate in multiple states, understanding each state's regulations is crucial. LLCs offer a flexible structure that can adapt to different state requirements more easily than some other business forms.

Balancing Work and Life

For many entrepreneurs, maintaining a balance between work and personal life is important. LLCs offer the flexibility to structure management and ownership in a way that aligns with your lifestyle goals. Whether you want to be actively involved in day-to-day operations or prefer a more hands-off approach, an LLC can accommodate your preferences.

Transitioning From a Sole Proprietorship or Partnership

If you are currently operating as a sole proprietorship or partnership and are considering expanding or formalizing your business structure, transitioning to an LLC can be a logical step. LLCs offer the same simplicity and flexibility while providing additional liability protection and tax benefits.

Protecting Intellectual Property

If your business relies heavily on intellectual property, such as patents, trademarks, or proprietary processes, forming an LLC can help protect these assets. While sole proprietorships and general partnerships offer no legal separation between personal and business assets, an LLC provides a distinct entity that can safeguard your intellectual property.

Minimizing Compliance Burden

For businesses that want to minimize the administrative burden associated with compliance, such as holding annual meetings or maintaining detailed corporate records, an LLC is often a preferable choice. LLCs have fewer formal requirements compared to corporations, allowing you to focus more on growing your business.

Maintaining Flexibility in Ownership and Management

LLCs offer unparalleled flexibility in ownership and management structures. Whether you want to have a single-member LLC with complete control or a multi-member LLC with shared decision-making, an LLC can accommodate your preferences. Additionally, LLCs allow for different classes of membership interests, enabling you to customize profit-sharing arrangements and voting rights.

Limiting Personal Liability

Perhaps one of the most compelling reasons to choose an LLC is the limited liability protection it offers. Unlike sole proprietorships and partnerships, where owners are personally liable for business debts and legal actions, LLC members are generally shielded from personal liability. This means that your personal assets, such as your home, savings, and investments, are protected in the event of a lawsuit or bankruptcy.

While every business is unique, forming an LLC offers significant advantages over other business structures in many scenarios. From limited liability protection to tax flexibility and simplified compliance, an LLC provides a versatile and accommodating framework for entre-preneurs. By understanding the differences between LLCs and other business structures and considering your specific business needs and goals, you can make an informed decision that sets your business up for long-term success. Whether you are just starting out or looking to expand your existing business, an LLC can be the ideal choice to protect your assets, minimize tax liabilities, and foster growth and innovation.

Current Trends and Future Outlook

Understanding the current trends in Limited Liability Company (LLC) formation and management is essential for staying ahead in today's dynamic business landscape. In this section, we'll explore the latest developments in LLCs and discuss potential future changes and regulatory considerations that could impact your business.

Current Trends in LLC Formation and Management

Surge in Entrepreneurship

The past decade has seen a significant rise in entrepreneurship, driven by factors such as technological advancements, changing consumer preferences, and the gig economy. As a result, more individuals are opting to start their own businesses, and many are choosing the LLC structure due to its flexibility, simplicity, and liability protection.

Increased Emphasis on Digital Transformation

The digital revolution has transformed the way businesses operate, and LLCs are no exception. From online LLC formation services to cloud-based management tools, technology has made it easier than ever to start and manage an LLC. Digital platforms also offer opportunities for remote work, collaboration, and customer engagement, allowing LLCs to reach a global audience with minimal overhead.

Growing Interest in Social Responsibility

Consumers are becoming increasingly conscious of social and environmental issues, and businesses are responding by integrating social responsibility into their operations. LLCs are leveraging their flexibility to adopt sustainable practices, support local communities, and engage in corporate social responsibility (CSR) initiatives. This trend is not only driven by ethical considerations but also by the desire to attract socially conscious consumers and investors.

Shift Towards Remote Work and Flexible Work Arrangements

The COVID-19 pandemic accelerated the shift towards remote work and flexible work arrangements, and many LLCs have embraced this trend. Remote work not only reduces overhead costs but also allows LLCs to access a wider talent pool and improve employee satisfaction and retention. As remote work becomes more normalized, LLCs are investing in digital infrastructure, cybersecurity measures, and collaboration tools to support remote teams effectively.

Focus on Diversity, Equity, and Inclusion (DEI)

Diversity, equity, and inclusion have become top priorities for businesses across industries, including LLCs. Companies are recognizing the importance of fostering diverse and inclusive workplaces to drive innovation, attract top talent, and better serve diverse customer bases. LLCs are implementing DEI initiatives, such as diversity training, inclusive hiring practices, and employee resource groups, to create more equitable and supportive environments.

Rise of E-commerce and Direct-to-Consumer (DTC) Brands

The rise of e-commerce and direct-to-consumer (DTC) brands has disrupted traditional retail models and created new opportunities for LLCs. With the proliferation of online marketplaces, social media platforms, and digital advertising tools, LLCs can now reach consumers directly, bypassing intermediaries and expanding their market reach. This trend has fueled the growth of niche products, personalized shopping experiences, and digitally native brands.

Embrace of Remote Services and Digital Nomadism

As remote work becomes more prevalent, LLCs are embracing remote services and digital nomadism. Digital nomads, who work remotely while traveling the world, represent a growing segment of the workforce, and many LLCs are adapting their operations to accommodate this lifestyle. From virtual assistants to online consultants, remote service providers are leveraging technology to deliver value to clients regardless of location.

Future Developments and Potential Changes in LLC Regulations and Business Environments

Evolving Regulatory Landscape

The regulatory environment for LLCs is constantly evolving, and businesses must stay informed about changes that could impact their operations. Future developments may include updates to tax laws, compliance requirements, and industry-specific regulations. LLCs should regularly review their legal and regulatory obligations and adapt their practices accordingly to ensure compliance and minimize risk.

Impact of Economic Trends

Economic trends, such as inflation, interest rates, and geopolitical events, can have a significant impact on LLCs and their business environments. Future economic developments may influence consumer spending habits, market demand, and access to capital. LLCs should monitor economic indicators, assess potential risks and opportunities, and adjust their strategies accordingly to navigate changing market conditions effectively.

Technological Advancements

Advancements in technology, such as artificial intelligence, automation, and blockchain, will continue to shape the future of LLCs. These technologies have the potential to streamline operations, improve efficiency, and unlock new business opportunities. LLCs that embrace digital innovation and invest in technology infrastructure will be better positioned to compete in the digital economy and drive sustainable growth.

Changing Workforce Dynamics

The workforce of the future will be characterized by greater diversity, mobility, and digital fluency. LLCs must adapt their recruitment, retention, and talent development strategies to attract and retain top talent in this dynamic environment. Flexible work arrangements, remote work options, and ongoing skills development will be essential for LLCs to build high-performing teams and foster a culture of innovation and collaboration.

Sustainability and Climate Change

Climate change and environmental sustainability are increasingly pressing concerns for businesses and society as a whole. LLCs will face growing pressure to reduce their environmental impact, adopt sustainable practices, and disclose their environmental performance. Future regulations may impose stricter emissions standards, carbon pricing mechanisms, and sustainability reporting requirements on LLCs, requiring them to integrate environmental considerations into their business strategies.

Globalization and International Expansion

Globalization presents both opportunities and challenges for LLCs seeking to expand internationally. Future developments may include changes in trade policies, currency exchange rates, and geopolitical dynamics that could impact cross-border business operations. LLCs must carefully evaluate market opportunities, assess regulatory and compliance requirements, and mitigate risks associated with global expansion to succeed in an increasingly interconnected world.

Conclusion

As LLCs navigate the current business landscape and prepare for the future, it's essential to stay informed about the latest trends, developments, and regulatory changes. By embracing innovation, adapting to changing market conditions, and prioritizing sustainability and social responsibility, LLCs can position themselves for long-term success in an increasingly competitive and dynamic environment.

Chapter 2
Industry-Specific Considerations

Tailoring Your LLC to Your Industry

The structure and management of your LLC can be significantly influenced by the sector in which you operate. Different industries have unique regulatory requirements, operational practices, and market dynamics that can shape how you should structure and manage your LLC. This section will explain how various industries might impact your LLC's formation and management and provide tips on tailoring your LLC to meet industry-specific needs and standards.

Industry-Specific Influences on LLC Structure and Management

Technology Sector

The technology industry is characterized by rapid innovation, scalability, and a high degree of competition. For LLCs in the tech sector, the following considerations are important:

Intellectual Property Protection:

Ensure that your LLC's structure allows for robust protection of intellectual property, including patents, trademarks, and copyrights. This might involve creating detailed operating agreements that outline the ownership and management of IP.

Scalability:

The tech industry often requires rapid scaling. Your LLC's structure should be flexible enough to accommodate growth, whether through additional funding rounds, mergers, or partnerships.

Investment and Funding:

Many tech startups seek venture capital or angel investment. Structuring your LLC to facilitate equity investment can be crucial. This might involve creating different classes of membership interests to attract investors while retaining control over the company.

Healthcare Sector

The healthcare industry is heavily regulated and demands a high degree of compliance and ethical standards. Key considerations for LLCs in this sector include:

Regulatory Compliance:

Healthcare businesses must comply with numerous federal and state regulations, such as HIPAA (Health Insurance Portability and Accountability Act) for patient privacy. Your LLC should have a compliance officer or legal advisor to ensure adherence to these regulations.

Licensing and Certifications:

Ensure that your LLC meets all licensing requirements and that staff members are appropriately certified. This can affect how you structure your LLC, particularly if you need to create specialized roles or departments.

Risk Management:

Healthcare involves significant liability risks. Structuring your LLC to include comprehensive liability protection and obtaining sufficient insurance coverage is essential.

Retail Sector

Retail businesses operate in a highly competitive and customer-focused environment. For LLCs in the retail sector, consider the following:

Location and Zoning:

The location of your retail business can significantly impact its success. Ensure your LLC complies with local zoning laws and secures the necessary permits for retail operations.

Customer Engagement:

Retail businesses must focus on customer service and engagement. Structuring your LLC to include dedicated roles for marketing, customer service, and sales can help meet these needs.

Inventory Management:

Efficient inventory management is crucial in retail. Your LLC should implement robust systems for tracking inventory, managing supply chains, and handling logistics.

Professional Services Sector

LLCs offering professional services, such as consulting, legal advice, or financial planning, need to prioritize expertise and client trust. Key considerations include:

Professional Licensing:

Ensure that all practitioners within your LLC hold the necessary licenses and certifications. This might involve creating specific roles or departments to oversee licensing and professional development.

Client Relationships:

Building and maintaining strong client relationships is vital. Structuring your LLC to include roles focused on client acquisition, retention, and satisfaction can enhance your service delivery.

Liability Protection:

Professional services often come with significant liability risks. Structuring your LLC to include comprehensive liability protection and obtaining professional liability insurance is essential.

Tips for Tailoring Your LLC to Meet Industry-Specific Needs and Standards

Understand Regulatory Requirements

Each industry has its own set of regulations and compliance standards. It's essential to thoroughly research the regulatory environment for your industry and ensure your LLC structure aligns with these requirements. This might involve:

Hiring Legal Advisors:

Engage with legal professionals who specialize in your industry to help navigate complex regulatory landscapes.

Compliance Officers:

Consider appointing a compliance officer within your LLC to oversee adherence to industry regulations and standards.

Develop Specialized Operating Agreements

Your LLC's operating agreement should reflect the specific needs of your industry. This includes outlining roles, responsibilities, and protocols that are relevant to your sector. For instance:

Healthcare:

Include clauses related to patient confidentiality, regulatory compliance, and staff certifications.

Technology:

Focus on intellectual property ownership, data security measures, and investment structures.

Retail:

Address inventory management, customer service standards, and location-specific requirements.

Implement Industry-Specific Best Practices

Adopting best practices that are specific to your industry can enhance the efficiency and effectiveness of your LLC. This includes:

Technology:

Invest in cybersecurity measures, adopt agile project management practices, and prioritize continuous innovation.

Healthcare:

Implement rigorous quality control protocols, prioritize patient safety, and maintain high ethical standards.

Retail:

Utilize data analytics for inventory management, focus on customer experience optimization, and stay abreast of retail trends.

Leverage Technology and Digital Tools

Incorporating technology and digital tools that are specific to your industry can streamline operations and improve performance. Examples include:

Technology:

Use project management software, version control systems, and collaboration tools to enhance productivity and innovation.

Healthcare:

Implement electronic health record (EHR) systems, telemedicine platforms, and medical billing software to improve patient care and operational efficiency.

Retail:

Utilize e-commerce platforms, customer relationship management (CRM) systems, and point-of-sale (POS) systems to enhance sales and customer engagement.

Focus on Talent Acquisition and Development

Building a skilled and knowledgeable team is crucial for the success of your LLC. Tailor your recruitment and development strategies to meet the needs of your industry:

Technology:

Hire software developers, data scientists, and IT professionals with expertise in the latest technologies and methodologies.

Healthcare:

Recruit licensed healthcare providers, administrative staff with healthcare experience, and compliance officers to ensure high standards of care and regulatory adherence.

Retail:

Employ experienced sales associates, inventory managers, and marketing professionals to drive sales and customer satisfaction.

Network and Build Industry Connections

Establishing connections within your industry can provide valuable insights, support, and opportunities for collaboration. Consider:

Joining Industry Associations:

Participate in industry-specific associations and organizations to stay informed about trends, regulations, and best practices.

Attending Conferences and Events:

Attend industry conferences, trade shows, and networking events to connect with peers, learn from experts, and discover new opportunities.

Engaging in Online Communities:

Participate in online forums, social media groups, and professional networks to share knowledge, ask questions, and build relationships with other industry professionals.

Monitor Industry Trends and Adapt

Staying informed about industry trends and adapting your LLC's strategies accordingly is essential for long-term success. This involves:

Conducting Market Research:

Regularly conduct market research to identify emerging trends, consumer preferences, and competitive dynamics.

Adapting Business Strategies:

Adjust your business strategies to align with industry trends, such as adopting new technologies, expanding product lines, or entering new markets.

Continuous Learning:

Encourage continuous learning and professional development within your LLC to ensure your team stays current with industry advancements and best practices.

"Tailoring your LLC to meet the specific needs and standards of your industry is a critical step in building a successful and sustainable business. By understanding how different industries influence the structure and management of an LLC, and by implementing industry-specific strategies and best practices, you can position your LLC for growth and resilience."

Case Studies and Success Stories

Understanding how successful LLCs operate can provide valuable insights and inspiration for your own business. This section shares real-life examples of LLCs in various industries, analyzing what they did right and how they overcame challenges. By examining these case studies, you can learn practical strategies and best practices to apply to your own LLC.

Technology Sector: Slack Technologies

Overview:

Slack Technologies, known for its popular messaging app Slack, is an exemplary case of a technology LLC that achieved rapid growth and widespread adoption. Founded in 2009, Slack quickly became a go-to platform for team communication and collaboration in workplaces around the world.

What They Did Right:

Identifying a Market Gap:

Slack's founders noticed the inefficiency in workplace communication and developed a product to address this gap. By providing a user-friendly and integrated messaging platform, Slack met a critical need in the market.

Focus on User Experience:

Slack prioritized creating an intuitive and enjoyable user experience. The platform's clean design, ease of use, and seamless integration with other tools contributed to its popularity.

Scalability:

Slack was designed to scale, accommodating the needs of both small teams and large enterprises. The company's infrastructure could handle rapid growth and increasing user demand without compromising performance.

Freemium Model:

Slack's freemium pricing strategy allowed users to start with a free version and upgrade to paid plans as their needs grew. This approach helped attract a large user base and convert many free users into paying customers.

Challenges and How They Overcame Them:

Competition:

The tech sector is highly competitive, with numerous messaging and collaboration tools available. Slack distinguished itself through superior user experience and continuous innovation, maintaining its competitive edge.

Data Security:

As a communication platform, Slack needed to ensure robust data security. The company invested heavily in cybersecurity measures and compliance with data protection regulations, building trust with users.

Integration:

Slack had to integrate with a wide range of third-party applications to provide a seamless experience. The company developed an extensive API and actively collaborated with other software providers to ensure compatibility and enhance functionality.

Healthcare Sector: One Medical

Overview:

One Medical is an innovative healthcare provider that operates as an LLC, offering a membership-based primary care service. Founded in 2007, One Medical has grown to serve numerous locations across the United States, providing high-quality, patient-centered care.

What They Did Right:

Patient-Centered Approach:

One Medical focused on improving the patient experience by offering convenient appointment scheduling, longer consultation times, and personalized care. This approach differentiated them from traditional healthcare providers.

Technology Integration:

One Medical leveraged technology to enhance care delivery. Their user-friendly app allowed patients to book appointments, access medical records, and communicate with their healthcare providers seamlessly.

Membership Model:

The membership-based model provided predictable revenue and encouraged patient loyalty. Members received access to premium services and personalized care, creating a strong value proposition.

Strategic Partnerships:

One Medical formed partnerships with employers, insurers, and health systems to expand their reach and integrate into the broader healthcare ecosystem. These partnerships facilitated growth and improved patient access to services.

Challenges and How They Overcame Them:

Regulatory Compliance:

The healthcare industry is heavily regulated. One Medical ensured compliance by hiring experienced legal and compliance professionals and investing in training and development to keep staff updated on regulations.

Scalability:

Expanding the practice while maintaining high-quality care was a challenge. One Medical implemented standardized protocols and invested in training and technology to ensure consistent service across all locations.

Competition:

One Medical faced competition from both traditional healthcare providers and new entrants. They focused on maintaining a superior patient experience and leveraging their technological advantage to stay ahead.

Retail Sector: Warby Parker

Overview:

Warby Parker, an eyewear retailer, operates as an LLC and has revolutionized the retail sector with its direct-to-consumer model. Founded in 2010, Warby Parker has grown into a successful brand known for affordable, stylish eyewear and innovative business practices.

What They Did Right:

Direct-to-Consumer Model:

By selling directly to consumers online, Warby Parker bypassed traditional retail channels and significantly reduced costs. This model allowed them to offer high-quality eyewear at competitive prices.

Social Responsibility:

Warby Parker's "Buy a Pair, Give a Pair" program, which donates a pair of glasses for every pair sold, resonated with socially conscious consumers. This commitment to social responsibility helped build a loyal customer base.

Brand Identity:

Warby Parker invested in creating a strong, recognizable brand with a focus on style, quality, and affordability. Their distinctive brand identity set them apart in the crowded eyewear market.

Omnichannel Strategy:

While starting as an online retailer, Warby Parker recognized the importance of physical presence and opened brick-and-mortar stores. This omnichannel approach provided customers with a seamless shopping experience, whether online or in-store.

Challenges and How They Overcame Them:

Consumer Trust:

Convincing consumers to buy eyewear online without trying it on was a significant hurdle. Warby Parker introduced a home try-on program, allowing customers to try frames at home before purchasing, which built trust and increased sales.

Logistics:

Managing logistics for both online and physical stores required efficient supply chain management. Warby Parker invested in logistics technology and partnerships to ensure smooth operations and timely delivery.

Scaling Operations:

Rapid growth posed challenges in maintaining quality and customer service. Warby Parker standardized processes, invested in employee training, and implemented scalable systems to support expansion.

Professional Services Sector: LegalZoom

Overview:

LegalZoom, an online legal services provider, operates as an LLC and has transformed the legal services industry. Founded in 2001, Legal-Zoom offers affordable, accessible legal services to individuals and small businesses.

What They Did Right:

Accessibility:

LegalZoom democratized legal services by providing an easy-to-use online platform. This accessibility made legal assistance affordable and convenient for a broader audience.

Technology Integration:

LegalZoom leveraged technology to automate and streamline legal processes. Their platform provided step-by-step guidance, ensuring users could complete legal documents accurately and efficiently.

Brand Trust:

Building a strong brand and earning consumer trust was crucial. Legal-Zoom invested in marketing and customer service to establish itself as a reliable and reputable provider of legal services.

Diverse Service Offerings:

LegalZoom expanded its services beyond document preparation to include attorney consultations, estate planning, and business formation services. This diversification attracted a wide range of clients.

Challenges and How They Overcame Them:

Regulatory Hurdles:

The legal industry is highly regulated, and LegalZoom faced scrutiny from state bar associations. They navigated these challenges by ensuring compliance, working with regulatory bodies, and advocating for changes in legal service delivery.

Consumer Trust:

Building trust in an industry traditionally dominated by face-to-face interactions was challenging. LegalZoom invested in transparent pricing, clear communication, and exceptional customer support to build credibility.

Scalability:

Managing rapid growth required robust technology infrastructure and efficient operations. LegalZoom continuously improved their platform and processes to scale effectively while maintaining high service standards.

E-commerce Sector: Shopify

Overview:

Shopify, a leading e-commerce platform, operates as an LLC and empowers entrepreneurs to start, run, and grow their online businesses. Founded in 2006, Shopify has become a cornerstone of the e-commerce industry.

What They Did Right:

User-Friendly Platform:

Shopify developed an intuitive and user-friendly platform that made it easy for anyone to set up and manage an online store. This accessibility attracted a large and diverse user base.

Ecosystem of Apps:

Shopify created an extensive ecosystem of apps and integrations, allowing users to customize their stores and add functionalities as needed. This flexibility made Shopify suitable for businesses of all sizes.

Support and Resources:

Shopify provided robust support and educational resources, including tutorials, webinars, and customer service, to help users succeed. This support was crucial in building customer loyalty and satisfaction.

Global Reach:

Shopify enabled businesses to sell globally, providing tools for international shipping, multiple currencies, and language support. This global reach helped businesses expand their markets and increase sales.

Challenges and How They Overcame Them:

Competition:

The e-commerce platform market is competitive, with many options available. Shopify distinguished itself through superior usability, extensive features, and exceptional customer support.

Scalability:

Supporting a growing number of merchants and their varying needs required scalable infrastructure. Shopify invested in technology and infrastructure to handle increasing demand and maintain performance.

Security:

Ensuring the security of transactions and customer data was paramount. Shopify implemented robust security measures and continuously updated their systems to protect against threats and maintain trust.

"These case studies illustrate how LLCs in various industries have successfully navigated challenges and leveraged opportunities to achieve significant growth and impact. By identifying market gaps, focusing on customer needs, embracing technology, and maintaining regulatory compliance, these businesses set themselves apart in their respective fields. As you build and manage your LLC, consider these success stories as sources of inspiration and practical insights. Adapt their strategies to your unique context, and stay committed to continuous improvement and innovation."

Challenges and Opportunities in Key Sectors

In this section, we will explore the common challenges faced by LLCs in various key industries, such as technology, healthcare, and retail. We will also highlight opportunities for growth and innovation within these sectors. Understanding these challenges and opportunities can help you better prepare for the specific demands of your industry and position your LLC for success.

Technology Sector

Challenges:

Rapid Technological Changes:

The technology sector is characterized by rapid advancements. Staying up-to-date with the latest developments and integrating new technologies can be challenging. LLCs in this sector must continuously innovate to remain competitive.

Cybersecurity Threats:

As technology companies often handle sensitive data, they are prime targets for cyberattacks. Ensuring robust cybersecurity measures and compliance with data protection regulations is essential to protect your business and maintain customer trust.

Talent Acquisition and Retention:

The demand for skilled tech professionals is high. Competing with larger companies for top talent can be difficult for smaller LLCs. Retaining employees requires creating a supportive work environment and offering competitive benefits.

Intellectual Property Protection:

Protecting intellectual property (IP) is crucial in the technology sector. Ensuring that your products and innovations are legally protected can prevent unauthorized use and safeguard your competitive advantage.

Opportunities:

Innovation and Disruption:

The fast-paced nature of the technology sector presents ample opportunities for innovation. LLCs can develop new products or services that address emerging needs or disrupt existing markets.

Global Reach:

Technology products and services can often be scaled globally with relative ease. Expanding your market internationally can lead to significant growth opportunities.

Collaborations and Partnerships:

Forming strategic partnerships with other tech companies, research institutions, or industry leaders can enhance your capabilities and open new avenues for growth.

SaaS and Subscription Models:

Software as a Service (SaaS) and subscription-based models provide recurring revenue streams. These models can improve financial stability and customer retention.

Healthcare Sector

Challenges:

Regulatory Compliance:

The healthcare sector is heavily regulated, and compliance with laws and regulations can be complex. Ensuring that your LLC adheres to all relevant regulations is critical to avoid legal issues and penalties.

Data Security and Privacy:

Protecting patient data is paramount in healthcare. Implementing stringent data security measures and ensuring compliance with regulations like HIPAA (Health Insurance Portability and Accountability Act) is essential.

High Operational Costs:

Running a healthcare business often involves significant operational costs, including equipment, facilities, and personnel. Managing these costs while maintaining high-quality care can be challenging.

Evolving Healthcare Policies:

Healthcare policies and reimbursement models frequently change. Keeping up with these changes and adjusting your business strategies accordingly is necessary to remain viable.

Opportunities:

Telemedicine:

The rise of telemedicine offers opportunities to expand your services and reach more patients. Implementing telehealth solutions can improve accessibility and convenience for patients.

Preventive Care and Wellness Programs:

Focusing on preventive care and wellness programs can differentiate your LLC and provide additional revenue streams. These programs can improve patient outcomes and reduce healthcare costs.

Health Technology Innovations:

Innovations in health technology, such as wearable devices, electronic health records (EHR), and artificial intelligence (AI), offer opportunities to enhance patient care and operational efficiency.

Community Outreach and Education:

Engaging with the community through health education and outreach programs can build your reputation and foster trust. These initiatives can attract new patients and strengthen your brand.

Retail Sector

Challenges:

Changing Consumer Preferences:

Consumer preferences in the retail sector are constantly evolving. Adapting to these changes and anticipating trends can be difficult but is essential for staying relevant.

Supply Chain Management:

Efficient supply chain management is critical in retail. Disruptions in the supply chain can lead to inventory shortages and impact customer satisfaction.

Intense Competition:

The retail sector is highly competitive, with both brick-and-mortar and online retailers vying for market share. Differentiating your LLC from competitors requires strategic planning and innovation.

E-commerce Integration:

Integrating e-commerce capabilities with traditional retail operations can be challenging. Ensuring a seamless customer experience across all channels is necessary to meet consumer expectations.

Opportunities:

Omnichannel Retailing:

Implementing an omnichannel retail strategy can enhance customer experience by providing multiple touchpoints, such as physical stores, online platforms, and mobile apps. This approach can increase sales and customer loyalty.

Sustainability Practices:

Adopting sustainable practices and offering eco-friendly products can attract environmentally conscious consumers. This focus on sustainability can differentiate your LLC and build brand loyalty.

Personalization:

Utilizing data analytics to offer personalized shopping experiences can boost customer satisfaction and sales. Personalization can include tailored recommendations, targeted marketing, and customized products.

Pop-up Stores and Experiential Retail:

Pop-up stores and experiential retail events can create buzz and attract new customers. These initiatives can provide unique experiences and enhance brand visibility.

Real Estate Sector

Challenges:

Market Volatility:

The real estate market can be highly volatile, influenced by economic conditions, interest rates, and government policies. Managing these fluctuations and making informed investment decisions is crucial.

Regulatory Requirements:

Real estate LLCs must comply with various zoning laws, building codes, and property regulations. Navigating these requirements and ensuring compliance can be complex.

Financing:

Securing financing for real estate projects can be challenging, especially for new LLCs. Building strong relationships with lenders and demonstrating financial stability is essential for obtaining funding.

Property Management:

Effective property management involves maintaining properties, addressing tenant issues, and ensuring compliance with lease agreements. This requires significant time and resources.

Opportunities:

Real Estate Technology:

Leveraging technology, such as property management software and virtual tours, can streamline operations and enhance the customer experience. Real estate tech innovations offer opportunities to improve efficiency and attract tech-savvy clients.

Sustainable Development:

Investing in sustainable and energy-efficient properties can appeal to environmentally conscious buyers and tenants. Green building practices can also reduce operational costs and increase property value.

Commercial Real Estate:

The commercial real estate sector offers opportunities for growth, particularly in areas like coworking spaces, retail developments, and industrial properties. Diversifying your portfolio can mitigate risks and capitalize on different market segments.

Community Development Projects:

Participating in community development projects can generate positive social impact and build your reputation. These projects often receive support from local governments and community organizations, providing additional resources and opportunities for growth.

Hospitality Sector

Challenges:

Seasonality and Demand Fluctuations:

The hospitality sector is often affected by seasonal variations and demand fluctuations. Managing these changes and ensuring steady revenue can be challenging.

Operational Costs:

High operational costs, including staffing, maintenance, and utilities, can impact profitability. Efficiently managing these costs while maintaining high service standards is crucial.

Customer Expectations:

Meeting and exceeding customer expectations is essential in the hospitality sector. Providing exceptional service and maintaining positive reviews can drive repeat business and attract new customers.

Health and Safety Regulations:

Ensuring compliance with health and safety regulations, especially in the context of the COVID-19 pandemic, is critical. Implementing robust safety protocols can protect guests and staff and build trust.

Opportunities:

Experiential Travel:

Offering unique and immersive experiences can differentiate your hospitality business. Experiential travel is increasingly popular, and creating memorable experiences can attract guests and encourage repeat visits.

Sustainability Initiatives:

Implementing sustainable practices, such as reducing energy consumption and minimizing waste, can appeal to eco-conscious travelers. Sustainability initiatives can also reduce operational costs and enhance your brand image.

Technology Integration:

Utilizing technology, such as online booking systems, mobile check-ins, and smart room features, can enhance the guest experience and streamline operations. Investing in technology can improve efficiency and customer satisfaction.

Local Partnerships:

Forming partnerships with local businesses, such as restaurants, tour operators, and cultural attractions, can enhance the guest experience and create additional revenue streams. These partnerships can also strengthen your connection to the local community.

Manufacturing Sector

Challenges:

Supply Chain Disruptions:

Supply chain disruptions, such as those caused by global events or natural disasters, can impact production and lead to delays. Building resilient supply chains and diversifying suppliers can mitigate these risks.

Regulatory Compliance:

The manufacturing sector is subject to various regulations, including safety standards, environmental regulations, and labor laws. Ensuring compliance with these regulations is essential to avoid penalties and maintain operations.

Technological Advancements:

Keeping up with technological advancements, such as automation and smart manufacturing, requires significant investment. Adopting new technologies can enhance efficiency but also involves training and transitioning challenges.

Skilled Labor Shortage:

Finding and retaining skilled labor can be difficult in the manufacturing sector. Investing in workforce development and creating attractive employment conditions is necessary to address this challenge.

Opportunities:

Industry 4.0:

Embracing Industry 4.0 technologies, such as the Internet of Things (IoT), artificial intelligence (AI), and robotics, can transform manufacturing processes. These technologies can improve efficiency, reduce costs, and enhance product quality.

Sustainable Manufacturing:

Implementing sustainable manufacturing practices, such as using renewable energy and reducing waste, can attract environmentally conscious customers and improve your brand reputation.

Customization and Personalization:

Offering customized and personalized products can meet the growing demand for unique and tailored solutions. Advanced manufacturing technologies, such as 3D printing, enable cost-effective customization.

Reshoring and Local Production:

The trend of reshoring and local production offers opportunities to reduce dependency on global supply chains and improve supply chain resilience. Local production can also meet the demand for locally made products.

Financial Services Sector

Challenges:

Regulatory Compliance:

The financial services sector is heavily regulated, and ensuring compliance with financial regulations, anti-money laundering (AML) laws, and data protection regulations is critical.

Cybersecurity Threats:

Financial services companies are prime targets for cyberattacks. Implementing robust cybersecurity measures to protect sensitive financial data is essential.

Market Volatility:

Market volatility and economic fluctuations can impact financial services companies. Managing these risks and maintaining financial stability requires careful planning and risk management.

Technological Integration:

Integrating new technologies, such as blockchain and fintech solutions, can be challenging. Adopting these technologies requires significant investment and can involve regulatory hurdles.

Opportunities:

Fintech Innovations:

The rise of fintech offers numerous opportunities for innovation in financial services. Embracing fintech solutions can enhance customer experience, improve efficiency, and create new revenue streams.

Digital Banking:

Digital banking services, such as mobile banking and online financial management tools, are increasingly popular. Offering these services can attract tech-savvy customers and enhance customer satisfaction.

Sustainable Finance:

Focusing on sustainable finance and green investments can appeal to socially conscious investors. Sustainable finance initiatives can also align with regulatory requirements and enhance your brand reputation.

Financial Inclusion:

Providing financial services to underserved populations and promoting financial inclusion can open new markets and create positive social impact. Developing products and services that meet the needs of these populations can drive growth.

"Each industry presents unique challenges and opportunities for LLCs. Understanding these factors and developing strategies to address challenges while leveraging opportunities can position your LLC for success. By staying informed about industry trends, investing in innovation, and maintaining a customer-centric approach, you can navigate the complexities of your sector and achieve sustainable growth."

Chapter 3
Navigating Legal and Regulatory Requirements

Legal Basics of Forming an LLC

Forming a Limited Liability Company (LLC) involves several key legal steps that provide the foundation for your business. These steps ensure that your LLC is recognized as a legal entity, offering you protection and flexibility. Here, we will detail the legal process required to establish an LLC, including drafting and filing Articles of Organization and creating an Operating Agreement.

Drafting and Filing Articles of Organization

The first step in forming an LLC is drafting and filing the Articles of Organization. This document, also known as the Certificate of Formation in some states, is a formal declaration to the state government about the establishment of your LLC. The process typically includes the following elements:

Business Name:

Choosing a unique name for your LLC is crucial. The name must comply with state regulations and include a designation like "LLC" or

"Limited Liability Company." This ensures that your business is distinguishable from other registered entities. It's advisable to conduct a name search through the state's business registry to ensure your chosen name is not already in use.

Principal Address:

You need to provide the primary address where your business operates. This address will be used for official correspondence and public records.

Registered Agent:

A registered agent is an individual or business entity designated to receive legal documents on behalf of your LLC. The registered agent must have a physical address in the state where the LLC is registered and be available during business hours. This role is critical for ensuring that your LLC receives important legal and tax documents in a timely manner.

Management Structure:

The Articles of Organization must specify whether your LLC will be member-managed or manager-managed. In a member-managed LLC, the owners (members) handle the day-to-day operations. In a manager-managed LLC, members appoint one or more managers to run the business, allowing members to take a more passive role.

Duration of LLC:

You must indicate whether your LLC will exist perpetually or for a specified duration. Most LLCs are set up to exist indefinitely, but if you plan to dissolve the LLC after achieving specific goals or within a certain timeframe, this should be clearly stated.

Purpose of the LLC:

Some states require a brief description of your business activities or the purpose of the LLC. This can be a general statement like "to engage in any lawful business activity," giving your LLC the flexibility to operate in various fields.

Signatures:

The Articles of Organization must be signed by the person(s) forming the LLC, often called the organizers. In some states, these signatures need to be notarized.

"Once the Articles of Organization are prepared, they must be filed with the appropriate state agency, usually the Secretary of State's office. Filing can often be done online, by mail, or in person. A filing fee, which varies by state, is typically required. Upon acceptance, the state will issue a certificate confirming the formation of your LLC, officially recognizing it as a legal entity."

Creating an Operating Agreement

An Operating Agreement is a crucial document that outlines the internal workings of your LLC. While not always legally required, having an Operating Agreement is highly recommended as it provides clarity and structure, reducing the potential for conflicts among members. The Operating Agreement typically covers the following areas:

Ownership Structure:

The Operating Agreement specifies the ownership interests of each member. This includes detailing each member's capital contributions, whether in the form of cash, property, or services. It also outlines the process for admitting new members and transferring ownership interests.

Management and Voting Rights:

This section delineates how the LLC will be managed and how decisions will be made. In a member-managed LLC, all members have equal rights to participate in decision-making unless otherwise specified. In a manager-managed LLC, the agreement should specify the roles and responsibilities of managers and the extent of their authority. Voting procedures, including the proportion of votes required to pass resolutions, should also be clearly defined.

Profit and Loss Allocation:

The Operating Agreement outlines how profits and losses will be distributed among members. This distribution does not necessarily have to match the members' ownership percentages. The agreement can specify any arrangement agreed upon by the members, providing flexibility to account for varying levels of involvement and contribution.

Meetings and Voting Procedures:

Regular meetings ensure that all members stay informed and involved in the business. The Operating Agreement should detail the frequency and notice requirements for meetings, as well as the procedures for voting on important matters. It's essential to establish clear rules for quorum and voting thresholds to ensure fair and efficient decision-making.

Dispute Resolution:

Conflicts among members are inevitable in any business. The Operating Agreement should include provisions for resolving disputes, such as mediation or arbitration, to prevent costly and time-consuming litigation. This section can also outline steps for addressing breaches of the agreement and other conflicts.

Dissolution and Liquidation:

The agreement should detail the process for dissolving the LLC and distributing its assets. This includes specifying the conditions under which the LLC can be dissolved, such as a unanimous vote by the members or the achievement of the LLC's objectives. It should also outline the steps for winding up the business, settling debts, and distributing any remaining assets to the members.

Amendments to the Agreement:

As your business evolves, the Operating Agreement may need to be updated. This section should outline the procedures for amending the agreement, including the voting requirements and notice procedures for proposed changes. Ensuring that all members have a clear understanding of how amendments can be made helps maintain the integrity of the agreement over time.

> *"Creating a comprehensive Operating Agreement helps prevent misunderstandings and conflicts by clearly defining the rights and responsibilities of each member. It also demonstrates to potential investors, lenders, and regulators that your LLC is well-organized and professionally managed."*

Additional Considerations in the Formation Process

Beyond drafting and filing the Articles of Organization and creating an Operating Agreement, there are other important considerations in forming an LLC:

Federal Employer Identification Number (EIN):

An EIN, also known as a Federal Tax Identification Number, is required for tax purposes. This number is used to identify your business entity and is necessary for opening a business bank account, hiring employees, and filing taxes. You can obtain an EIN from the Internal Revenue Service (IRS) by completing an online application.

State-Specific Requirements:

Each state has its own requirements for forming an LLC. Some states may require additional filings, such as initial reports or publication of a notice in a local newspaper. It's essential to familiarize yourself with your state's specific requirements to ensure compliance.

Business Licenses and Permits:

Depending on your industry and location, you may need to obtain various licenses and permits to operate legally. These can include local business licenses, health department permits, and professional licenses. Ensuring that you have all necessary licenses and permits helps prevent legal issues and fines.

Insurance:

Securing the appropriate insurance coverage is critical to protect your LLC from potential liabilities. Common types of insurance include general liability, professional liability, and workers' compensation. Assessing your specific risks and consulting with an insurance professional can help you determine the coverage you need.

Banking and Financial Accounts:

Keeping your personal and business finances separate is crucial for maintaining the limited liability protection offered by an LLC. Opening a dedicated business bank account and obtaining a business credit card can help you manage your finances more effectively and simplify tax preparation.

Compliance and Record-Keeping:

Maintaining thorough records of your LLC's activities, including meeting minutes, financial statements, and tax filings, is essential for compliance and transparency. Good record-keeping practices can help you stay organized, meet legal requirements, and provide valuable insights into your business's performance.

> *"By following these steps and considerations, you can successfully form an LLC and establish a strong legal foundation for your business. Taking the time to properly organize and document your LLC's structure and operations will pay off in the long run by providing clarity, reducing risks, and enhancing your business's credibility."*

> *"Forming an LLC involves careful planning and attention to detail. By understanding the legal requirements and taking proactive steps to address them, you can set your business up for success. Remember, each state may have unique requirements, so it's important to consult with legal and business professionals to ensure that you meet all necessary regulations and obligations. With a solid legal foundation in place, your LLC will be well-positioned to grow and thrive in its industry."*

Registering Your Business

Registering your LLC with the state is a crucial step in establishing your business as a legal entity. This process involves a series of steps that ensure your LLC is recognized by the state and can operate legally. This section will guide you through the detailed process of registering your LLC, emphasizing the importance of choosing a unique business name and the necessary steps to ensure its availability.

The process of registering an LLC varies slightly from state to state, but the fundamental steps remain consistent across the United States. Here's a comprehensive guide to help you navigate the registration process smoothly and efficiently.

Choosing Your LLC Name

The first step in registering your LLC is choosing a name for your business. This name must comply with your state's LLC naming rules and should be unique to avoid confusion with other businesses. Your LLC name is more than just a label; it represents your brand and can significantly impact your marketing efforts and customer perception.

Start by brainstorming a list of potential names. Think about your business's mission, values, and the image you want to project. Once you have a few options, you'll need to ensure that your chosen name is available and complies with state regulations. Most states require that the LLC name includes a designator such as "LLC," "L.L.C.," or "Limited Liability Company."

To check the availability of your desired name, you can use your state's business name database. This database is typically accessible through the Secretary of State's website. Enter your proposed name into the search tool to see if it's already in use. If the name is available, you can proceed with the registration. If it's not, you'll need to choose an alternative.

Reserving Your LLC Name

In some states, you have the option to reserve your LLC name before officially registering your business. This can be particularly useful if you need additional time to prepare your Articles of Organization or if you're not ready to file just yet but want to ensure that your chosen name isn't taken by someone else. The name reservation process usually involves submitting a form and paying a small fee. The reservation period varies by state but typically ranges from 30 to 120 days.

Designating a Registered Agent

A registered agent is a person or business entity designated to receive legal documents and official government communications on behalf of your LLC. This is a mandatory requirement in all states. Your registered agent must have a physical address in the state where your LLC is registered and be available during standard business hours.

You can choose to act as your own registered agent, appoint another member of your LLC, or hire a professional registered agent service. Using a professional service can offer added privacy and ensure that important documents are handled promptly and professionally.

Filing the Articles of Organization

The core step in registering your LLC is filing the Articles of Organization with the state. This document, sometimes referred to as the Certificate of Formation or Certificate of Organization, officially creates your LLC and includes essential details about your business. Here's what you'll typically need to include:

- **LLC Name and Designator**: Your chosen name, including the appropriate LLC designator.
- **Principal Address**: The primary address where your business operates. This address will be part of the public record.
- **Registered Agent Information**: The name and address of your registered agent.
- **Management Structure**: Indicate whether your LLC will be member-managed or manager-managed.
- **Purpose of the LLC**: A brief description of your business activities. Some states allow a general statement like "to engage in any lawful business activity."
- **Duration**: Specify whether your LLC will exist perpetually or for a specified duration.

You can usually file the Articles of Organization online, by mail, or in person. The filing fee varies by state, typically ranging from $50 to $500. Once filed, the state will review your submission and, upon approval, issue a certificate confirming the formation of your LLC.

Creating an Operating Agreement

Although not required in all states, creating an Operating Agreement is a critical step in establishing the internal structure and operating procedures of your LLC. This document outlines how your LLC will be managed, the roles and responsibilities of members, and the distribution of profits and losses. Having a well-crafted Operating Agreement can prevent misunderstandings and conflicts among members.

Your Operating Agreement should address the following areas:

- **Ownership Structure**: Detail the ownership percentages of each member.
- **Management and Voting Rights**: Define whether the LLC is member-managed or manager-managed and outline voting procedures.
- **Profit and Loss Distribution**: Specify how profits and losses will be allocated among members.
- **Meeting and Voting Procedures**: Establish rules for holding meetings and making decisions.
- **Dispute Resolution**: Include provisions for resolving conflicts.
- **Dissolution**: Outline the process for dissolving the LLC and distributing assets.

Creating this agreement early on helps ensure that all members are on the same page and that your business operates smoothly.

Obtaining an Employer Identification Number (EIN)

An Employer Identification Number (EIN) is necessary for tax purposes and is used to identify your business entity. You'll need an EIN to open a business bank account, hire employees, and file taxes. You can obtain an EIN from the Internal Revenue Service (IRS) by completing an online application. The process is straightforward and free of charge.

Registering for State Taxes

Depending on your state and the nature of your business, you may need to register for various state taxes. Common taxes include sales tax, use tax, and employer taxes. Sales tax registration is typically required if you sell physical goods or certain services. Employer taxes include unemployment insurance tax and workers' compensation insurance.

Check with your state's tax authority to determine which taxes apply to your LLC and ensure that you comply with all registration requirements.

Obtaining Business Licenses and Permits

In addition to registering your LLC, you may need to obtain various licenses and permits to operate legally. The requirements vary by state, locality, and industry. Common examples include general business licenses, health permits, building permits, and professional licenses.

Research the specific licenses and permits required for your business type and location. Failing to obtain the necessary permits can result in fines and other legal issues.

Complying With State-Specific Requirements

Each state has its own unique requirements for LLCs, which may include publishing a notice of formation, filing initial reports, or appointing a specific type of registered agent. It's crucial to familiarize yourself with your state's specific requirements to ensure full compliance.

For example, some states, like New York and Arizona, require LLCs to publish a notice of formation in a local newspaper. This process involves placing an advertisement in a designated newspaper for a specified period, usually six consecutive weeks. After completing the publication requirement, you'll need to file an affidavit of publication with the state.

Maintaining Ongoing Compliance

Once your LLC is registered, maintaining compliance with state regulations is essential. This typically involves filing annual reports, paying annual fees, and keeping accurate records. Annual reports update the state on key information about your LLC, such as its principal address, registered agent, and management structure.

Failing to file these reports or pay the required fees can result in penalties or the dissolution of your LLC. To stay compliant, create a calendar or reminder system for important deadlines and ensure that all necessary documents are submitted on time.

The Importance of Choosing a Unique Business Name

Choosing a unique business name is a critical aspect of forming an LLC. Your business name is the first impression potential customers will have of your company, and it plays a significant role in your branding and marketing efforts. A unique and memorable name can set your business apart from competitors and help attract and retain customers.

Ensuring Name Availability

To ensure your chosen name is available, you'll need to conduct a thorough search. Start by using your state's business name database to check if the name is already in use. It's important to note that each state maintains its own database, so you'll need to check the database of the state where you plan to register your LLC.

In addition to checking state databases, consider conducting a broader search to ensure that your name is not in use by businesses in other states, especially if you plan to operate or expand nationwide. Online search engines and business directories can help you identify potential conflicts.

Trademark Considerations

To further protect your business name, consider registering it as a trademark. A trademark provides legal protection for your brand and prevents others from using a similar name or logo in a way that could confuse customers. The U.S. Patent and Trademark Office (USPTO) handles trademark registrations. Conduct a trademark search through the USPTO's database to ensure your name is not already trademarked.

If your name is available, you can file a trademark application with the USPTO. This process involves submitting detailed information about your business and the name or logo you wish to trademark, along with a filing fee. Once approved, you'll have exclusive rights to use the name or logo in connection with your business activities.

Domain Name Considerations

In today's digital age, having an online presence is essential for most businesses. Securing a domain name that matches your business name is crucial for building a cohesive brand. Check the availability of your desired domain name using a domain registration service. If the domain is available, consider registering it as soon as possible to prevent others from claiming it.

If your preferred domain name is already taken, you may need to get creative. Consider alternative domain extensions (e.g., .net, .co) or variations of your business name that still align with your brand. Having a domain name that closely matches your business name enhances your online visibility and makes it easier for customers to find you.

Registering a Trade Name or DBA

In some cases, you might want to operate your LLC under a different name than the one registered with the state. This is known as a trade name or "Doing Business As" (DBA) name. Registering a DBA allows you to use a different name for branding and marketing purposes while maintaining your legal business name.

To register a DBA, you'll need to file the appropriate paperwork with your state or local government and pay a registration fee. The process varies by state but generally involves submitting a form that includes your LLC's legal name, the desired DBA name, and the principal address of your business. Once registered, you can legally operate under the DBA name.

Avoiding Common Naming Pitfalls

When choosing your business name, be mindful of potential pitfalls that could complicate your registration or branding efforts. Avoid names that are too similar to existing businesses, as this can lead to legal disputes and confusion among customers. Also, steer clear of names that are too generic or descriptive, as these may not be eligible for trademark protection.

Consider the long-term implications of your chosen name. Ensure that it aligns with your business goals and is adaptable to potential changes in your products, services, or target market. A name that is too specific to a particular product or geographic location might limit your ability to expand or diversify in the future.

Building a Strong Brand Identity

Your business name is a key component of your brand identity. It should reflect your company's values, mission, and unique selling points. Take the time to develop a name that resonates with your target audience and sets the right tone for your business.

Once you've chosen a name, invest in building a strong brand identity around it. This includes creating a professional logo, designing cohesive marketing materials, and establishing a consistent online presence. A well-defined brand identity helps build trust with customers and sets your business apart from competitors.

> *"Registering your LLC and choosing a unique business name are foundational steps in establishing a successful business. By following the outlined process and considering the various factors involved, you can ensure that your LLC is legally recognized and positioned for growth. Taking the time to carefully choose and protect your business name enhances your brand's visibility and credibility, setting the stage for long-term success."*

Compliance and Regulatory Considerations

Ensuring your LLC remains compliant with state and federal regulations is crucial for maintaining its legal standing and avoiding penalties. Compliance requirements can vary widely depending on your location and industry, but there are common elements that every LLC must address. This section will detail ongoing compliance requirements, such as annual reports and fees, and discuss the importance of staying updated on regulations affecting your business.

Ongoing Compliance Requirements

Once your LLC is registered, ongoing compliance is essential. These requirements typically involve submitting various reports, paying fees, and maintaining accurate records. Failing to meet these obligations can result in fines, penalties, and even the dissolution of your LLC.

Annual Reports

Most states require LLCs to file annual or biennial reports. These reports update the state on key information about your LLC, such as its principal address, registered agent, and the names and addresses of members or managers. The specific requirements and due dates vary by state, so it's important to familiarize yourself with the regulations in your jurisdiction.

The purpose of the annual report is to ensure that the state has current information about your business. This helps maintain transparency and allows the state to keep accurate records of active businesses. Filing the report usually involves completing a form and paying a filing fee. The fee can range from $20 to $500, depending on the state.

To stay compliant, mark the due date of your annual report on your calendar or set a reminder well in advance. Some states impose late fees or penalties for missing the deadline, and repeated failures to file can lead to administrative dissolution of your LLC.

Franchise Taxes

In addition to annual reports, some states require LLCs to pay a franchise tax. Despite its name, a franchise tax is not related to franchising a business but is a fee charged for the privilege of doing business in the state. The amount of the franchise tax can be a flat fee or based on the LLC's income, assets, or number of members.

States like California, Delaware, and Texas have notable franchise taxes. For example, California imposes a minimum franchise tax of $800 per year, while Delaware's tax is based on the number of authorized shares. Ensuring timely payment of franchise taxes is crucial to avoid penalties and interest.

State-Specific Requirements

Beyond annual reports and franchise taxes, some states have additional compliance requirements. For instance, certain states require LLCs to publish a notice of formation in a local newspaper. New York and Arizona are two states with such requirements. In New York, you must publish notices in two newspapers for six consecutive weeks and then file an affidavit of publication with the state.

Other states may require LLCs to file initial reports shortly after formation or to maintain specific types of insurance coverage. Understanding and meeting these state-specific requirements is essential to maintaining your LLC's good standing.

Operating Agreement Updates

While not always legally required, maintaining an updated Operating Agreement is a best practice. This internal document outlines the management structure and operating procedures of your LLC. Regularly reviewing and updating your Operating Agreement ensures that it reflects the current operations and ownership structure of your business.

Changes in membership, management roles, or business activities may necessitate updates to the Operating Agreement. Keeping this document current helps prevent misunderstandings among members and provides clear guidelines for decision-making and conflict resolution.

Record Keeping

Accurate and organized record keeping is fundamental to maintaining compliance and supporting the financial health of your LLC. Essential records include your Articles of Organization, Operating Agreement, tax documents, financial statements, and meeting minutes.

Most states require LLCs to keep certain records at their principal place of business. These records may include:

1. A current list of members and managers.
2. Copies of the LLC's tax returns and financial statements for the last few years.
3. Minutes of member and manager meetings.
4. Copies of any written consents for actions taken by members or managers.

Having these records readily available ensures that you can provide them if requested by state authorities, members, or potential investors. Proper record keeping also facilitates accurate financial reporting and tax filings.

Importance of Staying Updated on Regulations

The regulatory landscape for LLCs is dynamic, with changes occurring at both the state and federal levels. Staying updated on relevant regulations is critical for ensuring ongoing compliance and protecting your business from legal issues.

State Regulations

Each state has its own set of laws governing LLCs, and these laws can change periodically. Legislative changes may impact filing requirements, tax obligations, and operational rules. Regularly reviewing your state's business regulations and subscribing to updates from the Secretary of State's office or a professional organization can help you stay informed.

Joining local business associations or chambers of commerce can also provide valuable insights into regulatory changes. These organizations often offer resources, seminars, and networking opportunities that keep business owners informed about new laws and compliance strategies.

Federal Regulations

At the federal level, regulations affecting LLCs primarily involve tax laws, employment laws, and industry-specific regulations. The Internal Revenue Service (IRS) frequently updates tax rules and guidelines, which can impact how your LLC handles deductions, credits, and reporting requirements.

For example, changes in the tax code can alter the tax treatment of certain expenses or affect the eligibility criteria for various tax credits. Staying informed about these changes ensures that your LLC maximizes tax benefits and complies with reporting obligations.

Employment laws, such as those related to minimum wage, overtime pay, and workplace safety, are also subject to change. The U.S. Department of Labor provides resources and updates on federal employment laws. Ensuring compliance with these laws protects your LLC from potential lawsuits and penalties.

Industry-Specific Regulations

Depending on your industry, there may be additional regulations that your LLC must comply with. For example, healthcare providers must adhere to HIPAA regulations, financial services firms must comply with SEC rules, and food businesses must follow FDA guidelines.

Industry-specific regulations can be complex and frequently updated, making it essential to stay informed through industry associations, professional groups, and regulatory agencies. Regular training and continuing education for you and your employees can also help ensure compliance with industry standards.

Using Professional Services

Given the complexity of compliance requirements, many LLCs benefit from using professional services such as accountants, attorneys, and compliance specialists. These professionals can help you navigate the regulatory landscape, file necessary documents, and keep your business in good standing.

An accountant can assist with tax filings, financial reporting, and payroll compliance, ensuring that your LLC meets all tax obligations. An attorney can provide legal advice on regulatory changes, review contracts, and help with any legal disputes that arise.

Compliance specialists or firms offer services specifically focused on maintaining compliance with state and federal regulations. They can manage filings, track deadlines, and provide ongoing support to ensure your LLC remains compliant.

Adopting Compliance Tools and Software

Leveraging technology can streamline your compliance efforts and reduce the risk of missing important deadlines. Compliance management software can help you track filing requirements, maintain accurate records, and receive alerts for upcoming deadlines.

These tools often include features such as document storage, task management, and automated reminders. By adopting compliance tools, you can improve efficiency, ensure timely filings, and reduce the administrative burden of maintaining compliance.

Conducting Regular Compliance Audits

Regular compliance audits are an effective way to ensure that your LLC adheres to all regulatory requirements. An internal audit involves reviewing your records, processes, and filings to identify any gaps or areas of non-compliance.

During an audit, check that all required documents are filed correctly and on time, that your financial records are accurate, and that your Operating Agreement reflects your current operations. Address any issues identified during the audit promptly to prevent future compliance problems.

Educating Yourself and Your Team

Staying educated about compliance requirements is an ongoing process. As a business owner, it's crucial to invest time in learning about regulatory changes and best practices. Attend workshops, webinars, and conferences focused on compliance topics relevant to your LLC.

Educating your team is equally important. Ensure that your employees understand the compliance requirements that apply to their roles and provide training on any new regulations or procedures. A well-informed team can help maintain compliance and reduce the risk of violations.

Adapting to Changes

The business environment is constantly evolving, and your LLC must be adaptable to remain compliant. Legislative changes, economic shifts, and industry trends can all impact your compliance obligations. Regularly reviewing your business practices and staying flexible in your approach can help your LLC navigate these changes effectively.

For instance, if new state regulations require additional reporting or changes to your Operating Agreement, address these requirements promptly and adjust your internal processes accordingly. Staying proactive and adaptable ensures that your LLC remains in good standing and can continue to operate without interruptions.

The Consequences of Non-Compliance

Failing to comply with state and federal regulations can have serious consequences for your LLC. Understanding these risks underscores the importance of maintaining compliance.

Penalties and Fines

Non-compliance can result in financial penalties and fines. These can range from relatively small amounts for minor infractions to substantial sums for more significant violations. Penalties for late filings, unpaid taxes, or failure to maintain required licenses can quickly add up and strain your LLC's finances.

Administrative Dissolution

Repeated failure to comply with state requirements, such as not filing annual reports or paying franchise taxes, can lead to administrative dissolution. This means the state revokes your LLC's legal status, effectively shutting down your business. Reinstating a dissolved LLC can be a complicated and costly process, involving back payments of fees and penalties.

Legal Liability

Non-compliance with regulations can expose your LLC to legal liability. For example, failing to adhere to employment laws can result in lawsuits from employees, while violating industry-specific regulations can lead to enforcement actions by regulatory agencies. Legal disputes can be time-consuming, costly, and damaging to your business's reputation.

Loss of Good Standing

Maintaining good standing with the state is crucial for your LLC's credibility and ability to conduct business. Losing good standing can impact your ability to secure financing, enter into contracts, and attract customers. It can also affect your business's reputation and relationships with partners and suppliers.

Impact on Business Operations

Compliance issues can disrupt your business operations. For instance, if your LLC is not in good standing, it may be barred from obtaining permits, licenses, or renewing existing ones. This can hinder your ability to expand, launch new products, or operate in certain jurisdictions.

"Maintaining compliance is not just a legal obligation but a strategic necessity for the success and longevity of your LLC. By understanding ongoing compliance requirements, staying updated on regulatory changes, and leveraging professional services and tools, you can ensure that your LLC operates smoothly and avoids the pitfalls of non-compliance. Taking a proactive approach to compliance strengthens your business's foundation and positions it for long-term growth and success."

Intellectual Property Protection

Protecting your intellectual property (IP) is crucial for safeguarding the unique elements that give your LLC a competitive edge. Intellectual property encompasses creations of the mind, such as inventions, literary and artistic works, designs, symbols, names, and images used in commerce. By understanding the basics of trademarks, copyrights, and patents, and implementing strategies to protect these assets, you can secure your business's unique ideas and products from unauthorized use.

Trademarks

Trademarks are vital for distinguishing your business's goods or services from those of others. A trademark can be a word, phrase, symbol, design, or a combination of these, that identifies and distinguishes your products. Registering a trademark provides legal protection, enabling you to prevent others from using a similar mark that could confuse consumers.

To secure a trademark, you need to conduct a thorough search to ensure that your proposed mark is not already in use. The United States Patent and Trademark Office (USPTO) provides a searchable database for this purpose. After confirming that your mark is unique, you can file an application with the USPTO. The application process involves providing details about your mark, the goods or services it will represent, and specimens showing how the mark is used in commerce.

Once registered, a trademark offers several benefits. It grants you exclusive rights to use the mark nationwide in connection with your goods or services, provides legal presumption of ownership, and allows you to bring legal action against others who infringe on your mark. Moreover, a registered trademark can enhance your brand's credibility and value.

However, owning a trademark also involves ongoing responsibilities. You must use the mark in commerce and periodically renew the registration. Failure to do so can result in the loss of trademark protection. Additionally, monitoring the marketplace for potential infringements and taking action when necessary is crucial for maintaining your rights.

Copyrights

Copyrights protect original works of authorship, such as literary, musical, and artistic works, including books, music, films, software, and architectural designs. A copyright grants the creator exclusive rights to use and distribute the work, typically for the life of the author plus 70 years.

To obtain copyright protection, a work must be original and fixed in a tangible medium of expression. Unlike trademarks, copyrights do not require registration to be valid. However, registering your copyright with the U.S. Copyright Office provides significant advantages, such as the ability to file a lawsuit for infringement and the potential to recover statutory damages and attorney's fees.

The process of registering a copyright involves submitting an application, a copy of the work, and the appropriate fee to the U.S. Copyright

Office. The office will review your application and, if approved, issue a certificate of registration.

Protecting your copyrighted work involves more than just registration. You should clearly mark your work with a copyright notice, including the copyright symbol (©), the year of first publication, and your name. This notice informs others that the work is protected and discourages unauthorized use.

Monitoring the use of your copyrighted material and taking action against infringers is also crucial. This can include sending cease-and-desist letters, negotiating licensing agreements, or pursuing legal action if necessary.

Patents

Patents protect new, useful, and non-obvious inventions or discoveries. There are three main types of patents: utility patents, design patents, and plant patents. Utility patents are the most common and cover new processes, machines, manufactures, or compositions of matter. Design patents protect new, original, and ornamental designs for an article of manufacture, while plant patents cover new and distinct varieties of plants.

Securing a patent involves a rigorous application process with the USPTO. This process includes a detailed description of the invention, claims defining the scope of the patent, and often, drawings illustrating the invention. The application is then examined by a patent examiner to ensure that it meets all legal requirements.

A granted patent provides the holder with exclusive rights to make, use, sell, and import the invention for a limited period, typically 20 years from the filing date for utility patents. This exclusivity can provide a significant competitive advantage, allowing you to control the use of your invention and potentially generate revenue through licensing or sales.

However, maintaining a patent also involves responsibilities. You must pay maintenance fees to keep the patent in force, and you must monitor the market for potential infringements. Enforcing your patent rights may require legal action, which can be costly and time-consuming.

Safeguarding Your Business's Unique Ideas and Products

In addition to securing trademarks, copyrights, and patents, there are several strategies you can implement to protect your business's unique ideas and products.

Non-Disclosure Agreements (NDAs)

Non-disclosure agreements are legal contracts that prohibit parties from disclosing confidential information. When sharing sensitive information with employees, contractors, or business partners, an NDA can help ensure that your ideas and products remain protected. NDAs should clearly define the confidential information, the obligations of the receiving party, and the duration of confidentiality.

Employee Agreements

Including IP protection clauses in employee agreements is essential for ensuring that any inventions or creative works developed by employees as part of their job duties are owned by the LLC. These agreements should specify that all work-related IP created during employment belongs to the company and may include provisions for handling IP developed outside of work hours but related to the company's business.

Secure IT Systems

Protecting digital assets requires robust IT security measures. Implementing strong passwords, encryption, firewalls, and regular security audits can help prevent unauthorized access to your company's intellectual property. Additionally, limiting access to sensitive information to only those employees who need it can reduce the risk of leaks.

Continuous Monitoring and Enforcement

Regularly monitoring the market for potential IP infringements is crucial for protecting your rights. This can involve setting up alerts for trademark and patent filings, conducting periodic searches for unauthorized use of your works, and monitoring competitors' products and marketing materials. When infringements are identified, taking swift action through cease-and-desist letters or legal proceedings can help enforce your rights.

Educating Employees

Ensuring that your employees understand the importance of IP protection and their role in safeguarding it is vital. Conduct regular training sessions on IP policies, security practices, and the potential consequences of IP theft or infringement. An informed workforce is better equipped to protect your company's intellectual property.

IP Audits

Conducting regular IP audits can help you identify and protect all your intellectual property assets. An IP audit involves reviewing your company's creations, innovations, and branding materials to ensure that all eligible assets are properly protected through trademarks, copyrights, and patents. This process can also help you identify potential gaps in your IP strategy and take corrective action.

Legal Counsel

Working with an attorney specializing in intellectual property law can provide invaluable guidance and support. An IP attorney can assist with the registration process, draft legal agreements, advise on enforcement strategies, and represent your company in legal disputes. Having professional legal support can help ensure that your IP protection measures are comprehensive and effective.

Licensing and Joint Ventures

Licensing your intellectual property to other companies or entering into joint ventures can provide additional revenue streams while maintaining control over your IP. Licensing agreements should clearly outline the terms of use, royalties, and the scope of the license. Joint ventures can offer opportunities for collaboration and innovation while ensuring that your IP rights are protected.

Trade Secrets

Some intellectual property, such as formulas, processes, or methods that provide a competitive edge, can be protected as trade secrets. Unlike patents, trade secrets are not registered with the government. Instead, protection relies on maintaining strict confidentiality. Implementing policies and procedures to safeguard trade secrets, such as restricting access and using NDAs, is essential for protecting this type of IP.

Brand Protection Strategies

In addition to registering trademarks, implementing brand protection strategies can help maintain the integrity and reputation of your brand. This can include monitoring online marketplaces for counterfeit products, taking action against unauthorized sellers, and maintaining consistent branding across all platforms. Protecting your brand's image and reputation is critical for long-term success.

International IP Protection

If your business operates internationally or plans to expand into global markets, securing IP protection in other countries is essential. Intellectual property laws vary by country, and protections in the U.S. do not extend internationally. Applying for international trademarks, patents, and copyrights through mechanisms such as the Madrid Protocol (for trademarks) or the Patent Cooperation Treaty (for patents) can provide protection in multiple jurisdictions.

Public Disclosure and Timing

Timing your public disclosures and IP filings strategically can also play a role in protecting your intellectual property. For instance, disclosing an invention before filing a patent application can jeopardize your ability to secure a patent. Planning your IP filings and public announcements carefully ensures that you maximize protection and avoid unintentional disclosures.

Utilizing IP Insurance

Intellectual property insurance can provide financial protection against the costs associated with IP litigation, including defense costs and potential damages. IP insurance policies can cover various types of intellectual property and provide peace of mind that your business is protected against potential legal challenges.

"Protecting your LLC's intellectual property is a multifaceted process that involves understanding the basics of trademarks, copyrights, and patents, as well as implementing comprehensive strategies to safeguard your unique ideas and products. By securing legal protections, educating employees, and adopting best practices for IP management, you can ensure that your business's intellectual property remains a valuable asset and a source of competitive advantage. Staying proactive and vigilant in protecting your intellectual property helps secure your business's future and fosters innovation and growth."

Chapter 4
Tax Implications and Financial Management

Tax Advantages of LLCs

One of the most compelling reasons to choose a Limited Liability Company (LLC) as your business structure is the array of tax benefits it offers. Understanding these advantages can help you make informed decisions that optimize your business's financial health. LLCs provide significant flexibility in taxation, allowing you to tailor your tax strategy to best suit your business's needs. This section will explore the primary tax benefits of LLCs, including pass-through taxation and the flexibility to choose your tax status, and how these advantages can contribute to your LLC's success.

Pass-Through Taxation

Pass-through taxation is one of the hallmark features of an LLC, and it provides a significant tax advantage over other business structures like C-corporations. In a C-corporation, the company's profits are taxed at the corporate level, and then any distributions to shareholders (such as dividends) are taxed again at the individual level. This results in double taxation, which can significantly reduce the overall profitability of the business.

In contrast, LLCs are typically treated as pass-through entities for federal income tax purposes. This means that the LLC itself does not pay federal income taxes. Instead, the profits and losses of the LLC are passed through to the individual members, who report this income on their personal tax returns. This single layer of taxation can lead to substantial tax savings, especially for small business owners.

For example, if your LLC earns $100,000 in profit, you avoid paying corporate taxes on that amount. Instead, the profit is divided among the members according to their ownership interests, and each member includes their share of the profit on their personal tax return. This method not only simplifies the tax process but can also result in a lower overall tax burden.

Flexibility in Choosing Tax Status

One of the unique benefits of an LLC is its flexibility in choosing how it is taxed. By default, a single-member LLC is treated as a sole proprietorship for tax purposes, while a multi-member LLC is treated as a partnership. However, LLCs can elect to be taxed as a C-corporation or an S-corporation if it better suits their financial strategy.

Sole Proprietorship or Partnership Taxation:

When an LLC is taxed as a sole proprietorship or partnership, the income passes through to the owners, who then report it on their individual tax returns. This default taxation method benefits those who prefer a straightforward tax filing process without the additional complexities of corporate taxation.

S-corporation Election:

Electing to be taxed as an S-corporation can provide additional tax advantages, particularly concerning self-employment taxes. In a standard LLC, all net earnings are subject to self-employment taxes, which include Social Security and Medicare taxes. However, if you elect S-corporation status, you can divide your earnings into salary and distributions. Only the salary portion is subject to self-employment taxes, while distributions are not, potentially reducing your overall tax liability.

For instance, if your LLC earns $100,000, you might pay yourself a reasonable salary of $60,000 and take the remaining $40,000 as a distribution. You would only pay self-employment taxes on the $60,000 salary, which can result in significant tax savings.

C-corporation Election:

While less common, some LLCs may choose to be taxed as C-corporations. This election can be advantageous for businesses that plan to retain earnings within the company for growth or reinvestment, as corporate tax rates can sometimes be lower than individual tax rates. Additionally, C-corporations can offer fringe benefits to owners that are tax-deductible, such as health insurance and retirement plans.

However, it's essential to weigh the potential for double taxation in a C-corporation structure, as profits are taxed at the corporate level and then again at the individual level when distributed as dividends. This option is typically more suitable for larger LLCs with significant reinvestment strategies.

Deductible Business Expenses

Another significant tax advantage of LLCs is the ability to deduct ordinary and necessary business expenses from the company's income, which reduces the overall taxable income. Common deductible expenses include rent, utilities, salaries and wages, office supplies, and marketing costs. These deductions can lower your taxable income and, consequently, your tax liability.

For instance, if your LLC incurs $30,000 in deductible expenses over a year, and you earned $100,000 in revenue, you would only be taxed on the net income of $70,000. This ability to deduct a wide range of business expenses provides substantial tax relief and encourages reinvestment in the business.

Home Office Deduction

If you operate your LLC from a home office, you may be eligible for a home office deduction, which can significantly reduce your taxable income. To qualify, the space must be used exclusively and regularly for business purposes. The deduction can be calculated based on a simplified method, which allows a standard deduction of $5 per square foot of the home used for business, up to a maximum of 300 square feet, or through a more complex method that involves calculating actual expenses.

The actual expense method allows you to deduct a portion of your home's expenses, such as mortgage interest, property taxes, utilities, and repairs, based on the percentage of your home's square footage used for business. This can result in significant tax savings, particularly for small business owners operating from home.

Retirement Contributions

LLCs also provide opportunities for retirement savings, which can be tax-advantaged. Contributions to retirement plans, such as Simplified Employee Pension (SEP) IRAs, Savings Incentive Match Plan for Employees (SIMPLE) IRAs, or 401(k) plans, can be deducted from the LLC's taxable income. These retirement plans allow for substantial contributions, which not only prepare you for the future but also reduce current tax liabilities.

For example, a SEP IRA allows you to contribute up to 25% of your net earnings from self-employment, up to a maximum of $61,000 (for the 2024 tax year). These contributions are tax-deductible, which can significantly lower your taxable income and reduce your overall tax bill.

Health Insurance Deduction

If your LLC pays health insurance premiums for you as the owner, these premiums may be fully deductible. This deduction can be particularly beneficial if you are self-employed and paying for your own health insurance. The self-employed health insurance deduction allows you to deduct premiums paid for medical, dental, and long-term care insurance for yourself, your spouse, and your dependents, reducing your adjusted gross income and overall tax liability.

QBI Deduction

One of the recent tax advantages introduced by the Tax Cuts and Jobs Act of 2017 is the Qualified Business Income (QBI) deduction. This deduction allows eligible LLC owners to deduct up to 20% of their qualified business income, subject to certain limitations and thresholds. The QBI deduction can significantly reduce the effective tax rate on business income for many LLC owners.

For instance, if your LLC generates $100,000 in qualified business income, you may be eligible to deduct $20,000, reducing your taxable income to $80,000. This deduction is available to LLCs taxed as sole proprietorships, partnerships, or S-corporations and provides a substantial tax break for small business owners.

State and Local Tax Flexibility

LLCs also offer flexibility in handling state and local taxes. Each state has its own tax regulations for LLCs, which can vary widely. Some states impose franchise taxes or annual fees on LLCs, while others have no such requirements. Additionally, certain states allow LLCs to elect different tax treatments, providing opportunities to minimize state tax liabilities.

For example, in California, LLCs must pay an annual franchise tax and an LLC fee based on their income. However, states like Wyoming and South Dakota do not impose state income taxes or franchise taxes on

LLCs, making them attractive locations for forming an LLC. By understanding the state-specific tax requirements and planning accordingly, you can optimize your tax strategy to minimize your overall tax burden.

Flexibility in Profit Distribution

LLCs provide flexibility in how profits are distributed among members. Unlike corporations, which must distribute profits based on the percentage of ownership, LLCs can allocate profits and losses in a way that does not necessarily reflect ownership percentages. This flexibility allows LLC members to structure profit distributions in a manner that aligns with their financial and tax planning strategies.

For example, if you and your partner each own 50% of the LLC, but you agree that you will take on more operational responsibilities, you can allocate a larger share of the profits to yourself. This can be advantageous for tax planning purposes, allowing you to maximize deductions and minimize overall tax liability.

> *"The tax advantages of forming an LLC are substantial and can provide significant financial benefits to business owners. Pass-through taxation, flexibility in choosing tax status, and the ability to deduct business expenses are just a few of the benefits that make LLCs an attractive option. Additionally, opportunities for home office deductions, retirement contributions, health insurance deductions, and the QBI deduction further enhance the tax advantages of an LLC."*

Understanding Tax Obligations

Understanding the various tax obligations of your LLC is essential for maintaining compliance and optimizing your business's financial performance. Federal, state, and local taxes all play a significant role in how your LLC operates and plans its finances. Additionally, self-employment taxes and potential deductions can greatly impact your overall tax liability. In this section, we will thoroughly explore these tax obligations to provide you with a clear understanding of what is required and how to manage these responsibilities effectively.

Federal Tax Obligations

Federal taxes are a primary concern for any LLC. Unlike corporations, LLCs benefit from pass-through taxation, which can simplify tax processes and potentially lower tax burdens. The key federal tax obligations include income tax, self-employment tax, and employment taxes if you have employees.

Income Tax:

As an LLC, you generally do not pay federal income taxes at the company level. Instead, the business's income, deductions, and credits pass through to the individual members, who then report this information on their personal tax returns. This means that each member pays taxes on their share of the LLC's profits, based on their individual tax rates.

If your LLC has only one member, it is treated as a sole proprietorship by default for federal tax purposes, and the business income is reported on Schedule C of your personal tax return. For multi-member LLCs, the business is treated as a partnership, and the income is reported on Form 1065, with each member receiving a Schedule K-1 detailing their share of the profits.

Self-Employment Tax:

One of the significant federal tax obligations for LLC members is self-employment tax. This tax covers Social Security and Medicare contributions, which are critical for funding these social safety nets. For 2024, the self-employment tax rate is 15.3%, which includes 12.4% for Social Security and 2.9% for Medicare.

LLC members must pay self-employment tax on their share of the business income. For example, if your share of the LLC's profit is $50,000, you would be responsible for paying self-employment tax on that amount, which would be $7,650. It's important to note that you can deduct the employer-equivalent portion of your self-employment tax when calculating your adjusted gross income, which helps reduce your taxable income.

Employment Taxes:

If your LLC has employees, you must withhold and pay employment taxes, including federal income tax, Social Security, Medicare, and federal unemployment tax (FUTA). These taxes are reported using various forms, such as Form 941 for quarterly tax returns and Form 940 for annual FUTA tax.

To comply with federal employment tax obligations, you must obtain an Employer Identification Number (EIN) from the IRS, which serves as your business's tax identification number. You will also need to keep accurate records of employee wages, tax withholdings, and payments made to the IRS.

State Tax Obligations

In addition to federal taxes, your LLC must also comply with state tax obligations, which can vary significantly depending on your location. Common state taxes include income tax, sales tax, and franchise tax.

State Income Tax:

Most states require LLCs to pay state income tax on their earnings. Like federal taxes, state income taxes are typically passed through to the individual members, who report their share of the income on their state tax returns. However, some states impose additional taxes or fees on LLCs, so it is crucial to understand your state's specific requirements.

For example, in California, LLCs must pay an annual franchise tax and an LLC fee based on their total income. The franchise tax is a minimum of $800 per year, and the LLC fee varies depending on the LLC's income level. Other states, such as Texas and Florida, do not impose state income taxes on LLCs, making them attractive locations for business formation.

Sales Tax:

If your LLC sells goods or services, you may be required to collect and remit sales tax to the state. Sales tax rates and regulations vary by state and even by locality, so it is essential to understand the specific requirements for your business. You will need to register for a sales tax permit, collect sales tax from customers, and file regular sales tax returns.

For instance, if your LLC operates an online retail store, you may need to collect sales tax on sales made to customers in states where you have a significant presence, known as nexus. Nexus can be established through physical presence, such as a storefront or warehouse, or economic presence, based on the volume of sales or transactions in a state.

Franchise Tax:

Some states impose a franchise tax on LLCs for the privilege of doing business in the state. Franchise taxes can be based on various factors, such as the LLC's income, net worth, or capital stock. The rates and calculation methods vary by state, so it is important to understand the specific requirements in your state.

For example, in Delaware, LLCs are required to pay an annual franchise tax of $300, regardless of their income or activity level. In contrast, Tennessee imposes both a franchise tax based on the LLC's net worth and an excise tax based on the LLC's net earnings.

Local Tax Obligations

In addition to federal and state taxes, your LLC may also be subject to local taxes imposed by cities, counties, or other municipalities. Common local taxes include business licenses, property taxes, and local income taxes.

Business Licenses:

Many local governments require businesses to obtain a business license or permit to operate legally within their jurisdiction. The requirements and fees vary by location and industry, so it is essential to check with your local government to determine the specific requirements for your LLC.

For example, if your LLC operates a restaurant, you may need to obtain a food service permit, health department permit, and alcohol license, in addition to a general business license. These permits often require annual renewals and payment of associated fees.

Property Taxes:

If your LLC owns real property, such as land or buildings, you will be responsible for paying property taxes to the local government. Property tax rates and assessment methods vary by location, so it is important to understand your local property tax obligations and budget accordingly.

Additionally, some jurisdictions impose personal property taxes on business assets, such as equipment, furniture, and inventory. These taxes are typically based on the value of the assets and may require annual filings and payments.

Local Income Taxes:

Some cities and counties impose local income taxes on businesses operating within their jurisdiction. These taxes are usually based on the LLC's income or payroll and are in addition to federal and state income taxes. Local income tax rates and regulations vary, so it is essential to check with your local tax authority to determine your specific obligations.

For example, if your LLC operates in New York City, you will be subject to the city's Unincorporated Business Tax (UBT), which is imposed on unincorporated businesses, including LLCs, that conduct business within the city. The UBT rate is currently 4% of taxable income, with various deductions and credits available.

Self-Employment Taxes

One of the unique tax obligations for LLC members is self-employment tax. As an LLC member, you are considered self-employed, which means you are responsible for paying Social Security and Medicare taxes on your share of the business income. The self-employment tax rate is 15.3%, which includes 12.4% for Social Security and 2.9% for Medicare.

Self-employment tax is calculated on your net earnings from self-employment, which is your share of the LLC's income after deducting allowable business expenses. For example, if your share of the LLC's profit is $60,000, you would calculate self-employment tax on that amount, resulting in a tax liability of $9,180.

It is important to note that self-employment tax is in addition to any federal, state, and local income taxes you may owe. However, you can deduct the employer-equivalent portion of your self-employment tax when calculating your adjusted gross income, which helps reduce your overall tax liability.

To manage self-employment tax, you will need to make quarterly estimated tax payments to the IRS using Form 1040-ES. These payments cover both your income tax and self-employment tax obligations. Failing to make timely estimated tax payments can result in penalties and interest, so it is crucial to plan and budget for these payments throughout the year.

Potential Deductions

As an LLC, you are entitled to various deductions that can reduce your taxable income and overall tax liability. Understanding these deductions and how to maximize them is essential for effective tax planning and financial management.

Ordinary and Necessary Business Expenses:

The IRS allows you to deduct ordinary and necessary business expenses from your LLC's income. Ordinary expenses are those that are common and accepted in your industry, while necessary expenses are those that are helpful and appropriate for your business. Common deductible business expenses include rent, utilities, salaries and wages, office supplies, marketing costs, and professional services.

For example, if your LLC incurs $40,000 in deductible expenses over a year, and you earned $100,000 in revenue, you would only be taxed on the net income of $60,000. This ability to deduct a wide range of business expenses provides substantial tax relief and encourages reinvestment in the business.

Home Office Deduction:

If you operate your LLC from a home office, you may be eligible for a home office deduction, which can significantly reduce your taxable income. To qualify, the space must be used exclusively and regularly for business purposes. The deduction can be calculated based on a simplified method, which allows a standard deduction of $5 per square foot of the home used for business, up to a maximum of 300 square feet, or through a more complex method that involves calculating actual expenses.

The actual expense method allows you to deduct a portion of your home's expenses, such as mortgage interest, property taxes, utilities, and repairs, based on the percentage of your home's square footage used for business. This can result in significant tax savings, particularly for small business owners operating from home.

Vehicle Expenses:

If you use a vehicle for business purposes, you can deduct the costs associated with operating the vehicle. The IRS allows you to choose between two methods for calculating the deduction: the standard mileage rate or actual expenses. The standard mileage rate is a simplified method that allows you to deduct a fixed rate per mile driven for business purposes. For 2024, the standard mileage rate is 58.5 cents per mile.

The actual expense method involves calculating the total costs of operating the vehicle, including gas, maintenance, repairs, insurance, and depreciation, and then deducting the portion of these expenses attributable to business use. This method can result in a larger deduction if you have significant vehicle expenses.

Retirement Contributions:

LLCs also provide opportunities for retirement savings, which can be tax-advantaged. Contributions to retirement plans, such as Simplified Employee Pension (SEP) IRAs, Savings Incentive Match Plan for Employees (SIMPLE) IRAs, or 401(k) plans, can be deducted from the LLC's taxable income. These retirement plans allow for substantial contributions, which not only prepare you for the future but also reduce current tax liabilities.

For example, a SEP IRA allows you to contribute up to 25% of your net earnings from self-employment, up to a maximum of $61,000 (for the 2024 tax year). These contributions are tax-deductible, which can significantly lower your taxable income and reduce your overall tax bill.

Health Insurance Deduction:

If your LLC pays health insurance premiums for you as the owner, these premiums may be fully deductible. This deduction can be particularly beneficial if you are self-employed and paying for your own health insurance. The self-employed health insurance deduction allows you to deduct premiums paid for medical, dental, and long-term care insurance for yourself, your spouse, and your dependents, reducing your adjusted gross income and overall tax liability.

Qualified Business Income (QBI) Deduction:

One of the recent tax advantages introduced by the Tax Cuts and Jobs Act of 2017 is the Qualified Business Income (QBI) deduction. This deduction allows eligible LLC owners to deduct up to 20% of their qualified business income, subject to certain limitations and thresholds. The QBI deduction can significantly reduce the effective tax rate on business income for many LLC owners.

For instance, if your LLC generates $100,000 in qualified business income, you may be eligible to deduct $20,000, reducing your taxable income to $80,000. This deduction is available to LLCs taxed as sole proprietorships, partnerships, or S-corporations and provides a substantial tax break for small business owners.

"Understanding the various tax obligations of your LLC is crucial for maintaining compliance and optimizing your business's financial performance. Federal, state, and local taxes all play a significant role in how your LLC operates and plans its finances. Additionally, self-employment taxes and potential deductions can greatly impact your overall tax liability."

Financial Planning and Management Tips

Effective financial planning and management are crucial to the success of your LLC. Proper financial planning ensures that your business has the resources it needs to grow, while good financial management practices help you track and control your expenses, revenues, and profits. In this section, we'll explore strategies for effective financial planning and budgeting, and discuss the importance of maintaining accurate financial records and using accounting software.

Strategies for Effective Financial Planning and Budgeting

Financial planning is the process of setting financial goals, developing a plan to achieve them, and monitoring progress. It involves forecasting revenues and expenses, planning for future growth, and ensuring that your business has the necessary resources to achieve its objectives.

Setting Financial Goals:

The first step in financial planning is setting clear, measurable financial goals. These goals should align with your overall business objectives and provide a roadmap for your financial strategy. Financial goals can include increasing revenues, reducing costs, improving cash flow, and achieving profitability.

For example, if your goal is to increase revenues by 20% over the next year, you need to develop a plan to achieve this target. This might involve expanding your product line, entering new markets, or increasing your marketing efforts. By setting specific financial goals, you can create a focused plan to achieve them.

Developing a Budget:

A budget is a financial plan that outlines your expected revenues and expenses over a specific period. It serves as a roadmap for your business finances, helping you allocate resources, control costs, and monitor financial performance.

When developing a budget, start by estimating your revenues based on historical data, market trends, and sales forecasts. Next, estimate your expenses, including fixed costs (such as rent, salaries, and utilities) and variable costs (such as materials, marketing, and travel). Be sure to include a contingency plan for unexpected expenses or changes in revenue.

For example, if you anticipate $500,000 in revenue for the year, and your fixed costs are $200,000, you can allocate the remaining $300,000 to variable costs and contingencies. By creating a detailed budget, you can ensure that you have the resources to meet your financial goals and respond to changes in your business environment.

Cash Flow Management:

Cash flow management is critical to the financial health of your LLC. It involves monitoring and controlling the flow of cash into and out of your business to ensure that you have enough cash on hand to meet your obligations.

To manage cash flow effectively, start by creating a cash flow forecast that projects your expected cash inflows and outflows over a specific period. This forecast should include all sources of cash, such as sales, loans, and investments, as well as all uses of cash, such as expenses, loan repayments, and capital expenditures.

For example, if your cash flow forecast shows that you will have a shortfall in the next quarter, you can take steps to address this issue, such as accelerating collections, delaying payments, or securing additional financing. By regularly monitoring your cash flow, you can identify potential issues early and take proactive measures to maintain a healthy cash position.

Cost Control and Reduction:

Controlling and reducing costs is essential for improving profitability and maintaining financial stability. Cost control involves monitoring and managing your expenses to ensure that they stay within budget, while cost reduction involves finding ways to lower your expenses without compromising quality or performance.

To control costs, start by reviewing your expenses regularly and comparing them to your budget. Identify any areas where expenses are higher than expected and investigate the reasons for these variances. Look for opportunities to reduce costs by negotiating better terms with suppliers, finding more efficient ways to operate, or eliminating unnecessary expenses.

For example, if your marketing expenses are higher than budgeted, you might explore more cost-effective marketing strategies, such as social media advertising or email marketing, rather than traditional print advertising. By actively managing your costs, you can improve your profitability and ensure that your business remains financially healthy.

Capital Planning and Investment:

Capital planning involves making decisions about how to allocate your business's financial resources to support growth and achieve your long-term goals. This includes decisions about investing in new equipment, expanding facilities, hiring new employees, or entering new markets.

When making capital investment decisions, consider the potential return on investment (ROI) and the impact on your cash flow. Evaluate each investment opportunity based on its expected costs, benefits, and risks, and prioritize those that offer the highest potential returns and align with your business objectives.

For example, if you are considering purchasing new manufacturing equipment, calculate the expected increase in production capacity, the cost savings from improved efficiency, and the potential increase in revenues. Compare these benefits to the cost of the equipment and the impact on your cash flow to determine whether the investment is worthwhile.

The Importance of Maintaining Accurate Financial Records

Maintaining accurate financial records is essential for effective financial management and compliance with tax and regulatory requirements. Accurate records provide a clear picture of your business's financial health, support informed decision-making, and ensure that you can meet your legal and tax obligations.

Tracking Revenues and Expenses:

Accurate financial records allow you to track your revenues and expenses, providing a detailed view of your business's financial performance. This information is essential for budgeting, forecasting, and managing cash flow.

To track revenues and expenses effectively, maintain detailed records of all financial transactions, including sales, purchases, payments, and receipts. Use accounting software to record these transactions and generate financial reports, such as income statements, balance sheets, and cash flow statements.

For example, if your income statement shows that your revenues are increasing but your expenses are rising at a faster rate, you can investigate the reasons for this trend and take corrective action. By regularly reviewing your financial records, you can identify potential issues early and make informed decisions to improve your financial performance.

Supporting Tax Compliance:

Accurate financial records are essential for complying with tax regulations and preparing accurate tax returns. They provide the documentation needed to support your income, deductions, and credits, ensuring that you can accurately report your business's financial activity to tax authorities.

To support tax compliance, maintain detailed records of all income and expenses, including receipts, invoices, and bank statements. Use accounting software to organize and categorize these records, making it easier to prepare your tax returns and respond to any inquiries from tax authorities.

For example, if you are audited by the IRS, having accurate and organized financial records can help you provide the necessary documentation to support your tax return and avoid penalties. By maintaining accurate records, you can ensure that you meet your tax obligations and minimize the risk of errors or audits.

Facilitating Financial Analysis:

Accurate financial records are essential for conducting financial analysis and evaluating your business's performance. They provide the data needed to calculate key financial metrics, such as profitability, liquidity, and solvency, and support informed decision-making.

To facilitate financial analysis, use accounting software to generate financial reports and calculate key metrics. Regularly review these reports to assess your business's performance, identify trends, and make informed decisions about your financial strategy.

For example, if your profitability metrics show that your gross margin is declining, you can investigate the reasons for this trend and take corrective action, such as adjusting pricing, reducing costs, or improving operational efficiency. By conducting regular financial analysis, you can make data-driven decisions to improve your business's financial performance.

Ensuring Legal and Regulatory Compliance:

Maintaining accurate financial records is essential for complying with legal and regulatory requirements, such as filing annual reports, paying taxes, and meeting disclosure requirements. Accurate records provide the documentation needed to support your compliance efforts and avoid legal or regulatory issues.

To ensure legal and regulatory compliance, maintain detailed records of all financial transactions, including income, expenses, assets, and liabilities. Use accounting software to organize and categorize these records, making it easier to prepare and file required reports and meet your compliance obligations.

For example, if your state requires LLCs to file an annual report, having accurate financial records can help you complete the report accurately and on time. By maintaining accurate records, you can ensure that you meet your legal and regulatory obligations and avoid potential penalties or legal issues.

Using Accounting Software

Using accounting software is essential for maintaining accurate financial records, managing your business's finances, and supporting informed decision-making. Accounting software automates many financial tasks, reduces the risk of errors, and provides valuable insights into your business's financial performance.

Choosing the Right Accounting Software:

Selecting the right accounting software for your LLC is essential for effective financial management. Consider factors such as the size of your business, your industry, and your specific financial needs when choosing software.

Popular accounting software options for small businesses include QuickBooks, Xero, and FreshBooks. These platforms offer a range of features, such as invoicing, expense tracking, payroll processing, and financial reporting, to help you manage your business's finances.

For example, if you run a small retail business, QuickBooks may be a good choice due to its robust inventory management features and integration with point-of-sale systems. If you run a service-based business, FreshBooks may be more suitable due to its focus on invoicing and time tracking.

Automating Financial Tasks:

Accounting software automates many financial tasks, reducing the time and effort required to manage your business's finances. Automation can help you streamline processes, reduce the risk of errors, and ensure that your financial records are accurate and up-to-date.

For example, accounting software can automate tasks such as invoicing, expense tracking, payroll processing, and bank reconciliations. By automating these tasks, you can save time, reduce the risk of errors, and focus on growing your business.

Generating Financial Reports:

Accounting software generates financial reports that provide valuable insights into your business's financial performance. These reports help you monitor revenues and expenses, assess profitability, and make informed decisions about your financial strategy.

Common financial reports generated by accounting software include income statements, balance sheets, cash flow statements, and expense reports. By regularly reviewing these reports, you can track your business's financial performance, identify trends, and make data-driven decisions to improve your financial performance.

For example, if you notice that your expenses are increasing faster than your revenues, you can analyze the detailed expense report generated by your accounting software to identify areas where costs can be reduced or optimized. This could involve renegotiating contracts with suppliers, implementing cost-saving measures, or reallocating resources to more profitable areas of your business.

Streamlining Financial Processes:

Accounting software streamlines financial processes by centralizing financial data, automating routine tasks, and providing real-time insights into your business's financial health. This streamlining allows you to manage your finances more efficiently and effectively, reducing the time and effort required to perform routine financial tasks.

For instance, instead of manually entering data into spreadsheets or reconciling bank statements, accounting software automatically syncs with your bank accounts and categorizes transactions, saving you time and reducing the risk of errors. This allows you to focus on analyzing your financial data and making strategic decisions to improve your business's financial performance.

Enhancing Collaboration and Communication:

Accounting software enhances collaboration and communication by providing access to financial data and reports to multiple users within your organization. This allows team members to collaborate on financial tasks, share information, and make decisions based on real-time data.

For example, you can grant access to your accountant or financial advisor, allowing them to review your financial data, generate reports, and provide advice on financial strategy. This collaboration ensures that everyone involved in your business's finances has access to the information they need to make informed decisions and drive business success.

Ensuring Security and Compliance:

Accounting software ensures security and compliance by implementing robust security measures and adhering to industry regulations and standards. This includes measures such as data encryption, access controls, and regular software updates to protect your financial data from unauthorized access and ensure compliance with data protection laws.

For example, reputable accounting software providers implement industry-standard security measures, such as SSL encryption and multi-factor authentication, to protect your financial data from cyber threats. They also adhere to regulatory requirements, such as GDPR and

HIPAA, to ensure that your data is handled securely and in compliance with relevant regulations.

> *"Effective financial planning and management are essential for the success of your LLC. By implementing strategies for financial planning and budgeting, maintaining accurate financial records, and using accounting software, you can effectively manage your business's finances, make informed decisions, and achieve your financial goals. By taking a proactive approach to financial management, you can ensure the long-term success and sustainability of your LLC."*

Hiring Accountants and Financial Advisors

When it comes to managing the financial aspects of your LLC, you may find yourself facing complex tasks and decisions that require specialized expertise. While you may have a solid understanding of your business, navigating the intricate world of accounting, tax planning, and financial strategy can be challenging. This is where professional accountants and financial advisors can play a crucial role in helping you make informed decisions and optimize your financial performance.

Benefits of Working With Professional Accountants and Financial Advisors

Expertise and Knowledge:

Professional accountants and financial advisors bring years of experience and expertise to the table. They have a deep understanding of accounting principles, tax regulations, and financial strategies that can help you navigate complex financial issues with confidence. By leveraging their knowledge, you can make informed decisions that optimize your financial health and position your business for long-term success.

Time and Resource Savings:

Managing your business's finances can be time-consuming and resource-intensive, especially as your business grows. By outsourcing financial tasks to professional accountants and financial advisors, you can free up valuable time and resources that can be better spent on growing your business. Instead of getting bogged down in spreadsheets and tax forms, you can focus on strategic initiatives that drive revenue and profitability.

Compliance and Risk Management:

Navigating the ever-changing landscape of tax laws, regulations, and compliance requirements can be daunting. Professional accountants and financial advisors stay abreast of the latest developments in their field and can help ensure that your business remains compliant with all relevant regulations. They can also help you identify and mitigate financial risks, protecting your business from costly mistakes and penalties.

Strategic Financial Planning:

Professional accountants and financial advisors can help you develop and execute strategic financial plans that align with your business goals. Whether you're looking to expand into new markets, invest in new technology, or optimize your tax strategy, they can provide valuable insights and guidance that drive your business forward. By taking a proactive approach to financial planning, you can position your business for long-term growth and success.

Objective Advice and Perspective:

Running a business can be emotionally and mentally taxing, making it difficult to maintain objectivity when it comes to financial decisions. Professional accountants and financial advisors can provide an objective perspective on your business's financial health and performance.

They can offer unbiased advice and recommendations based on their expertise and experience, helping you make decisions that are in the best interest of your business.

Tips on Selecting the Right Financial Professionals for Your LLC

Define Your Needs:

Before hiring professional accountants or financial advisors, take the time to define your specific needs and objectives. Are you looking for help with day-to-day bookkeeping tasks, tax planning, financial forecasting, or strategic financial planning? By clearly articulating your needs, you can narrow down your search and find professionals who specialize in the areas most relevant to your business.

Evaluate Qualifications and Credentials:

When selecting financial professionals for your LLC, it's essential to evaluate their qualifications and credentials carefully. Look for accountants who are certified public accountants (CPAs) or chartered accountants (CAs) and financial advisors who are certified financial planners (CFPs) or chartered financial analysts (CFAs). These credentials indicate that the professionals have met rigorous education and experience requirements and adhere to ethical standards.

Consider Experience and Industry Knowledge:

Consider the experience and industry knowledge of the professionals you're considering hiring. Look for accountants and financial advisors who have experience working with businesses similar to yours in terms of size, industry, and financial needs. They will have a better understanding of the unique challenges and opportunities facing your business and can provide tailored advice and solutions.

Evaluate Communication and Compatibility:

Effective communication is essential when working with professional accountants and financial advisors. Look for professionals who communicate clearly, promptly, and effectively and who take the time to understand your business and financial goals. Additionally, consider compatibility and rapport when selecting financial professionals. You'll be working closely with them on important financial matters, so it's essential to choose professionals with whom you feel comfortable and confident.

Ask for References and Reviews:

Before making a final decision, ask for references and reviews from past or current clients. This will give you insight into the professionals' track record, reputation, and the quality of their services. Reach out to other business owners or professionals in your network for recommendations and feedback on their experiences working with the professionals you're considering.

Evaluate Fees and Pricing Structure:

Finally, consider the fees and pricing structure of the professionals you're considering hiring. Some accountants and financial advisors charge hourly rates, while others may work on a retainer or project basis. Evaluate the fees and pricing structure carefully to ensure that they align with your budget and expectations. Additionally, consider the value you'll receive in return for the fees charged, rather than focusing solely on the cost.

"Working with professional accountants and financial advisors can provide significant benefits for your LLC, from expert financial guidance and strategic planning to time and resource savings. By carefully selecting the right financial professionals for your business and leveraging their expertise, you can navi-

gate complex financial issues with confidence, optimize your financial performance, and position your business for long-term success."

Chapter 5
Building Your Brand and Marketing Your LLC

Defining Your Brand Identity

Your brand identity is the foundation of your LLC's image and reputation. It represents who you are, what you stand for, and how you differentiate yourself from competitors. A strong brand identity not only helps you attract customers but also fosters loyalty and trust among your target audience. In this section, we'll explore the importance of a strong brand identity and provide steps to help you define yours effectively.

Importance of a Strong Brand Identity:

Building a strong brand identity is not just about creating a logo or choosing a color scheme; it's about defining who you are as a business and how you want to be perceived by your target audience. Your brand identity sets the tone for all your marketing efforts and shapes the way customers perceive and interact with your LLC. Let's explore why a strong brand identity is crucial for the success of your business.

1. Differentiation:

In today's competitive marketplace, standing out from the crowd is more important than ever. A strong brand identity helps you differentiate yourself from competitors by clearly communicating what makes your LLC unique. By defining your unique value proposition and highlighting the benefits of your products or services, you can attract customers who resonate with your brand's message and offerings. Whether it's your innovative solutions, exceptional customer service, or commitment to sustainability, your brand identity should make it clear why customers should choose you over alternatives.

2. Recognition:

Consistency is key to building brand recognition and recall. A strong brand identity ensures that your LLC is easily recognizable across all touchpoints, from your website and social media profiles to your packaging and advertising materials. When customers encounter your brand consistently, they become familiar with your business and are more likely to remember you when making purchasing decisions. This familiarity breeds trust and confidence, making it easier to convert prospects into loyal customers. By investing in a strong brand identity, you can increase brand recognition and establish a strong presence in your industry.

3. Credibility:

A well-defined brand identity signals professionalism and reliability to your target audience. When customers see a cohesive brand identity, they perceive your business as trustworthy and reputable. This credibility is essential for building long-term relationships with customers and earning their loyalty and advocacy. A strong brand identity reassures customers that you are committed to delivering high-quality products or services and that you take their needs and preferences seriously. By consistently delivering on your brand promise, you can strengthen trust and confidence in your LLC and position yourself as a leader in your industry.

4. Emotional Connection:

Beyond the functional benefits of your products or services, a strong brand identity evokes emotions and associations that resonate with your target audience. By tapping into their values, aspirations, and desires, you can create a meaningful connection with customers that goes beyond transactional relationships. Whether it's a sense of belonging, pride, or inspiration, your brand identity should evoke positive emotions and foster a sense of loyalty and affinity among customers. This emotional connection not only drives repeat business but also encourages customers to advocate for your brand and recommend it to others.

Steps to Define Your Brand's Identity:

Defining your brand's identity is a critical step in establishing a strong and memorable presence in the marketplace. It involves digging deep into the core values, aspirations, and unique characteristics that set your LLC apart from competitors. By following these key steps, you can develop a clear and compelling brand identity that resonates with your target audience and drives the success of your business.

1. Clarify Your Mission:

Your brand's mission serves as the guiding force behind everything you do as a business. It encapsulates the overarching purpose or reason for your LLC's existence and defines the impact you aim to make on the world. To clarify your mission, ask yourself what problem you solve for your customers and what drives you as a business owner. Consider the needs and aspirations of your target audience and how your products or services address those needs. Your mission should reflect your core values and beliefs, providing a solid foundation for your brand's identity and direction.

For example, if you run a sustainable clothing brand, your mission might be to provide eco-friendly and ethically sourced apparel options that empower consumers to make environmentally conscious choices. Your mission statement could emphasize your commitment to sustainability, fair labor practices, and reducing the environmental impact of the fashion industry.

2. Craft Your Vision:

While your mission defines your present-day purpose, your brand's vision paints a picture of your desired future. It articulates your long-term goals and aspirations for your business and sets the direction for your growth and development. When crafting your vision, consider where you see your LLC in the years to come and the impact you hope to have on your industry or community.

Imagine the ideal future state of your business and the milestones you aim to achieve along the way. Your vision should inspire and motivate both you and your team, driving innovation and strategic decision-making. It should also resonate with your target audience, aligning with their values and aspirations.

Continuing with the example of the sustainable clothing brand, your vision might be to become a global leader in eco-friendly fashion, known for setting industry standards in sustainability and ethical manufacturing practices. You may envision expanding your product line, opening flagship stores in major cities worldwide, and partnering with environmental organizations to promote sustainable living.

3. Identify Your Values:

Your brand's values are the principles and beliefs that guide your actions and decisions as a business. They define what you stand for and represent the ethical standards you uphold in everything you do. Identifying your values requires introspection and reflection on the core principles that drive your business operations.

Consider the values that are most important to you personally and how they align with your business objectives. Think about the values that resonate with your target audience and reflect their priorities and preferences. Your values should serve as the guiding compass for your brand, influencing everything from product development and customer interactions to marketing messaging and corporate social responsibility initiatives.

For instance, if integrity and transparency are core values for your LLC, you may prioritize honesty in your communication with customers, suppliers, and employees. You might also commit to using ethically sourced materials and providing full transparency about your supply chain and production processes.

4. Define Your Unique Selling Proposition (USP):

Your unique selling proposition (USP) is what sets your LLC apart from competitors and makes your products or services stand out in the marketplace. It identifies the specific benefits or advantages you offer that address the needs or pain points of your target audience. To define your USP, consider what makes your products or services unique, desirable, and worth choosing over alternatives.

Think about the key features, benefits, or characteristics that differentiate your offerings from those of competitors. Consider the value you provide to customers and how your products or services solve their problems or fulfill their desires in ways that others don't. Your USP should be clear, concise, and compelling, communicating a distinct value proposition that resonates with your target audience.

In the case of the sustainable clothing brand, your USP might be your commitment to using organic, eco-friendly materials and sustainable production methods. You might emphasize the superior quality and durability of your garments, as well as their minimal environmental footprint. By highlighting these unique features and benefits, you differentiate your brand from conventional fashion brands and appeal to environmentally conscious consumers seeking ethically made apparel options.

> *"By following these steps, you can develop a clear and compelling brand identity that resonates with your target audience and sets your LLC apart from competitors. Remember to communicate your brand identity consistently across all touchpoints, including your website, marketing materials, and customer interactions, to build a strong and cohesive brand presence."*

Creating a Marketing Strategy

Crafting an effective marketing strategy is essential for reaching your target audience, generating leads, and ultimately driving sales for your LLC. A well-designed marketing strategy outlines the specific tactics and channels you'll use to promote your brand, engage with customers, and achieve your business objectives. In this section, we'll explore the key components of an effective marketing strategy and discuss various marketing channels and tactics you can leverage to maximize your reach and impact.

Components of an Effective Marketing Strategy:

Target Audience Identification:

The first step in creating a marketing strategy is to identify your target audience – the group of people most likely to be interested in your products or services. By understanding your audience's demographics, interests, and pain points, you can tailor your marketing efforts to resonate with their needs and preferences. Conduct market research, analyze customer data, and create buyer personas to gain insights into your target audience and inform your marketing strategy.

Clear Objectives:

Define clear and measurable objectives for your marketing efforts. Whether your goal is to increase brand awareness, drive website traffic, generate leads, or boost sales, having specific objectives allows you to track your progress and evaluate the effectiveness of your marketing activities. Align your marketing objectives with your overall business goals to ensure that your efforts contribute to your LLC's success.

Strategic Messaging:

Develop compelling and consistent messaging that communicates your brand's value proposition and resonates with your target audience. Your messaging should highlight the benefits of your products or services, address customer pain points, and differentiate your brand from competitors. Tailor your messaging to different stages of the buyer's journey, from awareness and consideration to decision-making, to guide prospects through the sales funnel effectively.

Integrated Channels and Tactics:

Identify the most effective marketing channels and tactics for reaching your target audience and achieving your objectives. Consider a mix of online and offline channels, such as digital marketing, social media, content marketing, email marketing, search engine optimization (SEO), paid advertising, events, and public relations. Integrate these channels and tactics into a cohesive marketing plan that maximizes your reach and engagement across multiple touchpoints.

Budget Allocation:

Allocate resources and budget to each marketing channel and tactic based on their potential impact and ROI. Consider factors such as audience size, reach, engagement, and conversion rates when determining your budget allocation. Monitor and adjust your budget allocation over time based on performance data and evolving market conditions to optimize your marketing investment and maximize results.

Measurement and Analytics:

Establish key performance indicators (KPIs) and metrics to track the success of your marketing efforts. Measure metrics such as website traffic, conversion rates, lead generation, customer acquisition cost (CAC), return on investment (ROI), and customer lifetime value (CLV) to evaluate the performance of your marketing campaigns. Use analytics tools and reporting dashboards to monitor progress, identify areas for improvement, and make data-driven decisions to optimize your marketing strategy.

Marketing Channels and Tactics:

Content Marketing:

Content marketing involves creating and distributing valuable, relevant, and consistent content to attract and engage your target audience. This can include blog posts, articles, videos, infographics, ebooks, whitepapers, podcasts, and more. Content marketing helps establish your brand as a thought leader in your industry, build trust with your audience, and drive organic traffic to your website.

Social Media Marketing:

Social media marketing involves using social media platforms such as Facebook, Instagram, Twitter, LinkedIn, and Pinterest to promote your brand, engage with your audience, and drive traffic to your website. Create compelling social media content, engage with your followers, run targeted advertising campaigns, and leverage social media analytics to measure performance and optimize your strategy.

Email Marketing:

Email marketing involves sending targeted and personalized emails to your subscribers to nurture leads, build relationships, and drive conversions. Segment your email list based on demographics, interests, and behaviors to deliver relevant content to your subscribers. Use email automation, personalization, and A/B testing to optimize your email campaigns and improve engagement and conversion rates.

Search Engine Optimization (SEO):

SEO involves optimizing your website and content to improve your organic search engine rankings and drive more traffic from search engines like Google. Conduct keyword research, optimize on-page elements such as title tags and meta descriptions, create high-quality content, build backlinks from authoritative websites, and monitor your site's performance with tools like Google Analytics and Google Search Console.

Paid Advertising:

Paid advertising involves paying for ad placements on various online platforms to reach your target audience and drive traffic to your website. This can include pay-per-click (PPC) advertising on search engines like Google and Bing, display advertising on websites and social media platforms, sponsored content, and influencer partnerships. Set clear objectives, target your ads effectively, and track key metrics to measure the effectiveness of your paid advertising campaigns.

Events and Sponsorships:

Events and sponsorships provide opportunities to engage with your target audience in-person and build brand awareness. Sponsor industry conferences and events, host workshops or webinars, participate in trade shows and exhibitions, or sponsor local community events. These activities allow you to connect with potential customers, showcase your products or services, and establish your brand as an authority in your industry. Collect feedback and data from event attendees to evaluate the impact of your participation and inform future event marketing strategies.

Public Relations (PR):

Public relations involves managing your brand's reputation and building relationships with the media, influencers, and other stakeholders. Develop compelling press releases, pitch story ideas to journalists and bloggers, and secure media coverage in relevant publications and online outlets. Engage with industry influencers and thought leaders to amplify your brand's reach and credibility.

Affiliate Marketing:

Affiliate marketing involves partnering with other businesses or individuals (affiliates) who promote your products or services in exchange for a commission on sales generated through their referral links. Identify potential affiliate partners with relevant audiences and complementary products or services, provide them with marketing materials and tracking links, and incentivize them to drive traffic and conversions for your LLC.

Referral Programs:

Referral programs encourage satisfied customers to refer their friends, family, or colleagues to your business in exchange for rewards or incentives. Develop referral programs that offer discounts, freebies, or exclusive perks to both referrers and new customers. Promote your referral program through email marketing, social media, and other channels to encourage participation and drive word-of-mouth referrals.

Community Engagement:

Engage with your target audience and build a sense of community around your brand by participating in online forums, social media groups, and community events. Listen to customer feedback, answer questions, and address concerns to demonstrate your commitment to customer satisfaction and build trust with your audience. Create user-generated content campaigns, host contests or challenges, and foster conversations that encourage community members to interact and share their experiences with your brand.

> *"Creating a comprehensive marketing strategy involves careful planning, strategic decision-making, and ongoing optimization to achieve your business objectives. By outlining clear objectives, identifying your target audience, and selecting the most effective channels and tactics, you can develop a cohesive marketing plan that drives results for your LLC. Continuously monitor performance, analyze data, and adapt your strategy based on insights and feedback to stay competitive in today's dynamic marketplace."*

Leveraging Digital Tools and Platforms

From building an online presence to engaging with customers and analyzing performance metrics, digital tools and platforms offer a wide range of capabilities to help you achieve your marketing goals. In this section, we'll explore key digital tools and platforms that can enhance your marketing efforts and discuss the importance of having a professional website and utilizing SEO best practices.

Key Digital Tools and Platforms:

Website Builder Platforms:

Building a professional website is essential for establishing your online presence and showcasing your products or services. Website builder platforms like WordPress, Wix, Squarespace, and Shopify offer user-friendly tools and templates that allow you to create and customize your website without any coding knowledge. Choose a platform that best suits your needs and preferences, and design a visually appealing and user-friendly website that reflects your brand identity and engages visitors.

Content Management Systems (CMS):

Content management systems like WordPress and Drupal provide powerful tools for creating, publishing, and managing digital content on your website. With a CMS, you can easily add and update blog posts, articles, product pages, and multimedia content to keep your website fresh and engaging. Take advantage of built-in features such as SEO optimization, mobile responsiveness, and social media integration to enhance your website's performance and user experience.

Email Marketing Platforms:

Email marketing platforms like Mailchimp, Constant Contact, and HubSpot allow you to create, send, and track email campaigns to nurture leads, engage with customers, and drive conversions. Use email marketing automation, personalization, and segmentation features to deliver targeted and relevant content to your subscribers. Monitor email open rates, click-through rates, and conversion rates to measure the effectiveness of your email campaigns and optimize performance over time.

Social Media Management Tools:

Social media management tools like Hootsuite, Buffer, and Sprout Social streamline the process of managing multiple social media accounts, scheduling posts, and analyzing performance metrics. These tools allow you to plan and execute your social media strategy more efficiently, engage with your audience in real-time, and track engagement, reach, and sentiment across different social media platforms.

Analytics Platforms:

Analytics platforms like Google Analytics, Adobe Analytics, and Facebook Insights provide valuable insights into your website traffic, user behavior, and marketing performance. Track key metrics such as website traffic, conversion rates, bounce rates, and referral sources to measure the impact of your marketing efforts and identify areas for improvement. Use analytics data to make data-driven decisions, optimize your marketing strategy, and allocate resources effectively.

Search Engine Optimization (SEO) Tools:

SEO tools like SEMrush, Moz, and Ahrefs help you optimize your website for search engines and improve your organic search rankings. Conduct keyword research, analyze competitor websites, and audit your website's SEO performance to identify opportunities for optimization. Implement on-page SEO techniques such as optimizing meta tags, headings, and content, as well as off-page SEO strategies such as link building and local SEO to increase your website's visibility and drive organic traffic.

Importance of Having a Professional Website and Utilizing SEO Best Practices:

A professional website serves as the foundation of your online presence and is often the first impression that potential customers have of your business. Here's why having a professional website and utilizing SEO best practices are essential for marketing your LLC:

Credibility and Trust:

A professionally designed and well-maintained website instills confidence in your brand and builds trust with visitors. A visually appealing and user-friendly website conveys professionalism and reliability, reassuring customers that they are dealing with a legitimate and reputable business.

24/7 Accessibility:

Unlike traditional brick-and-mortar stores with limited operating hours, a website provides round-the-clock accessibility to your products or services. Customers can visit your website at any time from anywhere, browse your offerings, and make purchases or inquiries, increasing convenience and accessibility for potential buyers.

Global Reach:

With an online presence, your LLC can reach a global audience beyond geographical boundaries. By optimizing your website for search engines and leveraging SEO best practices, you can attract organic traffic from around the world and expand your customer base beyond your local market.

Lead Generation and Conversion:

A professionally designed website with clear calls-to-action (CTAs), compelling content, and intuitive navigation helps generate leads and drive conversions. By providing valuable information, engaging visitors, and guiding them through the sales funnel, your website becomes a powerful tool for converting prospects into customers.

SEO Visibility:

Utilizing SEO best practices improves your website's visibility and rankings in search engine results pages (SERPs), increasing organic traffic and exposure for your brand. By optimizing your website for relevant keywords, creating high-quality content, and earning authoritative backlinks, you can improve your chances of ranking higher in search results and attracting qualified traffic to your website.

"Incorporating digital tools and platforms into your marketing strategy, maintaining a professional website, and implementing

SEO best practices are essential steps for effectively marketing your LLC in today's digital landscape. "

Measuring Marketing Effectiveness

Measuring the effectiveness of your marketing efforts is crucial for understanding what works, what doesn't, and how to optimize your strategies for better results. By tracking key metrics and analyzing data, you can gain valuable insights into the performance of your campaigns and make informed decisions to drive success for your LLC. In this section, we'll explore how to measure marketing effectiveness and provide tips on using analytics tools to make data-driven decisions.

Tracking and Measuring Marketing Effectiveness:

Define Key Performance Indicators (KPIs):

Start by identifying the key metrics that align with your marketing goals and objectives. These could include metrics such as website traffic, conversion rates, leads generated, sales revenue, customer acquisition cost (CAC), return on investment (ROI), and customer lifetime value (CLV). Define clear and specific KPIs that reflect the success criteria for your marketing campaigns.

Set Benchmarks and Goals:

Establish benchmarks and set achievable goals for each of your KPIs based on historical performance, industry standards, and business objectives. Determine what success looks like for your marketing efforts and track progress against these goals over time. Regularly review and adjust your benchmarks and goals as needed to reflect changes in market conditions and business priorities.

Track Attribution and Conversion Paths:

Use analytics tools to track the customer journey and understand how different marketing channels and touchpoints contribute to conversions. Analyze conversion paths to identify which channels and campaigns drive the most valuable leads and sales. Attribute conversions accurately to measure the impact of each marketing effort and allocate resources effectively across channels.

Monitor Website Analytics:

Utilize website analytics tools such as Google Analytics to track website traffic, user behavior, and conversion funnels. Monitor metrics such as traffic sources, bounce rates, time on page, and conversion rates to assess the performance of your website and individual landing pages. Identify areas for improvement and optimize your website to enhance user experience and drive conversions.

Track Campaign Performance:

Measure the performance of your marketing campaigns across various channels and platforms. Use campaign tracking parameters such as UTM parameters in URLs to differentiate between different marketing initiatives and track their effectiveness. Monitor key metrics such as click-through rates, conversion rates, cost per acquisition (CPA), and return on ad spend (ROAS) to evaluate the success of your campaigns and optimize performance.

Evaluate Engagement and Reach:

Assess the engagement and reach of your marketing efforts on social media platforms and other channels. Track metrics such as likes, shares, comments, followers, impressions, and reach to gauge the effectiveness of your content and audience engagement. Analyze audience demographics and behavior to better understand your target audience and tailor your messaging accordingly.

Measure Customer Satisfaction and Loyalty:

Monitor customer satisfaction and loyalty metrics such as Net Promoter Score (NPS), customer feedback, and repeat purchase rates to gauge the effectiveness of your marketing efforts in building long-term relationships with customers. Use surveys, reviews, and feedback mechanisms to collect actionable insights and address any issues or concerns raised by customers.

Tips for Using Analytics Tools and Making Data-Driven Decisions:

Choose the Right Analytics Tools:

Select analytics tools that align with your business needs, budget, and technical capabilities. Consider factors such as ease of use, scalability, integration with other platforms, and the availability of advanced features for data analysis and visualization.

Implement Tracking Mechanisms:

Ensure that tracking mechanisms are properly implemented across all marketing channels and touchpoints to capture accurate data. Use tracking codes, cookies, and pixels to monitor user interactions and attribute conversions across devices and platforms.

Regularly Monitor and Analyze Data:

Regularly monitor and analyze data to identify trends, patterns, and insights that can inform your marketing strategy. Use analytics dashboards and reports to visualize data and track progress towards your goals. Set up alerts and notifications to receive real-time updates on significant changes or anomalies in performance metrics.

A/B Test and Experiment:

Conduct A/B tests and experiments to compare different marketing tactics, messages, and creative elements and determine which ones resonate most with your audience. Test variables such as ad copy, visuals, calls-to-action, landing page designs, and targeting parameters to optimize campaign performance and maximize results.

Iterate and Optimize:

Use data-driven insights to iteratively optimize your marketing strategies and tactics. Identify areas for improvement based on performance metrics and user feedback, and implement changes to refine your approach over time. Continuously test new ideas, measure results, and iterate based on learnings to drive continuous improvement and innovation.

Stay Agile and Flexible:

Adapt your marketing strategy and tactics in response to changing market conditions, consumer behavior, and competitive landscape. Stay agile and flexible in your approach, and be prepared to pivot quickly based on emerging trends, opportunities, and challenges. Monitor industry developments and competitor activities to stay ahead of the curve and capitalize on new opportunities as they arise.

> *"By tracking and measuring the effectiveness of your marketing efforts, utilizing analytics tools, and making data-driven decisions, you can optimize your strategies, allocate resources efficiently, and achieve your business objectives. Continuously monitor performance, analyze data, and refine your approach based on insights to drive sustainable growth and success for your LLC."*

Chapter 6
Technology and Digital Transformation

Digital Tools for LLC Formation

In today's fast-paced digital landscape, establishing your Limited Liability Company (LLC) has never been more accessible, thanks to a myriad of online tools and services specifically designed to streamline the formation process. Let's delve into some of the essential digital tools and platforms that can assist you in setting up and managing your LLC efficiently, ensuring compliance and smooth operations from the start.

Online LLC Formation Services:

Services like LegalZoom, Incfile, and Rocket Lawyer provide comprehensive solutions tailored to your LLC formation needs. These platforms offer step-by-step guidance, document preparation, and filing services, eliminating the complexities associated with paperwork and legal formalities. By leveraging their expertise, you can expedite the formation process and ensure adherence to state regulations, saving valuable time and resources.

Document Preparation Tools:

Document preparation tools such as DocuSign and PandaDoc simplify the creation and customization of crucial legal documents required for LLC formation. From Articles of Organization to Operating Agreements, these platforms offer intuitive templates and electronic signature capabilities, facilitating seamless document generation and management. Say goodbye to tedious paperwork and hello to efficiency and accuracy.

Compliance Management Software:

Stay on top of compliance obligations with software solutions like ZenBusiness and GovDocFiling. These platforms automate compliance tracking, document storage, and deadline reminders, ensuring timely submissions and good standing with regulatory authorities. With compliance management software, you can navigate complex regulations effortlessly, mitigating risks and maintaining your LLC's legal status with ease.

Business Entity Management Platforms:

Platforms like Carta and Capbase provide centralized hubs for managing your LLC's corporate governance and ownership structure. From cap table management to decision-making support, these tools offer robust features to streamline administrative tasks and enhance transparency within your organization. With real-time insights and secure document storage, you can foster accountability and collaboration among LLC members effectively.

Accounting and Bookkeeping Software:

Optimize your financial management processes with accounting software solutions like QuickBooks and FreshBooks. These platforms offer invoicing, expense tracking, and financial reporting capabilities to simplify day-to-day operations. By automating routine tasks and providing actionable insights, accounting software empowers you to make informed decisions and drive financial growth for your LLC.

Collaboration and Communication Tools:

Facilitate seamless communication and collaboration with tools such as Slack, Microsoft Teams, and Google Workspace. These platforms offer instant messaging, file sharing, and project management features to enhance teamwork and productivity. Whether you're working remotely or in a traditional office setting, collaboration tools keep your team connected and engaged, fostering innovation and efficiency.

> *"Embrace the power of digital tools and platforms to streamline your LLC formation and management processes. From document preparation to compliance tracking and financial management, these tools empower you to navigate the complexities of entrepreneurship with confidence and ease."*

Online Legal Services and Documentation

Online legal services now offer efficient and accessible solutions for document preparation and filing, revolutionizing the way entrepreneurs establish their businesses. In this section, we'll explore the benefits of using online legal services for LLC documentation, empowering you to navigate the legal aspects of business formation with confidence and convenience.

Accessibility and Convenience:

One of the primary advantages of online legal services is their accessibility and convenience. With just a few clicks, you can access a wealth of legal resources and tools from the comfort of your home or office. Online platforms provide user-friendly interfaces and intuitive navigation, allowing you to complete essential tasks such as document preparation and filing at your convenience, without the need for lengthy appointments or visits to legal offices.

Cost-Effectiveness:

Compared to traditional legal services, online alternatives often offer more affordable pricing models. Many platforms provide fixed-rate packages or subscription plans that cater to various budgetary constraints. By leveraging online legal services for LLC documentation, you can significantly reduce upfront costs associated with legal fees, making it more accessible for entrepreneurs with limited financial resources to start their businesses.

Expert Guidance and Support:

Online legal services typically employ experienced attorneys and legal professionals who specialize in business law. These experts provide guidance and support throughout the LLC formation process, ensuring that your documents comply with state regulations and legal requirements. Whether you're drafting Articles of Organization or creating an Operating Agreement, you can rely on the expertise of online legal professionals to guide you through each step of the process.

Customization and Tailoring:

Online legal services offer customizable templates and document generators that cater to the specific needs of your LLC. You can tailor your legal documents to reflect your unique business structure, ownership arrangements, and operational preferences. Whether you're a single-member LLC or a multi-member organization, online platforms allow you to create personalized documents that align with your business goals and objectives.

Streamlined Document Preparation:

Gone are the days of wrestling with complex legal jargon and paperwork. Online legal services streamline the document preparation process, providing pre-populated templates and guided workflows that simplify the drafting and customization of essential documents. From

Articles of Organization to Member Resolutions, these platforms ensure accuracy and completeness, reducing the risk of errors or omissions in your LLC documentation.

Expedited Filing and Processing:

Online legal services offer expedited filing and processing options that accelerate the LLC formation timeline. Instead of waiting weeks for paper filings and manual processing, online platforms facilitate electronic submissions and digital signatures, expediting the approval process with state authorities. By leveraging online filing services, you can establish your LLC swiftly and efficiently, enabling you to focus on growing your business without unnecessary delays.

Compliance Assurance:

Compliance with state regulations and legal requirements is paramount for LLCs to maintain good standing and avoid potential penalties or liabilities. Online legal services ensure compliance assurance by staying up-to-date with changing regulations and requirements. These platforms provide built-in checks and validations to ensure that your documents meet the necessary criteria, minimizing the risk of compliance errors or oversights.

> *"Online legal services offer a convenient, cost-effective, and efficient solution for LLC documentation, empowering entrepreneurs to navigate the legal complexities of business formation with ease. From accessibility and affordability to expert guidance and compliance assurance, these platforms provide a comprehensive suite of tools and resources to streamline the LLC formation process."*

Cybersecurity Considerations

In today's digital age, cybersecurity has become a top priority for businesses of all sizes, including Limited Liability Companies (LLCs). As you embark on your entrepreneurial journey, understanding the importance of cybersecurity and implementing robust measures to protect your business from cyber threats is essential. In this section, we'll highlight the significance of cybersecurity for LLCs and provide actionable tips to fortify your defenses against potential cyberattacks.

Understanding the Cyber Threat Landscape:

Cyber threats pose a significant risk to businesses, ranging from data breaches and financial fraud to ransomware attacks and reputational damage. Hackers and cybercriminals are constantly evolving their tactics, exploiting vulnerabilities in technology and human behavior to infiltrate systems and steal sensitive information. As an LLC owner, it's crucial to recognize the evolving nature of cyber threats and proactively safeguard your business against potential risks.

Protecting Sensitive Data:

Your LLC likely handles a wealth of sensitive data, including customer information, financial records, and proprietary business data. Protecting this data from unauthorized access and misuse should be a top priority. Implement robust data encryption protocols to secure sensitive information both in transit and at rest. Utilize secure password management tools to strengthen access controls and enforce regular password updates to mitigate the risk of unauthorized access.

Securing Digital Assets:

In addition to protecting sensitive data, it's essential to secure your LLC's digital assets, including websites, online platforms, and cloud-based applications. Implement multi-factor authentication (MFA) across all digital assets to add an extra layer of security beyond passwords. Regularly update software and applications to patch known vulnerabilities and minimize the risk of exploitation by cyber attackers. Consider investing in cybersecurity solutions such as firewalls, intrusion detection systems, and endpoint protection to detect and prevent unauthorized access to your digital infrastructure.

Educating Employees:

Human error remains one of the leading causes of cybersecurity breaches. Educating your employees about cybersecurity best practices is critical to strengthening your LLC's defenses against potential threats. Provide comprehensive training on recognizing phishing attempts, social engineering tactics, and other common cyber threats. Encourage employees to exercise caution when accessing emails, downloading attachments, or clicking on links from unknown or suspicious sources. Foster a culture of cybersecurity awareness within your organization, where employees understand their role in protecting sensitive data and maintaining the integrity of your LLC's digital assets.

Implementing Incident Response Plans:

Despite your best efforts to prevent cyberattacks, it's essential to prepare for the possibility of a security breach. Develop and implement incident response plans that outline clear protocols for responding to cybersecurity incidents effectively. Define roles and responsibilities within your organization, establish communication channels for reporting incidents, and conduct regular drills and simulations to test the efficacy of your response procedures. By proactively planning for security incidents, you can minimize the impact of potential breaches and expedite recovery efforts to restore normal business operations.

Partnering With Trusted Vendors and Service Providers:

When outsourcing business functions or leveraging third-party services, choose vendors and service providers with strong cybersecurity practices and a demonstrated commitment to data protection. Conduct thorough due diligence to assess the security measures and protocols implemented by potential partners, including data encryption, access controls, and compliance with industry standards and regulations. Establish clear contractual agreements that outline the responsibilities of each party regarding data security and privacy, and regularly monitor and audit vendor compliance to ensure adherence to agreed-upon standards.

Staying Informed and Adapting to Emerging Threats:

Cyber threats are continually evolving, requiring businesses to stay informed and adapt to emerging risks and vulnerabilities. Keep abreast of the latest cybersecurity trends, threat intelligence reports, and industry developments to identify potential risks and vulnerabilities that may impact your LLC. Engage with cybersecurity professionals and industry experts to gain insights into emerging threats and best practices for mitigating risk. Leverage threat intelligence sharing platforms and information sharing partnerships to exchange knowledge and collaborate with other organizations in your industry to strengthen collective defenses against cyber threats.

> *"Cybersecurity is a critical aspect of running a successful LLC in today's digital landscape. By understanding the importance of cybersecurity and implementing robust measures to protect your business from cyber threats, you can safeguard sensitive data, secure digital assets, and mitigate the risk of potential breaches."*

Harnessing Technology for Growth and Innovation

In today's fast-paced business environment, technology plays a pivotal role in driving growth and fostering innovation for Limited Liability Companies (LLCs) across various industries. As you navigate the dynamic landscape of entrepreneurship, understanding how to harness technology effectively can provide your business with a competitive edge and unlock new opportunities for success. In this section, we'll explore the transformative potential of technology and discuss emerging trends and innovations that LLCs can leverage to fuel their growth and drive innovation.

Enhancing Operational Efficiency:

Technology offers LLCs the opportunity to streamline their operations, improve efficiency, and reduce costs across various business functions. By leveraging cloud-based productivity tools and project management platforms, you can optimize workflow processes, enhance collaboration among team members, and increase productivity levels. Implementing customer relationship management (CRM) systems allows you to centralize customer data, track interactions, and deliver personalized experiences, ultimately driving customer satisfaction and loyalty. Additionally, automation tools and software solutions can automate repetitive tasks, freeing up valuable time and resources to focus on strategic initiatives and business growth.

Expanding Market Reach:

Technology enables LLCs to expand their market reach and target audiences through digital channels and online platforms. By establishing a strong online presence, including a professional website and active presence on social media platforms, you can reach a broader audience of potential customers and engage with them effectively. E-commerce platforms and digital marketplaces provide opportunities to sell products and services globally, tapping into new markets and driving revenue growth. Moreover, leveraging search engine optimization (SEO) techniques and online advertising campaigns can increase visibility and attract qualified leads, driving traffic to your digital properties and converting prospects into customers.

Driving Innovation Through Data Analytics:

Data analytics empowers LLCs to make informed business decisions, identify market trends, and uncover actionable insights to drive innovation and growth. By collecting and analyzing data from various sources, including customer interactions, website traffic, and sales transactions, you can gain valuable insights into customer behavior, preferences, and emerging market trends. Utilizing advanced analytics tools and techniques, such as predictive analytics and machine learning algorithms, enables you to anticipate customer needs, optimize marketing strategies, and develop innovative products or services that meet evolving market demands. Additionally, data-driven decision-making fosters a culture of innovation within your organization, enabling you to iterate and refine your business strategies based on real-time feedback and performance metrics.

Embracing Emerging Technologies:

LLCs have the opportunity to leverage emerging technologies to drive innovation and gain a competitive edge in their respective industries. Blockchain technology, for example, offers secure and transparent transactional capabilities, enabling LLCs to streamline supply chain management, verify product authenticity, and facilitate peer-to-peer transactions with greater trust and efficiency. Internet of Things (IoT) devices and sensors allow businesses to collect and analyze real-time data from physical assets, enabling predictive maintenance, optimizing resource utilization, and enhancing operational efficiency. Artificial intelligence (AI) and machine learning (ML) technologies enable LLCs to automate routine tasks, personalize customer experiences, and extract insights from vast datasets, ultimately driving business growth and innovation.

Fostering Collaboration and Remote Work:

Technology facilitates collaboration and remote work, enabling LLCs to tap into a global talent pool, foster cross-functional teamwork, and adapt to evolving work environments. Collaboration tools such as video conferencing platforms, project management software, and document sharing platforms facilitate seamless communication and collaboration among remote teams, enabling LLCs to overcome geographical barriers and operate efficiently in a distributed workforce model. Additionally, cloud-based productivity tools and virtual workspaces provide employees with the flexibility to work from anywhere, empowering them to maintain productivity and collaboration regardless of their location or time zone.

"Technology presents LLCs with unprecedented opportunities for growth, innovation, and competitive advantage in today's digital economy. By harnessing the transformative power of technology, LLCs can streamline operations, expand market reach, drive innovation, and foster collaboration, ultimately positioning themselves for long-term success and sustainability."

Chapter 7
Social Responsibility and Sustainability

Incorporating Sustainable Practices Into Your LLC

Sustainability has become a cornerstone of modern business practices, and its importance cannot be overstated. As a business owner, you have a unique opportunity to integrate sustainable practices into your LLC's operations, not only to contribute to environmental preservation but also to enhance your company's reputation, attract conscientious consumers, and create long-term value. In this section, we'll explore the significance of sustainability in today's business world and provide detailed guidance on how you can incorporate sustainable practices into your LLC.

Understanding the Importance of Sustainability

Sustainability in business refers to conducting operations in a manner that is environmentally responsible, socially equitable, and economically viable. It involves making decisions that take into account the long-term impacts on the planet, people, and profits. Here are some reasons why sustainability is crucial for modern businesses:

Environmental Responsibility:

Businesses have a significant impact on the environment through their use of resources, energy consumption, waste production, and emissions. By adopting sustainable practices, you can reduce your ecological footprint and contribute to the preservation of natural resources and ecosystems.

Consumer Demand:

Today's consumers are more informed and concerned about environmental issues. They prefer to support companies that demonstrate a commitment to sustainability. By integrating sustainable practices, you can attract and retain environmentally conscious customers, thereby enhancing your brand loyalty and market share.

Regulatory Compliance:

Governments worldwide are increasingly enacting regulations to address environmental challenges such as climate change, pollution, and resource depletion. By proactively adopting sustainable practices, you can ensure compliance with current and future regulations, avoiding potential fines and legal issues.

Cost Savings:

Sustainable practices often lead to cost savings in the long run. Energy-efficient technologies, waste reduction strategies, and resource optimization can lower operational costs and improve your bottom line.

Innovation and Competitive Advantage:

Embracing sustainability can drive innovation within your business. By seeking out new technologies, materials, and processes, you can create more efficient and eco-friendly products or services, giving you a competitive edge in the market.

Employee Satisfaction and Retention:

Employees are increasingly looking to work for companies that align with their values. A strong commitment to sustainability can attract top talent, improve employee morale, and increase retention rates.

Integrating Sustainable Practices Into Your LLC

To successfully incorporate sustainability into your LLC's operations, you need to adopt a comprehensive approach that encompasses various aspects of your business. Here are some detailed tips to guide you through the process:

Conduct a Sustainability Audit

Begin by conducting a thorough sustainability audit of your current operations. Identify areas where your business has the most significant environmental impact, such as energy usage, waste generation, water consumption, and supply chain practices. This audit will provide a baseline for measuring progress and help you prioritize areas for improvement.

Set Clear Sustainability Goals

Based on the findings from your sustainability audit, set clear and measurable sustainability goals for your LLC. These goals should align with your business values and long-term vision. Examples of sustainability goals include reducing greenhouse gas emissions, achieving zero waste, conserving water, or sourcing 100% renewable energy. Establishing these goals will provide direction and motivation for your sustainability initiatives.

Implement Energy Efficiency Measures

Energy consumption is a major contributor to a business's environmental impact. Implementing energy-efficient measures can significantly reduce your carbon footprint and operational costs. Consider the following actions:

Upgrade Lighting:

Replace traditional incandescent or fluorescent bulbs with energy-efficient LED lighting. LED lights consume less energy, have a longer lifespan, and provide better illumination.

Optimize Heating and Cooling:

Invest in energy-efficient HVAC systems and programmable thermostats to regulate temperature settings and minimize energy waste. Proper insulation and weatherproofing can also reduce heating and cooling demands.

Use Energy-Efficient Equipment:

Choose energy-efficient appliances, machinery, and office equipment. Look for products with ENERGY STAR certification, which indicates superior energy performance.

Adopt Renewable Energy:

Explore options for sourcing renewable energy, such as installing solar panels or purchasing green energy credits. Transitioning to renewable energy sources can significantly reduce your reliance on fossil fuels.

Reduce, Reuse, and Recycle

Implementing waste reduction strategies can help minimize your environmental impact and contribute to a circular economy. Encourage your employees to adopt the principles of reduce, reuse, and recycle in their daily activities. Here are some practical steps:

Minimize Single-Use Items:

Reduce the use of single-use plastics and disposable products. Encourage employees to use reusable items, such as water bottles, coffee mugs, and shopping bags.

Optimize Packaging:

Evaluate your product packaging and explore eco-friendly alternatives. Use recyclable, biodegradable, or compostable materials, and design packaging that minimizes waste.

Implement Recycling Programs:

Set up recycling stations throughout your office or facility to collect paper, cardboard, glass, plastic, and electronic waste. Partner with local recycling facilities to ensure proper disposal and processing.

Promote a Paperless Environment:

Encourage digital documentation and communication to reduce paper consumption. Implement electronic filing systems and use digital signatures for contracts and agreements.

Sustainable Supply Chain Management

Your supply chain has a significant impact on your overall sustainability efforts. Collaborate with suppliers and partners who share your commitment to sustainability. Here are some strategies:

Evaluate Supplier Practices:

Assess the environmental and social practices of your suppliers. Choose suppliers who prioritize sustainability, ethical sourcing, and fair labor practices.

Local and Ethical Sourcing:

Whenever possible, source materials and products locally to reduce transportation-related emissions and support local economies. Ensure that your suppliers adhere to ethical and sustainable standards.

Transparency and Traceability:

Implement systems to track and verify the sustainability credentials of your suppliers. Transparency in your supply chain builds trust with customers and stakeholders.

Sustainable Product Design

Incorporating sustainability into your product design can enhance your brand's reputation and attract eco-conscious consumers. Consider the following:

Eco-Friendly Materials:

Use sustainable and non-toxic materials in your products. Avoid materials that are harmful to the environment or human health.

Design for Durability:

Create products that are durable and long-lasting, reducing the need for frequent replacements. Consider offering repair and maintenance services to extend product lifespan.

Eco-Design Principles:

Apply eco-design principles, such as lightweighting, modular design, and minimal packaging, to reduce resource consumption and environmental impact.

Employee Engagement and Education

Engaging your employees in sustainability initiatives is crucial for success. Foster a culture of sustainability within your organization by providing education, training, and opportunities for involvement. Here are some ways to engage your employees:

Sustainability Training:

Offer training sessions and workshops to educate employees about sustainability practices and their importance. Provide resources and tools to help them implement sustainable practices in their roles.

Green Teams:

Form sustainability or green teams composed of employees from different departments. These teams can brainstorm and implement sustainability initiatives, monitor progress, and promote a culture of environmental responsibility.

Incentives and Recognition:

Recognize and reward employees who contribute to sustainability efforts. Offer incentives for achieving sustainability goals, such as bonuses, awards, or public recognition.

Sustainable Transportation

Transportation is a significant source of greenhouse gas emissions. By promoting sustainable transportation options, you can reduce your carbon footprint and encourage eco-friendly commuting. Consider the following:

Remote Work:

Encourage remote work and telecommuting to reduce the need for daily commuting. Provide the necessary tools and technology to support remote work arrangements.

Carpooling and Public Transit:

Promote carpooling and the use of public transportation among employees. Provide incentives, such as subsidized transit passes or carpooling rewards.

Electric and Hybrid Vehicles:

If your business relies on a fleet of vehicles, consider transitioning to electric or hybrid vehicles. These vehicles produce fewer emissions and are more energy-efficient.

Sustainable Marketing and Communication

Communicating your sustainability efforts to customers, stakeholders, and the public is essential for building trust and credibility. Incorporate sustainability into your marketing and communication strategies:

Transparent Reporting:

Regularly report on your sustainability goals, progress, and achievements. Transparency builds trust and demonstrates your commitment to sustainability.

Sustainability Branding:

Highlight your sustainability initiatives in your branding and marketing materials. Use eco-friendly packaging, labels, and messaging to convey your commitment to sustainability.

Customer Engagement:

Engage with your customers on sustainability topics through social media, newsletters, and educational content. Encourage them to support your sustainability efforts and provide feedback.

Continuous Improvement and Innovation

Sustainability is an ongoing journey, and there is always room for improvement. Continuously evaluate and refine your sustainability practices to stay ahead of industry trends and emerging technologies. Here are some ways to foster continuous improvement:

Benchmarking:

Compare your sustainability performance with industry peers and best practices. Identify areas for improvement and set new sustainability goals.

Innovation:

Stay informed about emerging sustainability technologies and innovations. Experiment with new solutions and approaches to enhance your sustainability efforts.

Stakeholder Engagement:

Engage with stakeholders, including customers, employees, suppliers, and community members, to gather feedback and insights. Use their input to inform your sustainability strategy.

"Incorporating sustainable practices into your LLC's operations is not just a trend but a necessity in today's business landscape. By embracing sustainability, you can create a positive impact on the environment, attract conscientious consumers, and position your business for long-term success. Sustainability is a journey that requires commitment, creativity, and collaboration, but the rewards are well worth the effort."

Corporate Social Responsibility (CSR) Initiatives

Corporate Social Responsibility (CSR) is an increasingly critical aspect of modern business. It encompasses a company's efforts to conduct business in an ethical, socially responsible manner, balancing profitability with actions that benefit society and the environment. As a business owner, understanding and implementing CSR initiatives can significantly enhance your company's reputation, attract loyal customers, and contribute to long-term success. In this section, we will explore the concept of CSR, its benefits, and provide detailed examples of CSR initiatives that your LLC can implement.

Understanding the Concept of CSR

CSR refers to the responsibility of businesses to contribute positively to society and the environment while achieving their economic objectives. It involves going beyond the legal obligations and engaging in activities that promote social good, environmental sustainability, and ethical business practices. CSR is based on the idea that businesses have a broader role in society than simply generating profits for shareholders.

CSR can be divided into several key areas:

1. **Environmental Responsibility**: Companies take steps to minimize their environmental impact by reducing waste, conserving energy, and adopting sustainable practices.
2. **Social Responsibility**: Businesses contribute to the well-being of communities through philanthropy, volunteerism, and support for social causes.
3. **Economic Responsibility**: Companies engage in fair trade practices, support economic development, and create job opportunities.
4. **Ethical Responsibility**: Businesses uphold high ethical standards, ensuring transparency, fairness, and integrity in their operations.

Benefits of CSR

Implementing CSR initiatives offers numerous benefits to businesses, including:

Enhanced Reputation:

A strong CSR program can significantly boost your company's reputation. Customers, employees, and stakeholders are more likely to support a business that demonstrates a commitment to social and environmental causes.

Customer Loyalty:

Consumers are increasingly choosing to buy from companies that align with their values. CSR initiatives can foster loyalty and attract a dedicated customer base.

Employee Engagement:

CSR programs can improve employee morale, job satisfaction, and retention. Employees are proud to work for companies that contribute to the greater good.

Risk Management:

By addressing social and environmental issues, companies can mitigate risks and avoid potential legal and reputational pitfalls.

Innovation and Growth:

CSR can drive innovation by encouraging businesses to develop new products, services, and processes that meet social and environmental needs.

Attracting Investors:

Investors are increasingly considering CSR factors in their investment decisions. A strong CSR program can attract socially responsible investors.

Examples of CSR Initiatives for LLCs

To effectively implement CSR, your LLC can undertake various initiatives across the key areas of responsibility. Here are some detailed examples:

1. Environmental Responsibility Initiatives

Reducing your company's environmental footprint is a fundamental aspect of CSR. Here are several ways your LLC can promote environmental sustainability:

Energy Efficiency:

Invest in energy-efficient technologies and practices. Upgrade to LED lighting, use energy-efficient HVAC systems, and encourage energy-saving behaviors among employees.

Renewable Energy:

Transition to renewable energy sources such as solar, wind, or geothermal power. Install solar panels on your office building or purchase green energy credits.

Waste Reduction:

Implement a comprehensive waste reduction program. Promote recycling, composting, and the use of reusable materials. Reduce single-use plastics and encourage employees to bring their own reusable containers.

Sustainable Sourcing:

Source materials and products from suppliers who prioritize sustainability. Choose eco-friendly, biodegradable, or recycled materials whenever possible.

Green Office Practices:

Adopt green office practices such as reducing paper usage, promoting digital communication, and encouraging remote work to minimize commuting emissions.

2. Social Responsibility Initiatives

Contributing to the well-being of communities and supporting social causes are essential components of CSR. Here are some ways your LLC can engage in social responsibility:

Philanthropy:

Donate a portion of your profits to charitable organizations or social causes that align with your company's values. Consider establishing a corporate foundation to manage your philanthropic efforts.

Volunteer Programs:

Encourage employees to volunteer their time and skills to support local community projects. Offer paid volunteer days and organize company-wide volunteer events.

Employee Welfare:

Prioritize the well-being of your employees by providing a safe and healthy work environment, offering competitive benefits, and promoting work-life balance.

Education and Training:

Invest in the education and professional development of your employees. Offer training programs, scholarships, and opportunities for career advancement.

Community Support:

Partner with local organizations to address community needs. Support local schools, healthcare facilities, and social services through donations, sponsorships, and volunteerism.

3. Economic Responsibility Initiatives

Economic responsibility involves contributing to the economic development and prosperity of the communities where you operate. Here are some initiatives your LLC can undertake:

Fair Trade Practices:

Engage in fair trade practices by sourcing products and materials from suppliers who provide fair wages and safe working conditions. Support fair trade certification programs.

Job Creation:

Create job opportunities within your community, particularly for under-represented or disadvantaged groups. Offer internships, apprenticeships, and entry-level positions to help individuals gain valuable work experience.

Local Economic Development:

Support local businesses by sourcing products and services locally. Participate in local economic development initiatives and collaborate with other businesses to strengthen the local economy.

Supplier Diversity:

Promote supplier diversity by working with minority-owned, women-owned, and small businesses. Establish programs to identify and support diverse suppliers.

4. Ethical Responsibility Initiatives

Maintaining high ethical standards is crucial for building trust and credibility. Here are some ethical responsibility initiatives your LLC can implement:

Transparency:

Ensure transparency in your business operations by providing clear and accurate information to customers, employees, and stakeholders. Publish regular reports on your CSR activities and performance.

Fair Labor Practices:

Uphold fair labor practices by providing fair wages, safe working conditions, and respecting workers' rights. Ensure that your suppliers and partners also adhere to ethical labor standards.

Anti-Corruption Measures:

Implement anti-corruption measures and policies to prevent bribery, fraud, and unethical behavior. Train employees on ethical conduct and establish whistleblower protection mechanisms.

Customer Rights:

Respect and protect customer rights by ensuring the privacy and security of their personal information. Provide excellent customer service and address customer concerns promptly and fairly.

Case Studies of Successful CSR Initiatives

To further illustrate the impact of CSR, let's examine a few case studies of companies that have successfully implemented CSR initiatives:

1. Patagonia

Patagonia, an outdoor clothing and gear company, is renowned for its commitment to environmental sustainability. The company has implemented several innovative CSR initiatives:

1% for the Planet:

Patagonia donates 1% of its sales to environmental causes. This program has contributed millions of dollars to grassroots environmental organizations.

Worn Wear:

Patagonia encourages customers to repair, reuse, and recycle their clothing through its Worn Wear program. The company offers repair services and sells used Patagonia products at discounted prices.

Environmental Campaigns:

Patagonia actively campaigns for environmental protection and conservation. The company has supported various environmental initiatives, including efforts to protect public lands and combat climate change.

2. Ben & Jerry's

Ben & Jerry's, an ice cream company, is known for its strong social and environmental commitment. Some of their notable CSR initiatives include:

Fairtrade Certification:

Ben & Jerry's sources Fairtrade-certified ingredients to support farmers and workers in developing countries. This ensures fair wages and safe working conditions.

Climate Change Action:

The company is committed to reducing its carbon footprint and addressing climate change. Ben & Jerry's has implemented renewable energy projects and advocates for climate action through campaigns and partnerships.

Social Justice:

Ben & Jerry's actively supports social justice causes, including LGBTQ+ rights, racial equality, and refugee rights. The company uses its platform to raise awareness and drive positive social change.

3. TOMS Shoes

TOMS Shoes is a footwear company that has integrated social responsibility into its business model. Their notable CSR initiatives include:

One for One:

TOMS operates on a "One for One" model, where for every pair of shoes sold, the company donates a pair to a child in need. This program has provided millions of shoes to children worldwide.

Eyewear Program:

In addition to shoes, TOMS has an eyewear program where each purchase of TOMS eyewear helps restore sight to individuals through medical treatment, prescription glasses, or surgery.

Impact Grants:

TOMS provides grants to social entrepreneurs and organizations working on issues such as clean water, safe birth, and bullying prevention. These grants support impactful projects and initiatives.

Tips for Implementing CSR Initiatives in Your LLC

Implementing CSR initiatives requires careful planning and execution.

Here are some tips to help you successfully integrate CSR into your LLC's operations:

Align CSR With Your Business Values

Ensure that your CSR initiatives align with your company's core values and mission. Choose causes and activities that resonate with your business philosophy and goals. This alignment will make your CSR efforts more authentic and meaningful.

Engage Stakeholders

Involve your employees, customers, suppliers, and community members in your CSR initiatives. Seek their input, feedback, and support. Engaging stakeholders creates a sense of ownership and fosters collaboration.

Set Clear Objectives and Metrics

Define clear objectives and metrics for your CSR initiatives. Establish key performance indicators (KPIs) to measure the impact and success of your efforts. Regularly track and evaluate your progress to ensure continuous improvement.

Communicate Your Efforts

Communicate your CSR initiatives and achievements to your stakeholders. Use various communication channels, such as your website, social media, newsletters, and annual reports, to share your progress and impact. Transparency builds trust and credibility.

Start Small and Scale Up

Start with small, manageable CSR initiatives and gradually scale up your efforts. Pilot projects can help you test and refine your approach before expanding to larger initiatives. This incremental approach ensures sustainability and minimizes risks.

Collaborate With Partners

Partner with nonprofit organizations, government agencies, and other businesses to amplify the impact of your CSR initiatives. Collaborations can provide additional resources, expertise, and reach, making your efforts more effective.

Celebrate Successes

Celebrate your CSR successes and recognize the contributions of your employees and stakeholders. Publicly acknowledging achievements reinforces the importance of CSR and motivates continued participation.

Foster a CSR Culture

Embed CSR into your company culture by integrating it into your policies, practices, and values. Encourage employees to embrace CSR principles in their daily work and decision-making processes. A strong CSR culture ensures long-term commitment.

Future Trends in CSR

As societal expectations and environmental challenges evolve, CSR practices will continue to advance. Here are some emerging trends in CSR that businesses should be aware of:

Corporate Activism

Companies are increasingly taking public stances on social and political issues. Corporate activism involves advocating for causes such as climate action, human rights, and social justice. Businesses use their influence to drive change and support advocacy efforts.

Sustainable Development Goals (SDGs)

The United Nations' Sustainable Development Goals (SDGs) provide a framework for addressing global challenges such as poverty, inequality, and environmental degradation. Companies are aligning their CSR initiatives with the SDGs to contribute to global sustainability efforts.

Circular Economy

The circular economy model focuses on reducing waste and promoting the reuse, recycling, and regeneration of materials. Companies are adopting circular economy principles to create closed-loop systems that minimize resource consumption and environmental impact.

Impact Investing

Impact investing involves directing capital towards businesses and projects that generate positive social and environmental outcomes alongside financial returns. Companies are increasingly exploring impact investing opportunities to support sustainable development.

Inclusive Business Models

Inclusive business models aim to create economic opportunities for marginalized and underserved communities. Companies are developing products, services, and business practices that promote inclusivity and address social inequalities.

Technology and Innovation

Advancements in technology are enabling new and innovative CSR practices. Companies are leveraging technologies such as blockchain, artificial intelligence, and data analytics to enhance transparency, efficiency, and impact in their CSR initiatives.

"Corporate Social Responsibility (CSR) is a vital aspect of modern business that goes beyond profit-making to address social, environmental, and ethical concerns. By implementing CSR initiatives, your LLC can enhance its reputation, attract loyal customers, engage employees, and contribute positively to society and the environment."

Engaging With Local Communities

Community engagement is a cornerstone of responsible business practice and a key component of a successful, sustainable business strategy. By actively participating in and contributing to your local community, your LLC can build stronger relationships with stakeholders, enhance its reputation, and foster a positive impact on society. This section explores the importance of community engagement and offers detailed tips on how to build strong, lasting relationships with local communities and stakeholders.

The Importance of Community Engagement

Engaging with your local community is not just a moral obligation but also a strategic business practice. When you invest time and resources in your community, you build a foundation of trust and goodwill that can yield numerous benefits for your LLC. Here are several reasons why community engagement is essential:

Building Trust and Credibility

When your LLC actively participates in community activities and supports local causes, it demonstrates a commitment to the well-being of the community. This helps build trust and credibility with local residents, customers, and other stakeholders. Trust is a crucial element in any business relationship, and by showing that you care about more than just profits, you can earn the loyalty and respect of the community.

Enhancing Brand Reputation

A strong brand reputation is vital for business success, and community engagement can significantly enhance your brand's image. By being seen as a positive force in the community, your LLC can attract more customers and retain existing ones. People prefer to support businesses that are responsible and contribute positively to society.

Fostering Customer Loyalty

Customers are more likely to remain loyal to a business that they perceive as socially responsible and community-oriented. By engaging with the community, you can create emotional connections with your customers, making them more likely to choose your products or services over those of competitors.

Attracting and Retaining Employees

Employees want to work for companies that share their values and demonstrate a commitment to making a difference. Community engagement can enhance your company's appeal as an employer, helping you attract and retain talented individuals who are motivated by more than just financial incentives. Engaged employees are more productive and have higher job satisfaction.

Networking and Collaboration

Engaging with your local community provides opportunities to network and collaborate with other businesses, nonprofits, government agencies, and community groups. These connections can lead to valuable partnerships, new business opportunities, and shared resources that can benefit your LLC.

Supporting Local Economic Development

By supporting local initiatives and contributing to the community's economic development, your LLC can help create a more vibrant and prosperous environment. This, in turn, can lead to a more robust customer base, better infrastructure, and a thriving local economy that benefits everyone.

Tips on Building Strong Relationships With Local Communities and Stakeholders

Building strong relationships with local communities and stakeholders requires a strategic and thoughtful approach. Here are some detailed tips to help you effectively engage with your community:

Understand the Community's Needs and Priorities

Before you can effectively engage with your community, it's essential to understand its needs, priorities, and challenges. Conducting community assessments, surveys, and focus groups can provide valuable insights into what matters most to local residents and stakeholders. This information will help you tailor your engagement efforts to address the community's specific concerns and interests.

Be Present and Visible

Active participation in community events and activities is crucial for building relationships. Attend local meetings, sponsor events, and participate in community projects. Being visible in the community shows that you are genuinely interested in its well-being and are willing to invest time and resources to support it.

Establish Open Lines of Communication

Effective communication is key to building strong relationships with the community. Establish open lines of communication by creating platforms for dialogue and feedback. This can include regular newsletters, social media channels, community forums, and town hall meetings. Encourage community members to share their thoughts, concerns, and suggestions, and be responsive to their input.

Support Local Causes and Initiatives

Identify local causes and initiatives that align with your company's values and mission, and actively support them. This can include sponsoring local events, donating to charities, volunteering, and providing in-kind support. By aligning your business with causes that matter to the community, you can demonstrate your commitment to making a positive impact.

Collaborate With Community Organizations

Partnering with local nonprofits, schools, government agencies, and other community organizations can amplify your impact and help you reach a broader audience. Collaborative efforts can lead to more effective solutions to community challenges and provide opportunities for your LLC to contribute expertise, resources, and manpower.

Encourage Employee Volunteerism

Encourage your employees to get involved in community activities and volunteer their time and skills. This not only benefits the community but also fosters a sense of pride and engagement among your employees. Consider implementing volunteer programs, offering paid volunteer days, and organizing company-wide volunteer events.

Measure and Communicate Your Impact

It's important to track and measure the impact of your community engagement efforts. Use key performance indicators (KPIs) to evaluate the effectiveness of your initiatives and assess the benefits to both the community and your business. Communicate your impact through regular updates, reports, and success stories. Transparency builds trust and demonstrates accountability.

Adapt and Evolve Your Engagement Strategy

Community needs and priorities can change over time, so it's important to regularly review and adapt your engagement strategy. Stay informed about emerging issues and trends, and be willing to adjust your approach to address new challenges and opportunities. Continuous improvement ensures that your efforts remain relevant and impactful.

Foster a Culture of Community Engagement

Integrate community engagement into your company's culture and values. Encourage employees at all levels to embrace the importance of giving back and being active members of the community. Recognize and celebrate the contributions of employees and teams who go above and beyond in their community involvement.

Examples of Community Engagement Initiatives

To illustrate how these tips can be put into practice, here are some examples of community engagement initiatives that your LLC can implement:

Community Development Projects

Invest in community development projects that address critical needs such as affordable housing, infrastructure improvements, and public spaces. Partner with local government and organizations to support projects that enhance the quality of life for residents.

Educational Support Programs

Support local schools and educational programs by providing resources, mentorship, and financial assistance. This can include sponsoring scholarships, funding school supplies, and organizing tutoring programs. Education is a powerful tool for community empowerment, and your support can make a significant difference.

Health and Wellness Initiatives

Promote health and wellness in your community by supporting health-care facilities, organizing health fairs, and funding wellness programs. Encourage healthy lifestyles through initiatives such as fitness challenges, nutrition workshops, and mental health awareness campaigns.

Environmental Sustainability Efforts

Engage in environmental sustainability efforts by organizing community clean-up events, planting trees, and promoting recycling programs. Partner with local environmental organizations to address issues such as pollution, conservation, and climate change.

Economic Empowerment Programs

Support economic empowerment programs that provide job training, entrepreneurship support, and financial literacy education. Help local residents develop the skills and knowledge they need to achieve economic independence and success.

Cultural and Arts Programs

Invest in cultural and arts programs that enrich the community and celebrate local heritage. Sponsor art exhibitions, cultural festivals, and performances that showcase the talents and diversity of local artists and performers.

Disaster Relief and Emergency Support

In times of crisis, such as natural disasters or pandemics, provide immediate support to the community through donations, volunteer efforts, and emergency services. Collaborate with local agencies to ensure a coordinated and effective response to emergencies.

Community Grants and Sponsorships

Establish a community grants program to provide funding for local projects and initiatives. Offer sponsorships for community events, sports teams, and cultural activities. These contributions can have a significant impact on community development and well-being.

Employee-Driven Initiatives

Empower your employees to lead community engagement initiatives. Create employee-led committees or task forces to identify and organize community projects. Provide support and resources to help employees turn their ideas into action.

Measuring the Impact of Community Engagement

To ensure that your community engagement efforts are effective and impactful, it's important to measure and evaluate their outcomes. Here are some key steps to measuring the impact of your community engagement initiatives:

Set Clear Objectives

Define clear and specific objectives for your community engagement initiatives. These objectives should align with your company's values and mission and address the needs and priorities of the community. Setting measurable goals will help you track progress and assess the success of your efforts.

Identify Key Performance Indicators (KPIs)

Identify KPIs that will help you measure the impact of your initiatives. These indicators can include metrics such as the number of people served, funds raised, volunteer hours contributed, and improvements in community well-being. Choose KPIs that are relevant to your objectives and can provide meaningful insights.

Collect and Analyze Data

Collect data on your community engagement activities and their outcomes. This can include quantitative data such as participation numbers, financial contributions, and environmental impact, as well as qualitative data such as feedback from community members and stakeholders. Analyze the data to identify trends, successes, and areas for improvement.

Solicit Feedback From Stakeholders

Gather feedback from community members, employees, and other stakeholders to gain insights into the effectiveness of your initiatives. Conduct surveys, focus groups, and interviews to understand their perspectives and experiences. Use this feedback to refine your approach and address any concerns or suggestions.

Report on Your Impact

Regularly report on the impact of your community engagement efforts. Share updates and success stories through various communication channels, such as newsletters, social media, and annual reports. Transparency builds trust and demonstrates accountability to your stakeholders.

Adjust and Improve Your Strategy

Based on your evaluation and feedback, make adjustments to your community engagement strategy to enhance its effectiveness. Continuously seek ways to improve your initiatives and maximize their impact. Adapting your approach ensures that your efforts remain relevant and responsive to community needs.

Future Trends in Community Engagement

As society evolves, so do the ways in which businesses engage with their communities. Here are some emerging trends in community engagement that businesses should be aware of:

Digital Engagement

Advancements in technology are transforming community engagement. Digital platforms and tools enable businesses to connect with communities in new and innovative ways. Virtual events, online forums, social media campaigns, and digital collaboration tools can enhance engagement and reach a broader audience.

Impact Measurement and Reporting

There is an increasing emphasis on measuring and reporting the impact of community engagement efforts. Businesses are adopting more sophisticated methods to assess their initiatives' social, environmental, and economic outcomes. Impact measurement frameworks and reporting standards are becoming more prevalent.

Collaborative Partnerships

Collaborative partnerships between businesses, nonprofits, government agencies, and community organizations are becoming more common. These partnerships leverage the strengths and resources of each partner to address complex social and environmental challenges more effectively.

Employee-Led Initiatives

Employee-led community engagement initiatives are gaining popularity. Companies are empowering their employees to take the lead in identifying and organizing community projects. This approach fosters a sense of ownership and engagement among employees.

Sustainable Development Goals (SDGs)

Many businesses are aligning their community engagement efforts with the United Nations' Sustainable Development Goals (SDGs). The SDGs provide a comprehensive framework for addressing global challenges and promoting sustainable development. Businesses are adopting the SDGs as a guide for their community engagement initiatives.

Social Innovation

Social innovation involves developing new and creative solutions to social and environmental challenges. Businesses are increasingly investing in social innovation projects that address issues such as poverty, inequality, and climate change. These projects often involve collaboration with stakeholders and the use of cutting-edge technologies.

Conclusion

Community engagement is a vital aspect of responsible and sustainable business practice. By actively participating in and contributing to your local community, your LLC can build strong relationships with stakeholders, enhance its reputation, and create a positive impact on society. The tips and examples provided in this section offer a comprehensive guide to building and maintaining effective community engagement initiatives.

Remember that successful community engagement requires a genuine commitment to understanding and addressing the needs and priorities of the community. By being present, communicating openly, supporting local causes, collaborating with partners, and measuring your impact, you can build lasting and meaningful relationships with your community.

As you continue to engage with your local community, stay informed about emerging trends and be willing to adapt and evolve your strategy.

Embrace the opportunities to make a difference, and recognize that every action, no matter how small, can contribute to the greater good. Through community engagement, your LLC can achieve not only business success but also contribute to the well-being and sustainability of the community it serves.

Building a Purpose-Driven Brand

Creating a purpose-driven brand can be one of the most impactful strategies for your LLC. A brand anchored in social and environmental causes not only fosters customer loyalty and engagement but also drives business success through a deep connection with your audience. This chapter will explore the benefits of having a purpose-driven brand and provide detailed steps on how to align your brand with meaningful causes.

Benefits of a Purpose-Driven Brand

A purpose-driven brand can transform your business in several profound ways. Here are some key benefits:

Enhanced Customer Loyalty and Trust

Customers today are more conscious about the impact of their purchasing decisions. They seek brands that align with their values and contribute positively to society. By building a purpose-driven brand, you show your commitment to these values, thereby fostering a deep sense of trust and loyalty among your customers. When customers believe in your mission, they are more likely to support your business consistently and recommend it to others.

Differentiation in a Crowded Market

In a highly competitive market, standing out can be challenging. A strong brand purpose can differentiate your business from competitors. When your brand represents more than just products or services—

when it stands for something meaningful—you attract customers who share your values and are looking for brands that contribute to the greater good.

Increased Employee Engagement and Retention

A purpose-driven brand can attract and retain talented employees who are passionate about making a difference. Employees are more engaged and motivated when they feel their work contributes to a larger cause. This sense of purpose can lead to higher job satisfaction, improved productivity, and lower turnover rates, as employees are more likely to stay with a company that shares their values.

Improved Brand Reputation

A brand committed to social and environmental causes tends to enjoy a better reputation. Positive brand reputation can lead to increased customer trust, media attention, and overall business growth. When people see your brand as a force for good, they are more likely to support it and advocate for it.

Greater Financial Performance

Studies have shown that purpose-driven companies often outperform their peers financially. By aligning your business with a purpose, you can drive long-term growth and profitability. Customers are willing to pay a premium for products and services from brands that reflect their values, and purpose-driven companies often enjoy higher customer retention rates.

Opportunities for Innovation

A clear brand purpose can inspire innovation. When your business is driven by a mission, you are more likely to seek out creative solutions to societal and environmental challenges. This can lead to the development of new products, services, and business models that differentiate your brand and drive growth.

Steps to Align Your Brand With Social and Environmental Causes

Aligning your brand with social and environmental causes requires a strategic approach. Here are detailed steps to help you build a purpose-driven brand:

Define Your Brand Purpose

Start by defining your brand purpose. Your purpose should go beyond making profits and focus on the positive impact you want to make in the world. Consider the following questions:

- What societal or environmental issues are you passionate about?
- How can your business contribute to solving these issues?
- What impact do you want to have on your community, industry, or the world?

Your brand purpose should be clear, authentic, and aligned with your core values. It should inspire and guide all aspects of your business.

Identify Relevant Causes

Once you have defined your brand purpose, identify specific social and environmental causes that align with it. Choose causes that resonate with your brand values and are relevant to your industry and audience. Research different issues and organizations to understand where your support can make the most impact.

For example, if your brand is focused on sustainability, you might support causes related to climate change, renewable energy, or waste reduction. If your brand is centered on community empowerment, you might focus on education, healthcare, or economic development.

Integrate Purpose Into Your Business Strategy

To truly be purpose-driven, your brand purpose must be integrated into your overall business strategy. This involves embedding your purpose into your company's mission, vision, and values, as well as your business operations, culture, and decision-making processes. Ensure that every aspect of your business reflects and supports your brand purpose.

Mission and Vision:

Your brand purpose should be reflected in your mission statement, which defines your company's overarching goals and the impact you aim to make. Your vision statement should outline your long-term aspirations and how your brand purpose will shape the future of your business.

Values:

Establish core values that align with your brand purpose. These values should guide your actions and decisions, ensuring consistency and authenticity in your efforts.

Operations:

Implement business practices that support your brand purpose. This could include sustainable sourcing, ethical labor practices, or environmentally friendly production methods. Ensure that your operations reflect your commitment to the causes you support.

Communicate Your Purpose

Effectively communicating your brand purpose is essential for building trust and engagement with your audience. Use various channels to share your purpose and the actions you are taking to support it. Be transparent and authentic in your communications, providing clear and compelling messages about your commitment to social and environmental causes.

Website:

Create a dedicated section on your website that outlines your brand purpose, the causes you support, and the impact you are making. Share stories, updates, and testimonials to illustrate your efforts.

Social Media:

Use social media platforms to engage with your audience and raise awareness about your brand purpose. Share content that highlights your initiatives, partnerships, and progress. Encourage your followers to join you in supporting your causes.

Marketing Materials:

Incorporate your brand purpose into your marketing campaigns, advertisements, and promotional materials. Use compelling visuals and narratives to convey your commitment to making a positive impact.

Employee Communication:

Ensure that your employees are informed and aligned with your brand purpose. Provide training and resources to help them understand and communicate your purpose effectively.

Partner With Like-Minded Organizations

Collaborating with like-minded organizations can amplify your impact and enhance your credibility. Partner with nonprofits, social enterprises, and other businesses that share your values and are committed to similar causes. These partnerships can provide valuable resources, expertise, and support, helping you achieve your goals more effectively.

For example, if your brand purpose is to promote environmental sustainability, you might partner with environmental organizations to support conservation projects or advocate for policy changes. Collaborate on joint initiatives, co-host events, and leverage each other's networks to maximize your impact.

Engage Your Employees

Your employees play a crucial role in bringing your brand purpose to life. Engage them in your efforts by providing opportunities for involvement and recognizing their contributions. Foster a sense of ownership and pride among your employees by involving them in decision-making and encouraging them to support your initiatives.

Volunteer Programs:

Implement volunteer programs that allow employees to contribute their time and skills to the causes you support. Offer paid volunteer days and organize company-wide volunteer events.

Employee Initiatives:

Encourage employees to propose and lead their own initiatives related to your brand purpose. Provide support and resources to help them turn their ideas into action.

Recognition and Rewards:

Recognize and reward employees who go above and beyond in supporting your brand purpose. Celebrate their achievements and highlight their contributions in company communications.

Measure and Report Your Impact

Measuring and reporting your impact is essential for demonstrating accountability and transparency. Use key performance indicators (KPIs) to track your progress and assess the effectiveness of your initiatives. Regularly report on your impact to your stakeholders, including customers, employees, and partners.

Impact Metrics:

Define specific metrics to measure your impact, such as the number of people served, funds raised, carbon emissions reduced, or resources conserved. Choose metrics that are relevant to your brand purpose and the causes you support.

Progress Reports:

Regularly publish progress reports that provide updates on your initiatives and their outcomes. Use these reports to share success stories, lessons learned, and future goals.

Stakeholder Engagement:

Engage with your stakeholders to gather feedback and insights on your impact. Use surveys, focus groups, and interviews to understand their perspectives and identify areas for improvement.

Stay Committed and Adaptable

Building a purpose-driven brand is an ongoing process that requires long-term commitment and adaptability. Stay committed to your brand purpose and continuously seek ways to improve and expand your efforts. Be willing to adapt your strategy in response to new challenges and opportunities.

Continuous Improvement:

Regularly review and assess your initiatives to identify areas for improvement. Use feedback and data to refine your approach and enhance your impact.

Innovate and Experiment:

Embrace innovation and experimentation to find new and creative ways to support your brand purpose. Stay informed about emerging trends and best practices in social and environmental responsibility.

Sustainability and Resilience:

Ensure that your efforts are sustainable and resilient in the face of changing circumstances. Plan for long-term success by building a solid foundation and investing in resources and partnerships that can support your initiatives over time.

"Building a purpose-driven brand can transform your LLC into a force for good, creating positive social and environmental impact while driving business success. By defining your brand purpose, aligning with relevant causes, integrating purpose into your business strategy, communicating your commitment, partnering with like-minded organizations, engaging your employees, measuring your impact, and staying committed and adaptable, you can build a brand that resonates deeply with your audience and makes a meaningful difference in the world."

Chapter 8
Personal Development and Entrepreneurial Mindset

Developing an Entrepreneurial Mindset

Cultivating an entrepreneurial mindset is crucial for success in business. This mindset involves a specific set of characteristics and attitudes that enable entrepreneurs to identify opportunities, overcome challenges, and achieve their goals. Understanding these characteristics and how to develop them can significantly enhance your entrepreneurial journey.

Characteristics of a Successful Entrepreneur

Successful entrepreneurs share several key characteristics that distinguish them from others. These traits enable them to navigate the complexities of business and achieve their goals.

Vision and Passion

A successful entrepreneur has a clear vision for their business and is deeply passionate about their work. This vision guides their decisions and actions, helping them to stay focused and motivated. Passion drives them to work hard and persevere through challenges, ensuring that they remain committed to their goals.

Resilience and Perseverance

Entrepreneurs often face setbacks and failures. The ability to bounce back from these challenges and continue pursuing their goals is essential. Resilience involves maintaining a positive attitude, learning from mistakes, and finding new ways to overcome obstacles. Perseverance ensures that entrepreneurs remain determined and do not give up easily.

Creativity and Innovation

Innovation is at the heart of entrepreneurship. Successful entrepreneurs are creative thinkers who constantly seek new solutions and opportunities. They are not afraid to challenge the status quo and are always looking for ways to improve their products, services, or business processes. This creativity drives growth and sets them apart from competitors.

Adaptability and Flexibility

The business environment is constantly changing, and successful entrepreneurs must be able to adapt to these changes. They are flexible in their approach and can pivot when necessary. This adaptability allows them to respond effectively to new opportunities and challenges, ensuring the long-term success of their business.

Risk-Taking and Decision-Making

Entrepreneurship involves taking calculated risks. Successful entrepreneurs are willing to take risks when the potential rewards justify them. They are also decisive, able to make informed decisions quickly and confidently. This combination of risk-taking and decision-making enables them to seize opportunities and navigate uncertainties.

Self-Motivation and Discipline

Entrepreneurs must be self-motivated and disciplined to succeed. They set their own goals and hold themselves accountable for achieving them. This self-discipline ensures that they stay on track and manage their time effectively. Self-motivation keeps them driven and focused, even when facing challenges or setbacks.

Networking and Relationship-Building

Building a strong network is crucial for entrepreneurs. Successful entrepreneurs understand the importance of relationships and actively seek to build connections with others. These relationships can provide valuable resources, support, and opportunities for collaboration. Effective networking helps entrepreneurs to grow their business and achieve their goals.

Tips on Cultivating an Entrepreneurial Mindset

Developing an entrepreneurial mindset involves adopting these characteristics and incorporating them into your daily life. Here are some tips to help you cultivate this mindset:

Set Clear Goals

Establishing clear, achievable goals is essential for staying focused and motivated. Break down your long-term vision into smaller, actionable steps. This will help you to stay on track and measure your progress. Regularly review and adjust your goals to ensure that they remain relevant and attainable.

Embrace Continuous Learning

Entrepreneurs must constantly seek new knowledge and skills to stay competitive. Commit to lifelong learning by reading books, attending workshops, and seeking out mentors. Stay informed about industry trends and best practices. This continuous learning will help you to innovate and adapt to changing circumstances.

Develop a Positive Attitude

A positive attitude is crucial for overcoming challenges and maintaining motivation. Focus on your strengths and achievements, and learn to view setbacks as opportunities for growth. Surround yourself with positive influences, such as supportive friends, mentors, and peers. This positive mindset will help you to stay resilient and persevere through difficulties.

Practice Creative Thinking

Encourage creativity by exploring new ideas and perspectives. Set aside time for brainstorming and experimentation. Challenge yourself to think outside the box and consider unconventional solutions. This creative thinking will drive innovation and help you to identify new opportunities.

Build a Strong Network

Invest time in building and maintaining relationships with others. Attend industry events, join professional organizations, and participate in online communities. Seek out mentors and advisors who can provide guidance and support. Building a strong network will open up new opportunities and resources for your business.

Take Calculated Risks

Entrepreneurship involves taking risks, but these should be calculated and well-informed. Evaluate the potential rewards and drawbacks of each decision. Develop a risk management plan to mitigate potential challenges. Being willing to take calculated risks will help you to seize opportunities and drive growth.

Stay Adaptable

Embrace change and remain flexible in your approach. Be open to new ideas and willing to pivot when necessary. Regularly assess your business strategies and make adjustments as needed. This adaptability will help you to respond effectively to new opportunities and challenges.

Cultivate Self-Discipline

Develop strong self-discipline by establishing routines and managing your time effectively. Set daily, weekly, and monthly goals, and hold yourself accountable for achieving them. Create a structured work environment and minimize distractions. This discipline will ensure that you stay focused and productive.

Seek Feedback

Regularly seek feedback from customers, employees, and peers. Use this feedback to improve your products, services, and business processes. Being open to feedback and willing to make changes will help you to continuously improve and stay competitive.

Reflect and Learn From Experiences

Take time to reflect on your experiences, both successes and failures. Analyze what went well and what could be improved. Use these insights to inform your future decisions and strategies. Learning from your experiences will help you to grow as an entrepreneur and avoid repeating mistakes.

"Developing an entrepreneurial mindset is essential for achieving success in business. By understanding and adopting the characteristics of successful entrepreneurs, you can navigate the complexities of entrepreneurship and achieve your goals. Setting clear goals, embracing continuous learning, developing

a positive attitude, practicing creative thinking, building a strong network, taking calculated risks, staying adaptable, cultivating self-discipline, seeking feedback, and reflecting on experiences are all crucial steps in cultivating this mindset."

Goal Setting and Time Management

Setting clear, achievable goals and managing your time effectively are crucial components of personal and business success. In this section, we will explore the importance of goal setting and provide strategies for effective time management and productivity.

The Importance of Setting Clear, Achievable Goals

Goals serve as the foundation for your efforts and provide direction and motivation. Clear, achievable goals help you focus on what truly matters, measure your progress, and stay motivated. Understanding why goal setting is important will inspire you to take the process seriously.

Direction and Focus

Goals provide a clear sense of direction. Without them, it is easy to become overwhelmed by the many tasks and decisions that arise daily. Goals help you prioritize your efforts, ensuring that you spend your time and resources on activities that move you closer to your objectives. This focus prevents you from getting sidetracked by less important tasks and keeps you aligned with your long-term vision.

Motivation and Commitment

Setting goals gives you something to strive for and keeps you motivated. When you have a clear target, you are more likely to stay committed to your efforts, even when faced with challenges. Goals provide a sense of purpose and urgency, driving you to take action and make progress. The satisfaction of achieving a goal also boosts your confidence and motivates you to set and pursue new objectives.

Measurement and Accountability

Goals provide a benchmark for measuring progress. By setting specific, measurable goals, you can track your achievements and see how far you have come. This measurement helps you stay accountable to yourself and others, ensuring that you remain on track and make necessary adjustments. Regularly reviewing your goals and progress allows you to identify areas for improvement and celebrate your successes.

Clarity and Decision-Making

Having clear goals simplifies decision-making. When faced with choices, you can evaluate options based on how well they align with your goals. This clarity helps you make more informed decisions and avoid distractions that do not contribute to your objectives. Goals also provide a framework for setting priorities, making it easier to determine what tasks and activities are most important.

Strategies for Effective Goal Setting

To set clear, achievable goals, you need to follow a structured approach. Here are some strategies to help you establish meaningful goals and ensure that you stay on track to achieve them.

Define Specific and Measurable Goals

Your goals should be specific and measurable. Instead of setting vague goals like "increase sales," define clear targets such as "increase sales by 20% in the next six months." This specificity helps you understand exactly what you need to achieve and how you will measure success. Measurable goals provide a concrete way to track progress and stay motivated.

Set Realistic and Attainable Goals

While it is important to challenge yourself, your goals should also be realistic and attainable. Setting overly ambitious goals can lead to frustration and disappointment. Consider your current resources, constraints, and capabilities when setting goals. Break down larger goals into smaller, manageable steps to make them more achievable. This approach allows you to build momentum and maintain motivation as you progress.

Establish Time-Bound Goals

Goals should have a clear timeframe for completion. Setting deadlines creates a sense of urgency and helps you stay focused. Time-bound goals also enable you to track progress and make adjustments as needed. When setting deadlines, be realistic about the time required to achieve your goals and consider potential obstacles that may arise.

Align Goals With Your Values and Vision

Your goals should align with your core values and long-term vision. This alignment ensures that your efforts are meaningful and fulfilling. Reflect on what is truly important to you and how your goals contribute to your overall purpose. This connection between your goals and values will keep you motivated and committed to achieving them.

Write Down Your Goals

Writing down your goals increases your commitment and accountability. It also provides a tangible reminder of what you are working towards. Keep your written goals in a visible place, such as your workspace or planner, to reinforce your focus and motivation. Regularly review and update your written goals to reflect your progress and any changes in your priorities.

Create an Action Plan

An action plan outlines the specific steps you need to take to achieve your goals. Break down each goal into smaller tasks and milestones, and establish a timeline for completing them. This detailed plan helps you stay organized and focused, ensuring that you make steady progress. Regularly review and adjust your action plan as needed to stay on track.

Strategies for Effective Time Management and Productivity

Effective time management is essential for achieving your goals and maintaining productivity. By adopting the right strategies, you can make the most of your time and accomplish more with less stress. Here are some key strategies to help you manage your time effectively and boost productivity.

Prioritize Your Tasks

Prioritizing your tasks is crucial for effective time management. Identify the most important and urgent tasks that need to be completed and focus on them first. Use a prioritization method, such as the Eisenhower Matrix, to categorize tasks based on their urgency and importance. This approach helps you allocate your time and energy to the tasks that have the greatest impact on your goals.

Create a Daily Schedule

A well-structured daily schedule helps you stay organized and focused. Plan your day in advance by listing the tasks you need to complete and allocating specific time blocks for each task. Be realistic about the time required for each task and include breaks to avoid burnout. Stick to your schedule as closely as possible, but be flexible enough to accommodate unexpected changes.

Set Time Limits for Tasks

Setting time limits for tasks helps you stay focused and avoid spending too much time on any one activity. Use techniques like the Pomodoro Technique, which involves working in focused intervals (typically 25 minutes) followed by short breaks. This method helps maintain concentration and productivity while preventing fatigue.

Minimize Distractions

Distractions can significantly impact your productivity. Identify common distractions in your work environment and take steps to minimize them. This might include turning off notifications, setting boundaries with others, and creating a dedicated workspace. Use tools like website blockers and focus apps to help you stay on task.

Delegate and Outsource

Delegating tasks to others can free up your time for more important activities. Identify tasks that can be handled by others and delegate them to team members or consider outsourcing. Effective delegation involves clear communication, setting expectations, and providing necessary resources and support. This approach helps you focus on high-priority tasks and leverages the skills and expertise of others.

Use Time Management Tools

There are numerous tools and apps available to help you manage your time more effectively. Consider using task management apps like Todoist, Trello, or Asana to organize your tasks and track progress. Calendar apps like Google Calendar or Microsoft Outlook can help you schedule and manage your time. Time tracking tools like Toggl or Clockify can provide insights into how you spend your time and identify areas for improvement.

Batch Similar Tasks

Batching similar tasks involves grouping related activities together and completing them in a single time block. This approach minimizes context switching and increases efficiency. For example, you can batch tasks like responding to emails, making phone calls, or working on similar projects. This method helps you maintain focus and complete tasks more quickly.

Practice the Two-Minute Rule

The two-minute rule, popularized by productivity expert David Allen, suggests that if a task can be completed in two minutes or less, you should do it immediately. This approach helps you quickly handle small tasks and prevent them from accumulating. By addressing these quick tasks right away, you can keep your to-do list manageable and stay focused on more significant activities.

Review and Reflect

Regularly reviewing and reflecting on your time management practices is essential for continuous improvement. At the end of each day or week, evaluate what went well and identify areas for improvement. Adjust your strategies and schedule as needed to enhance your productivity. Reflecting on your progress helps you stay accountable and make informed decisions about how to manage your time more effectively.

Maintain a Healthy Work-Life Balance

Balancing work and personal life is crucial for long-term productivity and well-being. Overworking can lead to burnout and decreased efficiency. Ensure that you allocate time for personal activities, hobbies, and relaxation. Set boundaries between work and personal time to maintain a healthy balance. Taking regular breaks and vacations can also help you recharge and stay productive in the long run.

Conclusion

Setting clear, achievable goals and managing your time effectively are fundamental components of personal and business success. Goals provide direction, motivation, and a framework for measuring progress. By defining specific, measurable, realistic, and time-bound goals, you can stay focused and committed to your objectives.

Effective time management involves prioritizing tasks, creating a structured schedule, setting time limits, minimizing distractions, delegating tasks, using time management tools, batching similar tasks, practicing the two-minute rule, reviewing and reflecting on your practices, and maintaining a healthy work-life balance. By adopting these strategies, you can make the most of your time, enhance your productivity, and achieve your goals.

Incorporating these practices into your daily routine will help you stay organized, focused, and motivated. As you develop these skills, you will find that you can accomplish more with less stress and create a more balanced and fulfilling life.

Overcoming Challenges and Resilience

Entrepreneurship is filled with unique challenges and opportunities that can test your resolve and resilience. From financial constraints to market competition, the road to building a successful business is often fraught with obstacles. Understanding these common challenges and developing strategies to overcome them is essential for any entrepreneur. Additionally, building resilience and staying motivated are crucial for long-term success.

Common Challenges Faced by Entrepreneurs and How to Overcome Them

Financial Constraints

One of the most significant challenges entrepreneurs face is securing adequate funding. Startups often require substantial capital to cover initial expenses, such as product development, marketing, and operational costs. Limited financial resources can hinder growth and restrict your ability to scale the business.

To overcome financial constraints, consider exploring multiple funding options. Traditional bank loans, venture capital, angel investors, and crowdfunding platforms are all viable sources of capital. Developing a solid business plan and demonstrating potential for profitability can attract investors and lenders. Additionally, managing your finances prudently by maintaining a detailed budget and tracking expenses can help you make informed decisions and stretch your resources further.

Market Competition

In a competitive market, standing out can be challenging. Established companies with more resources and brand recognition often dominate the market, making it difficult for new entrants to gain a foothold.

To overcome market competition, focus on identifying and leveraging your unique selling proposition (USP). Understand your target audience's needs and preferences and tailor your products or services to meet those demands better than your competitors. Effective branding and marketing strategies can help you build a strong brand identity and create a loyal customer base. Networking with industry peers and participating in relevant events can also provide valuable insights and opportunities for collaboration.

Uncertain Market Conditions

Economic fluctuations, changing consumer preferences, and unforeseen events can create uncertainty and disrupt business operations. Navigating these uncertainties requires adaptability and strategic planning.

To mitigate the impact of uncertain market conditions, conduct regular market research to stay informed about industry trends and customer behavior. Diversifying your product or service offerings can reduce dependence on a single revenue stream and increase resilience. Developing contingency plans and maintaining financial reserves can also help you weather economic downturns and other unexpected challenges.

Hiring and Retaining Talent

Attracting and retaining skilled employees is crucial for business growth but can be challenging for startups with limited resources. High turnover rates can disrupt operations and increase recruitment costs.

To attract and retain talent, focus on creating a positive work environment and offering competitive compensation and benefits. Providing opportunities for professional development and career advancement can also enhance employee satisfaction and loyalty. Building a strong company culture that aligns with your values and mission can foster a sense of belonging and commitment among your team members.

Time Management

Entrepreneurs often wear multiple hats and juggle various responsibilities, leading to time management challenges. Balancing strategic planning with day-to-day operations can be overwhelming and impact productivity.

To improve time management, prioritize tasks based on their importance and urgency. Create a structured schedule and allocate specific time blocks for different activities. Delegating tasks to capable team members can free up your time for higher-level strategic planning. Using time management tools and techniques, such as the Pomodoro Technique or time blocking, can also help you stay focused and organized.

Maintaining Work-Life Balance

The demands of entrepreneurship can blur the lines between work and personal life, leading to burnout and reduced well-being. Maintaining a healthy work-life balance is essential for long-term success and overall happiness.

To achieve a better work-life balance, set clear boundaries between work and personal time. Schedule regular breaks and allocate time for hobbies, family, and relaxation. Prioritizing self-care, such as regular exercise, healthy eating, and sufficient sleep, can improve your physical and mental well-being. Developing a support network of friends, family, and mentors can also provide valuable emotional support and guidance.

Customer Acquisition and Retention

Acquiring new customers and retaining existing ones are ongoing challenges for any business. Effective customer acquisition and retention strategies are essential for sustainable growth.

To attract new customers, invest in targeted marketing campaigns that reach your ideal audience. Utilize digital marketing channels, such as social media, search engine optimization (SEO), and content marketing, to increase visibility and engagement. Providing exceptional customer service and building strong relationships with your customers can enhance loyalty and encourage repeat business. Collecting and analyzing customer feedback can also help you identify areas for improvement and tailor your offerings to meet customer needs.

Navigating Regulatory and Legal Requirements

Compliance with regulatory and legal requirements is essential but can be complex and time-consuming. Non-compliance can result in fines, legal issues, and reputational damage.

To navigate regulatory and legal requirements, stay informed about relevant laws and regulations in your industry. Consider consulting with legal professionals or hiring a compliance officer to ensure that your business adheres to all necessary standards. Implementing robust internal policies and procedures can also help you maintain compliance and mitigate risks.

Building Resilience and Staying Motivated

Building resilience and staying motivated are essential for overcoming challenges and achieving long-term success. Resilience allows you to bounce back from setbacks and adapt to changing circumstances, while motivation keeps you focused and driven. Here are some tips for developing resilience and maintaining motivation.

Develop a Growth Mindset

A growth mindset is the belief that your abilities and intelligence can be developed through effort and learning. Embracing a growth mindset encourages you to view challenges as opportunities for growth rather than obstacles.

To cultivate a growth mindset, focus on learning from your experiences and seeking feedback. Embrace challenges and view failures as valuable learning opportunities. Setting incremental goals and celebrating small achievements can also reinforce a growth mindset and build confidence.

Practice Self-Compassion

Entrepreneurship can be demanding, and self-criticism can undermine your confidence and motivation. Practicing self-compassion involves treating yourself with kindness and understanding, especially during difficult times.

To practice self-compassion, acknowledge your efforts and recognize that setbacks are a natural part of the entrepreneurial journey. Avoid harsh self-criticism and instead focus on constructive self-reflection. Practicing mindfulness and stress-reduction techniques, such as meditation or deep breathing, can also help you stay centered and resilient.

Build a Support Network

A strong support network can provide valuable emotional and practical support. Surrounding yourself with mentors, peers, friends, and family members who understand your challenges and can offer guidance and encouragement is essential.

To build a support network, seek out networking opportunities and join professional associations or entrepreneurial communities. Participating in mentorship programs can also connect you with experienced entrepreneurs who can provide valuable insights and advice. Regularly reaching out to your support network for feedback and encouragement can help you stay motivated and resilient.

Set Realistic Expectations

Setting realistic expectations helps you avoid unnecessary stress and disappointment. While it's important to aim high, recognizing the limitations of your resources and time is equally important.

To set realistic expectations, break down larger goals into smaller, manageable tasks. Create a timeline that considers potential obstacles and allows for flexibility. Regularly reassess your goals and adjust your expectations based on your progress and changing circumstances.

Maintain a Positive Outlook

A positive outlook can significantly impact your resilience and motivation. While challenges are inevitable, maintaining a positive attitude helps you stay focused on solutions rather than problems.

To cultivate a positive outlook, practice gratitude by regularly reflecting on your accomplishments and the positive aspects of your entrepreneurial journey. Surround yourself with positive influences, such as inspirational books, podcasts, or mentors. Engaging in activities that bring you joy and fulfillment can also boost your overall well-being and outlook.

Stay Physically and Mentally Healthy

Your physical and mental health directly impacts your resilience and motivation. Taking care of your body and mind is essential for maintaining the energy and focus needed to overcome challenges.

To stay physically healthy, prioritize regular exercise, a balanced diet, and sufficient sleep. Incorporating physical activity into your daily routine can boost your energy levels and reduce stress. To stay mentally healthy, practice stress-reduction techniques, such as mindfulness, meditation, or journaling. Seeking professional support from therapists or counselors can also help you manage stress and build resilience.

Embrace Flexibility and Adaptability

Flexibility and adaptability are crucial traits for overcoming challenges and thriving in a dynamic business environment. Being open to change and willing to adjust your strategies can help you navigate unexpected obstacles.

To develop flexibility and adaptability, regularly assess your business environment and be prepared to pivot when necessary. Embrace new technologies and innovative approaches that can enhance your operations and competitiveness. Encouraging a culture of adaptability within your team can also foster resilience and creativity.

Celebrate Achievements

Celebrating your achievements, both big and small, can boost your motivation and morale. Recognizing your progress and successes reinforces your efforts and inspires you to keep moving forward.

To celebrate achievements, set milestones and reward yourself and your team when you reach them. Acknowledging your hard work and progress can provide a sense of accomplishment and encourage continued effort. Sharing your successes with your support network can also strengthen your relationships and foster a positive environment.

Stay Focused on Your Vision

Keeping your vision at the forefront of your mind can provide a constant source of motivation and direction. Your vision represents your long-term goals and the impact you want to make through your business.

To stay focused on your vision, regularly revisit your mission statement and long-term objectives. Visualize the outcomes you want to achieve and remind yourself why you started your entrepreneurial journey. Aligning your daily activities with your vision can help you stay motivated and committed to your goals.

Seek Continuous Learning and Improvement

Continuous learning and improvement are essential for staying competitive and resilient. The business landscape is constantly evolving, and staying informed about industry trends and best practices can help you adapt and grow.

To seek continuous learning and improvement, invest in professional development opportunities, such as courses, workshops, or certifications. Stay updated on industry news and advancements by reading relevant publications and attending conferences. Encouraging a culture of learning within your team can also foster innovation and resilience.

"Overcoming challenges and building resilience are critical components of entrepreneurial success. Entrepreneurs face a myriad of obstacles, including financial constraints, market competition, uncertain conditions, hiring and retaining talent, time management, maintaining work-life balance, customer acquisition and retention, and navigating regulatory and legal requirements. By understanding these challenges and developing effective strategies, you can navigate the entrepreneurial landscape with confidence."

Balancing Work and Life as an Entrepreneur

As an entrepreneur, you are likely passionate about your business and fully committed to its success. However, it's essential to recognize the importance of maintaining a healthy balance between your work and personal life. Achieving a balance allows you to avoid burnout, maintain your overall well-being, and foster meaningful relationships outside of work. In this section, we'll explore the significance of work-life balance and provide strategies for effectively managing your time and energy.

The Importance of Work-Life Balance

Maintaining a healthy work-life balance is crucial for several reasons. First and foremost, it contributes to your overall well-being and happiness. Constantly prioritizing work over personal life can lead to stress, exhaustion, and burnout, ultimately impacting your physical and mental health. Additionally, neglecting personal relationships and hobbies can lead to feelings of isolation and loneliness, negatively impacting your quality of life.

Furthermore, achieving work-life balance allows you to be more productive and effective in your work. Taking regular breaks and engaging in activities outside of work rejuvenates your mind and body, enabling you to approach tasks with renewed energy and focus. It also provides valuable perspective, allowing you to step back and reassess your priorities and goals.

Finally, maintaining a healthy balance between work and personal life is essential for long-term sustainability and success. Avoiding burnout and maintaining your well-being ensures that you can continue to pursue your entrepreneurial endeavors with passion and enthusiasm over the long term. It also sets a positive example for your team members and encourages a culture of work-life balance within your organization.

Strategies for Maintaining Work-Life Balance

Achieving work-life balance requires intentional effort and commitment. Here are some strategies to help you effectively manage your time and energy:

Set Boundaries

Establish clear boundaries between your work and personal life. Define specific work hours and stick to them as much as possible. Avoid checking work emails or taking business calls outside of these designated hours. Similarly, set boundaries around personal time and prioritize activities that recharge and rejuvenate you.

Prioritize Tasks

Identify your most important tasks and prioritize them based on urgency and importance. Focus on completing high-priority tasks during peak productivity hours and delegate less critical tasks when possible. Remember to set realistic expectations for what you can accomplish within a given timeframe.

Practice Time Management Techniques

Implement time management techniques to maximize productivity and efficiency. Break tasks into smaller, manageable chunks and allocate specific time blocks for each task. Utilize tools such as calendars, to-do lists, and productivity apps to help you stay organized and on track.

Delegate Responsibilities

Recognize that you can't do everything yourself and delegate tasks to capable team members or outsourced professionals. Trusting others to handle certain responsibilities allows you to focus on higher-level strategic tasks and frees up time for personal pursuits.

Schedule Regular Breaks

Take regular breaks throughout the day to rest and recharge. Step away from your work environment, go for a walk, or engage in a brief mind-fulness practice to clear your mind and reduce stress. Incorporate longer breaks, such as vacations or extended weekends, to disconnect from work completely and rejuvenate your energy.

Prioritize Self-Care

Make self-care a priority by taking care of your physical, mental, and emotional well-being. Engage in regular exercise, eat nutritious meals, and prioritize sufficient sleep. Practice stress-reduction techniques such as meditation, yoga, or deep breathing exercises to manage stress and promote relaxation.

Set Personal Goals

In addition to professional goals, set personal goals that align with your values and interests. Whether it's pursuing a hobby, spending time with loved ones, or traveling, having personal goals outside of work provides a sense of fulfillment and balance.

Establish Rituals and Routines

Create rituals and routines that help you transition between work and personal life. Establish a morning routine to set the tone for the day and an evening routine to unwind and relax. Incorporate rituals such as journaling, reading, or practicing gratitude to promote mindfulness and self-reflection.

Learn to Say No

Practice saying no to commitments and requests that don't align with your priorities or values. Recognize that it's okay to decline opportunities that will stretch you too thin or detract from your work-life balance. Set boundaries around your time and energy and prioritize activities that align with your goals and values.

Seek Support

Don't hesitate to seek support from friends, family members, or mentors when needed. Surround yourself with a supportive network of individuals who understand the demands of entrepreneurship and can offer encouragement and perspective. Lean on your support system during challenging times and celebrate successes together.

"Achieving work-life balance is essential for your overall well-being, productivity, and long-term success as an entrepreneur. By setting boundaries, prioritizing tasks, practicing time management techniques, delegating responsibilities, scheduling regular breaks, prioritizing self-care, setting personal goals, establishing rituals and routines, learning to say no, and seeking support, you can effectively manage your time and energy and maintain a healthy balance between your work and personal life."

Chapter 9
Global Perspectives and Expansion Strategies

Expanding Your LLC Internationally

Expanding your LLC into international markets can offer significant opportunities for growth and profitability. However, it also comes with its own set of challenges and complexities. In this section, we'll discuss the benefits and challenges of international expansion and provide steps for successfully expanding your LLC into global markets.

Benefits of International Expansion

Expanding your LLC internationally can provide several benefits, including:

Increased Market Potential:

Venturing into global markets exposes your business to a larger customer base, unlocking new opportunities for growth and revenue generation.

Diversification:

International expansion allows you to diversify your revenue streams and reduce dependence on a single market, making your business more resilient to economic downturns and market fluctuations.

Access to Talent and Resources:

Operating in global markets provides access to a broader pool of talent, resources, and expertise, enabling you to tap into new ideas, skills, and capabilities.

Enhanced Competitive Advantage:

Expanding internationally can strengthen your competitive position by allowing you to gain market share, access new technologies, and leverage economies of scale.

Brand Visibility and Recognition:

Establishing a presence in international markets enhances your brand's visibility and recognition on a global scale, bolstering your reputation and credibility.

Challenges of International Expansion

While the benefits of international expansion are compelling, it's essential to acknowledge and address the challenges associated with venturing into global markets:

Cultural and Language Differences:

Operating in diverse cultural and linguistic environments requires sensitivity and adaptability to local customs, norms, and communication styles.

Legal and Regulatory Compliance:

Navigating complex international legal and regulatory frameworks can be daunting, requiring thorough research and compliance with diverse requirements.

Logistical and Supply Chain Challenges:

Managing logistics, supply chains, and distribution networks across borders presents logistical challenges such as transportation, customs clearance, and inventory management.

Currency Fluctuations and Financial Risks:

Exposure to currency fluctuations, exchange rate risks, and economic volatility in foreign markets can impact profitability and financial stability.

Competitive Pressures:

Entering global markets exposes your business to intensified competition from local and international rivals, requiring you to differentiate your offerings and adapt to competitive pressures.

Steps for Expanding Your LLC Into Global Markets

Successfully expanding your LLC into global markets requires careful planning, strategic decision-making, and execution. Here are the steps to guide you through the process:

Market Research and Analysis:

Conduct comprehensive market research to identify viable international markets with demand for your products or services. Evaluate market size, growth potential, competition, regulatory environment, and consumer preferences.

Develop a Market Entry Strategy:

Based on your market research, develop a market entry strategy tailored to each target market. Consider factors such as market entry barriers, distribution channels, pricing strategies, and localization requirements.

Establish Legal and Regulatory Compliance:

Familiarize yourself with the legal and regulatory requirements of each target market. Ensure compliance with local laws, regulations, tax obligations, import/export regulations, and intellectual property protection.

Build Strategic Partnerships:

Form strategic partnerships with local distributors, suppliers, agents, or joint venture partners to facilitate market entry and navigate cultural and operational challenges.

Adapt Products and Services:

Adapt your products or services to meet the needs and preferences of international customers. Consider factors such as language localization, packaging, branding, and product features to enhance market acceptance.

Invest in Marketing and Branding:

Invest in marketing and branding initiatives to raise awareness of your brand and offerings in target markets. Tailor your marketing messages, channels, and campaigns to resonate with local audiences.

Develop a Global Supply Chain:

Establish a robust global supply chain to ensure seamless sourcing, production, and distribution of your products or services. Optimize logistics, transportation, and inventory management to minimize costs and maximize efficiency.

Leverage Technology:

Leverage technology and digital tools to support international expansion efforts. Utilize e-commerce platforms, digital marketing channels, and analytics tools to reach global customers and track performance metrics.

Provide Excellent Customer Support:

Provide excellent customer support and service to build trust and loyalty among international customers. Offer multilingual customer support, responsive communication channels, and seamless transaction experiences.

Monitor and Adapt:

Continuously monitor market trends, consumer preferences, and competitive dynamics in international markets. Remain agile and adaptable, making necessary adjustments to your strategy, products, and operations based on feedback and insights.

By following these steps and addressing the challenges associated with international expansion, you can successfully grow your LLC into global markets and capitalize on new opportunities for business growth and success. Remember to approach international expansion with careful planning, flexibility, and a commitment to delivering value to customers worldwide.

Navigating Global Business Regulations

Navigating global business regulations can be a complex and challenging task for any company looking to expand its operations internationally. Each country has its own set of laws, regulations, and compliance requirements, making it essential for businesses to understand and adhere to these legal frameworks. In this section, we'll highlight key considerations for complying with international business regulations and provide tips on managing legal and regulatory requirements in different countries.

Understanding International Business Regulations

When expanding your LLC into global markets, it's crucial to familiarize yourself with the legal and regulatory landscape of each target country. Here are some key considerations to keep in mind:

Legal Structures and Business Entities:

Different countries may have varying legal structures and business entity options available for foreign businesses. Research and understand the options available, such as subsidiaries, branches, joint ventures, or representative offices, and choose the structure that best aligns with your business goals and objectives.

Taxation and Financial Regulations:

Tax laws and financial regulations can vary significantly from one country to another. Be aware of tax rates, filing requirements, and compliance obligations in each target market. Consider consulting with tax experts or international business advisors to ensure compliance and optimize tax planning strategies.

Employment Laws and Labor Regulations:

Labor laws and employment regulations may differ across countries, impacting hiring practices, employee rights, wages, benefits, and working conditions. Understand the local employment laws and labor standards to avoid potential legal risks and liabilities related to workforce management.

Intellectual Property Protection:

Intellectual property (IP) laws and regulations safeguard patents, trademarks, copyrights, and trade secrets, protecting your business's intangible assets. Prioritize IP protection by registering trademarks and patents in target markets and implementing strategies to prevent infringement and unauthorized use of intellectual property.

Trade and Import/Export Regulations:

International trade regulations govern the movement of goods and services across borders, including import/export restrictions, tariffs, customs duties, and trade agreements. Comply with trade regulations, obtain necessary licenses and permits, and stay informed about changes in trade policies and agreements that may impact your business operations.

Data Privacy and Security:

Data privacy laws and regulations govern the collection, processing, and storage of personal data, imposing obligations on businesses to protect individuals' privacy rights. Ensure compliance with data protection regulations such as the European Union's General Data Protection Regulation (GDPR) and implement robust data privacy and security measures to safeguard sensitive information.

Tips for Managing Legal and Regulatory Requirements

Managing legal and regulatory requirements in different countries requires careful planning, diligence, and attention to detail. Here are some tips to help you navigate global business regulations effectively:

Conduct Comprehensive Due Diligence:

Before entering a new market, conduct thorough due diligence to assess legal and regulatory risks, understand compliance requirements, and identify potential legal obstacles or challenges. Consider engaging legal advisors or consultants with expertise in international business law to assist with due diligence efforts.

Establish a Legal Compliance Program:

Develop a comprehensive legal compliance program to ensure adherence to applicable laws, regulations, and industry standards in each target market. Designate a compliance officer or team responsible for monitoring regulatory changes, implementing compliance policies and procedures, and conducting regular audits to assess compliance effectiveness.

Seek Expert Guidance:

Engage legal counsel, regulatory experts, or local advisors with knowledge of the legal and regulatory environment in target countries. Collaborate with professionals who can provide guidance on legal matters, interpret complex regulations, and navigate bureaucratic processes effectively.

Customize Contracts and Agreements:

Tailor contracts, agreements, and legal documents to reflect the specific requirements and nuances of each jurisdiction. Ensure that contracts are drafted in accordance with local laws, language preferences, and cultural norms to minimize legal risks and ambiguities.

Stay Informed and Updated:

Keep abreast of changes in international business regulations, legal developments, and emerging compliance trends that may impact your operations. Subscribe to legal updates, regulatory alerts, and industry publications, and actively participate in professional networks and forums to stay informed and exchange knowledge with peers and experts.

Foster Relationships With Regulatory Authorities:

Establish positive relationships with regulatory authorities, government agencies, and industry regulators in target markets. Proactively engage with regulatory stakeholders, seek clarification on regulatory requirements, and demonstrate a commitment to compliance and ethical business practices.

Monitor Legal and Compliance Risks:

Continuously monitor legal and compliance risks associated with international operations and take prompt action to address any issues or concerns that may arise. Conduct regular risk assessments, implement controls to mitigate legal risks, and respond effectively to compliance incidents or regulatory inquiries.

By prioritizing legal compliance, staying informed about regulatory requirements, and seeking expert guidance when needed, you can effectively manage legal and regulatory challenges in international markets and position your LLC for sustainable growth and success.

Cross-Cultural Communication and Management

Global business expansion offers immense opportunities for growth and success. However, effective cross-cultural communication and management are essential for navigating the complexities of international markets and building successful relationships with diverse stakeholders. In this section, we'll discuss the importance of cultural awareness in global business and provide strategies for fostering effective cross-cultural communication and management.

Importance of Cultural Awareness in Global Business

Cultural awareness plays a pivotal role in global business, influencing how companies interact with customers, partners, employees, and other stakeholders worldwide. Here's why cultural awareness is crucial:

Understanding Cultural Differences:

Cultures vary significantly across different regions, impacting communication styles, business practices, social norms, and values. By understanding cultural differences, you can avoid misunderstandings, misinterpretations, and cultural faux pas that may hinder effective communication and collaboration.

Building Trust and Relationships:

Cultural awareness fosters trust and rapport with stakeholders from diverse cultural backgrounds. By demonstrating respect for cultural norms, customs, and traditions, you can build stronger relationships, establish credibility, and enhance collaboration with international partners and clients.

Enhancing Communication Effectiveness:

Cultural awareness improves communication effectiveness by enabling you to adapt your communication approach to the cultural preferences and expectations of your audience. By using culturally appropriate language, tone, and gestures, you can convey your message more clearly and avoid potential communication barriers.

Resolving Conflicts and Negotiating Differences:

In cross-cultural business settings, conflicts and disagreements may arise due to cultural differences in communication styles, decision-making processes, and conflict resolution approaches. Cultural awareness equips you with the skills and insights needed to navigate conflicts constructively, negotiate differences, and find mutually acceptable solutions.

Leveraging Diversity as a Competitive Advantage:

Embracing cultural diversity enables companies to leverage it as a competitive advantage. By fostering an inclusive work environment that values diversity and promotes cultural sensitivity, organizations can tap into the collective knowledge, perspectives, and creativity of a diverse workforce to drive innovation and business growth.

Strategies for Effective Cross-Cultural Communication and Management

To succeed in global business, it's essential to adopt strategies for effective cross-cultural communication and management. Here are some tips to help you navigate cultural differences and foster productive relationships in international settings:

Educate Yourself About Different Cultures:

Take the time to learn about the cultural norms, values, beliefs, and customs of the countries where you conduct business. Invest in cultural awareness training, read books, attend cultural events, and engage with people from diverse backgrounds to broaden your cultural knowledge and perspective.

Practice Empathy and Open-Mindedness:

Approach cross-cultural interactions with empathy, curiosity, and an open mind. Be willing to listen, learn, and adapt to different cultural practices and perspectives. Avoid making assumptions or judgments based on stereotypes, and strive to understand the underlying cultural context of your interactions.

Adapt Your Communication Style:

Adjust your communication style to accommodate the cultural preferences of your audience. Pay attention to nonverbal cues, such as body language, facial expressions, and eye contact, which may vary across cultures. Use clear, simple language, avoid slang or idiomatic expressions that may not translate well, and be mindful of differences in communication etiquette, such as directness versus indirectness.

Show Respect and Cultural Sensitivity:

Demonstrate respect for cultural differences and show sensitivity to cultural norms and taboos. Avoid behaviors or actions that may be perceived as disrespectful or offensive in other cultures. Take the time to greet people using appropriate cultural greetings, show appreciation for local customs, and adapt your behavior to conform to cultural expectations.

Build Trust Through Relationship Building:

Cultivate trust and rapport with international partners and clients through relationship building efforts. Invest time in getting to know your counterparts on a personal level, building mutual respect, and fostering long-term relationships based on trust, integrity, and reliability. Be patient and understanding, and be prepared to invest the necessary time and effort to nurture relationships over time.

Seek Feedback and Clarification:

In cross-cultural interactions, seek feedback and clarification to ensure mutual understanding. Encourage open communication, ask questions to confirm comprehension, and be proactive in addressing any misunderstandings or misconceptions that may arise. Clarify expectations, goals, and responsibilities upfront to minimize confusion and ambiguity.

Develop Cross-Cultural Leadership Skills:

Cultivate cross-cultural leadership skills that enable you to effectively lead and manage diverse teams across geographical and cultural boundaries. Foster a culture of inclusivity, promote diversity and equity, and lead by example through your actions and behaviors. Encourage open dialogue, embrace diverse perspectives, and celebrate cultural differences as strengths that contribute to organizational success.

By embracing cultural awareness and adopting effective cross-cultural communication and management strategies, you can navigate the complexities of global business environments, build meaningful relationships, and drive sustainable success in international markets.

Case Studies of Successful International Expansion

By examining case studies of LLCs that have achieved successful international expansion, we can glean valuable insights into the strategies and practices that contributed to their success. In this section, we'll explore some notable examples of companies that have expanded internationally and analyze the key factors behind their achievements.

Case Study 1: Airbnb

Overview: Founded in 2008, Airbnb has revolutionized the travel and hospitality industry by providing a platform for individuals to rent out their homes or properties to travelers seeking unique and authentic accommodations. Today, Airbnb operates in over 220 countries and regions worldwide, offering a diverse range of lodging options to millions of users.

Strategies and Practices:

Localized Market Entry:

Airbnb's success in international expansion can be attributed in part to its localized market entry strategy. Rather than adopting a one-size-fits-all approach, Airbnb customized its offerings and marketing efforts to suit the preferences and needs of each market. For example, the company tailored its listings, pricing, and promotional campaigns to resonate with the local culture and preferences of users in different countries.

Cultural Sensitivity and Adaptation:

Airbnb prioritized cultural sensitivity and adaptation in its expansion efforts, recognizing the importance of understanding and respecting local customs, traditions, and regulations. By engaging with local communities, forging partnerships with local businesses, and adapting its services to align with cultural norms, Airbnb was able to build trust and credibility in new markets.

Investment in Technology and Innovation:

Airbnb's relentless focus on technology and innovation played a crucial role in its international expansion. The company leveraged cutting-edge digital tools, data analytics, and machine learning algorithms to optimize user experiences, enhance search and discovery capabilities, and personalize recommendations for users in different regions. By continuously innovating and refining its platform, Airbnb stayed ahead of competitors and maintained its position as a leader in the sharing economy.

Strategic Partnerships and Collaborations:

Airbnb forged strategic partnerships and collaborations with local governments, tourism boards, and hospitality industry stakeholders to facilitate its expansion into new markets. By working closely with regulatory authorities and addressing concerns related to housing regulations, tax compliance, and safety standards, Airbnb demonstrated its commitment to responsible business practices and earned the trust and support of key stakeholders.

Case Study 2: Netflix

Overview: Netflix, the world's leading streaming entertainment service, has successfully expanded its presence beyond its home market in the United States to become a global powerhouse in the entertainment industry. With a presence in over 190 countries, Netflix offers a vast library of original and licensed content to millions of subscribers worldwide.

Strategies and Practices:

Content Localization:

A key factor in Netflix's international success has been its emphasis on content localization. The company invests heavily in producing and acquiring content tailored to the preferences and tastes of audiences in different regions. By offering a diverse array of localized content, including original series, movies, and documentaries in multiple languages, Netflix has been able to attract and retain subscribers across diverse cultural backgrounds.

Flexible Pricing and Subscription Models:

Netflix adopts flexible pricing and subscription models to cater to the varying purchasing power and preferences of consumers in different markets. The company offers tiered subscription plans with different pricing levels and features, allowing users to choose the option that best suits their needs and budget. Additionally, Netflix periodically adjusts its pricing strategies and promotional offers to remain competitive and appeal to new audiences.

Investment in Technology and Infrastructure:

Netflix's robust technology infrastructure and scalable streaming platform have been instrumental in supporting its global expansion efforts. The company leverages cloud-based technologies, content delivery networks (CDNs), and advanced encoding algorithms to deliver high-quality streaming experiences to users worldwide. By investing in network optimization, data analytics, and machine learning capabilities, Netflix continuously improves its content recommendation algorithms and personalization features, enhancing user engagement and retention.

Strategic Partnerships and Distribution Deals:

Netflix forms strategic partnerships and distribution deals with local telecommunications companies, media outlets, and content producers to extend its reach and distribution capabilities in international markets. By collaborating with local partners, Netflix gains access to new audiences, secures favorable licensing agreements, and navigates regulatory complexities more effectively. These partnerships also enable Netflix to leverage local expertise and insights to tailor its content offerings and marketing strategies to specific regions.

Analysis and Insights:

From the case studies of Airbnb and Netflix, several common themes emerge that contributed to their successful international expansion:

Adaptability and Flexibility:

Both companies demonstrated adaptability and flexibility in their approach to international expansion, recognizing the need to customize their offerings, strategies, and operations to suit the unique characteristics of each market.

Technology and Innovation:

Investment in technology and innovation played a critical role in enabling Airbnb and Netflix to deliver superior user experiences, optimize their platforms, and stay ahead of competitors in rapidly evolving global markets.

Cultural Sensitivity and Localization:

Airbnb and Netflix prioritized cultural sensitivity and localization in their expansion efforts, acknowledging the importance of understanding and respecting local customs, preferences, and regulations.

Strategic Partnerships and Collaborations:

Strategic partnerships and collaborations with local stakeholders, including governments, businesses, and content producers, were key enablers of international expansion for both companies. These partnerships helped Airbnb and Netflix navigate regulatory complexities, gain access to new markets, and establish credibility and trust with local communities.

By studying these case studies and understanding the strategies and practices that contributed to their success, you can gain valuable insights and inspiration for your own international expansion efforts.

Chapter 10
Future Trends and Innovations

Emerging Technologies Shaping the Future of LLCs

In the rapidly evolving landscape of business, emerging technologies play a pivotal role in shaping the future trajectory of LLCs. As an entrepreneur or business owner, it's essential to stay abreast of these technological advancements and leverage them to drive innovation, enhance efficiency, and gain a competitive edge. In this section, we'll explore some of the key emerging technologies that are likely to impact LLCs in the future and provide actionable tips on how you can stay ahead of these trends.

Emerging Technologies Shaping the Future of LLCs

Artificial Intelligence (AI) and Machine Learning:

Artificial intelligence and machine learning are poised to revolutionize various aspects of business operations, from customer service and marketing to supply chain management and decision-making. AI-powered tools and algorithms can analyze vast amounts of data, uncover valuable insights, automate repetitive tasks, and personalize interactions with customers. To stay ahead of the curve, consider integrating AI and machine learning technologies into your LLC's operations. Invest in AI-powered analytics platforms, chatbots for customer support, and predictive analytics tools to optimize business processes and drive growth.

Internet of Things (IoT):

The Internet of Things (IoT) refers to the network of interconnected devices and sensors that collect and exchange data over the internet. In the context of LLCs, IoT technologies offer opportunities to improve operational efficiency, monitor assets in real-time, and enhance the customer experience. By leveraging IoT-enabled devices such as smart sensors, connected appliances, and wearable gadgets, you can gather valuable data insights, automate workflows, and deliver personalized services to customers. To capitalize on IoT trends, explore IoT solutions tailored to your industry and invest in infrastructure that supports IoT integration.

Blockchain Technology:

Blockchain technology, best known as the underlying technology behind cryptocurrencies like Bitcoin, has far-reaching implications for LLCs, particularly in the realms of finance, supply chain management, and digital identity verification. Blockchain's decentralized and tamper-proof ledger system can streamline transactions, enhance security, and facilitate transparent record-keeping. Consider exploring blockchain-based solutions for payment processing, supply chain tracking, and digital contracts to improve transparency, reduce costs, and mitigate risks in your business operations.

Augmented Reality (AR) and Virtual Reality (VR):

Augmented reality (AR) and virtual reality (VR) technologies have the potential to revolutionize customer engagement, employee training, and product visualization for LLCs. AR and VR applications can create immersive experiences that enable customers to interact with products virtually, visualize designs in real-world environments, and participate in virtual training simulations. To harness the power of AR and VR, consider developing branded AR/VR experiences, incorporating AR-enabled product demonstrations, and leveraging VR for employee training and collaboration.

Quantum Computing:

Quantum computing, still in its nascent stages, holds promise for tackling complex computational problems that are beyond the capabilities of classical computers. While quantum computing is currently limited to research labs and specialized applications, its potential impact on industries such as finance, healthcare, and cybersecurity cannot be overlooked. Keep an eye on advancements in quantum computing technology and explore potential applications for your LLC, such as optimizing supply chain logistics, enhancing cybersecurity protocols, or accelerating data analysis tasks.

Tips for Staying Ahead of Technological Trends and Innovations

Continuous Learning and Education:

Stay informed about emerging technologies and industry trends by attending conferences, webinars, and workshops, enrolling in online courses, and reading industry publications. Invest in ongoing learning and professional development to expand your knowledge base and stay ahead of the curve.

Networking and Collaboration:

Build a network of industry peers, mentors, and experts who can provide valuable insights and guidance on emerging technologies. Collaborate with technology partners, startups, and research institutions to explore innovative solutions and potential collaborations that can drive business growth.

Experimentation and Pilot Projects:

Embrace a culture of experimentation and innovation within your LLC by encouraging employees to explore new technologies and ideas. Pilot test emerging technologies in controlled environments to assess their feasibility, scalability, and impact on business outcomes before scaling up implementation.

Strategic Partnerships and Alliances:

Forge strategic partnerships and alliances with technology vendors, startups, and research institutions to gain access to cutting-edge technologies, expertise, and resources. Collaborate with industry leaders and innovators to co-create solutions tailored to your business needs and market demands.

Agility and Adaptability:

Maintain agility and adaptability in your business strategies and operations to respond effectively to changing technological landscapes and market dynamics. Foster a culture of innovation, creativity, and agility within your organization to embrace change and capitalize on new opportunities as they arise.

By embracing emerging technologies and adopting a proactive approach to innovation, you can position your LLC for long-term success and competitiveness in an increasingly digital and dynamic business environment. Stay curious, stay adaptable, and stay ahead of the curve to thrive in the future of business.

Regulatory Developments and Policy Trends

As an entrepreneur or business owner, it's crucial to stay informed about potential changes in regulations and policies that may affect your LLC and develop strategies to adapt to these developments effectively. In this section, we'll explore some of the key regulatory developments and policy trends that may impact LLCs and provide actionable strategies for navigating and adapting to regulatory changes.

Potential Changes in Regulations and Policies Affecting LLCs

Taxation Policies:

Taxation policies, both at the national and international levels, are subject to constant changes and revisions. Potential changes in tax laws, including corporate tax rates, deductions, and incentives, can significantly impact the financial planning and tax obligations of LLCs. Stay updated on proposed tax reforms, legislative changes, and international tax treaties that may affect your LLC's tax liabilities, compliance requirements, and overall financial strategy.

Data Privacy and Security Regulations:

With the increasing prevalence of data breaches and privacy concerns, governments around the world are enacting stringent data privacy and security regulations to protect consumer data and ensure transparency and accountability in data handling practices. Keep an eye on evolving data protection laws, such as the General Data Protection Regulation (GDPR) in the European Union and the California Consumer Privacy Act (CCPA) in the United States, and assess their potential impact on your LLC's data management processes, compliance efforts, and risk mitigation strategies.

Environmental Regulations:

Environmental regulations and sustainability initiatives are gaining prominence globally as governments seek to address climate change, pollution, and resource depletion. Anticipate potential changes in environmental regulations, such as emissions standards, waste management requirements, and renewable energy incentives, that may impact your LLC's operations, supply chain practices, and corporate social responsibility efforts. Proactively assess your environmental footprint, adopt sustainable practices, and comply with applicable regulations to minimize risks and capitalize on emerging opportunities in the green economy.

Employment Laws and Workplace Regulations:

Labor laws and workplace regulations govern various aspects of employment, including wages, working conditions, employee rights, and diversity and inclusion initiatives. Stay abreast of changes in labor laws, such as minimum wage increases, overtime regulations, and anti-discrimination policies, that may affect your LLC's hiring practices, employee benefits, and human resource management policies. Implement fair and inclusive employment practices, foster a positive work culture, and comply with relevant labor regulations to attract and retain top talent and mitigate legal risks.

Trade Policies and Tariffs:

Trade policies and tariffs have a significant impact on global supply chains, trade relations, and market dynamics. Monitor developments in trade negotiations, trade agreements, and tariff structures that may affect your LLC's import/export activities, international trade partnerships, and procurement strategies. Assess the potential impact of trade disputes, tariff changes, and trade barriers on your supply chain costs, competitiveness, and market access. Diversify your supply chain, explore alternative sourcing options, and develop contingency plans to mitigate risks arising from trade policy changes and geopolitical tensions.

Strategies for Adapting to Regulatory Developments

Stay Informed and Proactive:

Stay abreast of regulatory developments, policy changes, and industry trends by monitoring government websites, regulatory publications, industry associations, and news sources. Establish a proactive approach

226

to compliance by conducting regular assessments of regulatory requirements, conducting impact analyses, and developing action plans to address emerging regulatory challenges.

Engage With Regulatory Authorities:

Engage with regulatory authorities, industry regulators, and legal experts to seek guidance, clarification, and interpretation of regulatory requirements. Participate in industry forums, regulatory consultations, and stakeholder engagements to voice your concerns, provide feedback, and influence the development of regulatory policies that affect your business operations.

Invest in Compliance and Risk Management:

Invest in robust compliance programs, risk management systems, and internal controls to ensure adherence to regulatory requirements, mitigate compliance risks, and safeguard your LLC's reputation and integrity. Implement compliance training programs, conduct regular audits, and establish reporting mechanisms to monitor and address compliance violations effectively.

Embrace Technology and Automation:

Leverage technology and automation tools to streamline compliance processes, enhance regulatory reporting capabilities, and improve data accuracy and integrity. Invest in compliance management software, data analytics tools, and digital platforms that facilitate real-time monitoring, reporting, and decision-making to navigate regulatory complexities efficiently.

Foster a Culture of Compliance and Ethics:

Promote a culture of compliance, ethics, and integrity within your LLC by establishing clear policies, codes of conduct, and ethical guidelines that govern business conduct and decision-making. Educate employees about their responsibilities, ethical obligations, and compliance requirements, and encourage open communication, transparency, and accountability at all levels of the organization.

By staying vigilant, proactive, and adaptive in your approach to regulatory compliance, you can effectively navigate regulatory developments, mitigate compliance risks, and position your LLC for long-term success and sustainability in a dynamic and evolving regulatory landscape.

Anticipating Future Challenges and Opportunities

Anticipating future challenges and opportunities is a critical aspect of strategic planning for Limited Liability Companies (LLCs). As the business landscape continues to evolve rapidly, LLCs must proactively identify potential challenges and develop effective strategies to address them while also capitalizing on emerging opportunities. In this section, we will explore some of the potential future challenges that LLCs might face and provide actionable tips on how you can anticipate and prepare for these challenges.

Potential Future Challenges for LLCs

Economic Uncertainty:

Economic volatility, market disruptions, and geopolitical tensions can pose significant challenges for LLCs, affecting consumer confidence, market demand, and business operations. Anticipate potential economic downturns, recessions, or market fluctuations that may impact your industry or target market. Maintain financial resilience by diversifying revenue streams, optimizing costs, and building cash reserves to weather economic uncertainties and sustain business operations during challenging times.

Technological Disruption:

Rapid advancements in technology, automation, and artificial intelligence (AI) are reshaping industries, disrupting traditional business models, and creating both opportunities and challenges for LLCs. Anticipate technological disruptions in your industry, such as the rise of e-commerce, digital transformation, and the proliferation of smart technologies. Embrace innovation, invest in emerging technologies, and adapt your business processes and operations to leverage technological advancements effectively.

Regulatory Changes:

Regulatory frameworks, laws, and policies are subject to constant changes and revisions, posing compliance challenges and legal risks for LLCs. Anticipate potential regulatory changes, amendments, or new legislations that may affect your industry, operations, and market competitiveness. Stay informed about evolving regulatory requirements, engage with regulatory authorities, and proactively adapt your compliance programs and practices to ensure adherence to applicable laws and regulations.

Talent Acquisition and Retention:

The global talent landscape is evolving, with increased competition for skilled professionals, demographic shifts, and changing workforce preferences. Anticipate challenges in talent acquisition, recruitment, and retention, including skill shortages, talent gaps, and employee turnover. Develop proactive talent management strategies, foster a positive work culture, and invest in employee development, training, and career advancement opportunities to attract and retain top talent.

Environmental and Social Risks:

Environmental sustainability, social responsibility, and corporate citizenship are becoming increasingly important considerations for businesses worldwide. Anticipate potential environmental risks, social impacts, and ethical concerns associated with your business operations, supply chain practices, and corporate activities. Adopt sustainable business practices, implement responsible sourcing policies, and engage in community initiatives to mitigate environmental and social risks and enhance your brand reputation.

Tips for Anticipating and Preparing for Future Challenges

Conduct Scenario Planning:

Conduct scenario planning exercises to anticipate and prepare for potential future challenges and uncertainties. Identify various plausible scenarios, assess their likelihood and impact on your business, and develop contingency plans and strategies to address each scenario effectively. Scenario planning enables you to enhance your strategic foresight, mitigate risks, and capitalize on emerging opportunities.

Foster Innovation and Adaptability:

Foster a culture of innovation, agility, and adaptability within your LLC to respond effectively to changing market dynamics and evolving business environments. Encourage creativity, experimentation, and continuous improvement across all levels of the organization. Embrace change, embrace change, and empower your teams to proactively identify and implement innovative solutions to address future challenges and drive sustainable growth.

Build Strategic Partnerships:

Forge strategic partnerships and collaborations with industry peers, academic institutions, research organizations, and technology providers to access expertise, resources, and opportunities for innovation and growth. Collaborate with external stakeholders to share knowledge, exchange best practices, and co-create solutions to address common challenges and capitalize on emerging trends and opportunities in your industry.

Invest in Resilience and Sustainability:

Invest in building resilience and sustainability into your business operations, supply chain, and corporate strategy to mitigate risks and future-proof your LLC. Implement risk management frameworks, business continuity plans, and sustainability initiatives that prioritize environmental stewardship, social responsibility, and long-term value creation. Embrace sustainable practices, such as resource efficiency, waste reduction, and renewable energy adoption, to enhance your resilience and competitiveness in a changing world.

Stay Agile and Responsive:

Stay agile, responsive, and proactive in your approach to business management and decision-making. Monitor market trends, customer preferences, and competitor actions closely to identify emerging opportunities and threats early. Maintain open channels of communication with stakeholders, solicit feedback, and adapt your strategies and tactics accordingly to address changing market dynamics and stakeholder expectations.

By anticipating future challenges, embracing innovation, and adopting proactive strategies, you can position your LLC for long-term success and resilience in an uncertain and dynamic business environment. Continuously assess your business landscape, adapt to changing conditions, and seize opportunities to innovate, grow, and thrive in the face of future challenges and uncertainties.

Positioning Your LLC for Long-Term Success

Positioning your LLC for long-term success requires a strategic approach that encompasses various aspects of business management, innovation, and adaptability. In this section, we'll explore key strategies and tips to ensure the sustained growth and viability of your LLC in a dynamic and competitive business landscape.

Strategies for Ensuring Long-Term Success

Develop a Clear Vision and Mission:

Establish a clear vision and mission for your LLC that articulates its long-term objectives, values, and purpose. Your vision should provide a roadmap for where you want your business to go, while your mission defines its fundamental reason for existence. By aligning your business activities with your vision and mission, you can create a sense of direction and purpose that guides decision-making and drives growth.

Build Strong Organizational Culture:

Cultivate a strong organizational culture that fosters collaboration, innovation, and employee engagement. Your company culture shapes the attitudes, behaviors, and values of your team members, influencing their performance and satisfaction. Encourage transparency, open communication, and mutual respect within your organization, and empower employees to contribute their ideas and insights to the company's success.

Foster Innovation and Creativity:

Embrace a culture of innovation and creativity within your LLC to stay ahead of the competition and adapt to changing market demands. Encourage experimentation, risk-taking, and creative thinking among your team members, and provide them with the resources and support they need to explore new ideas and solutions. Foster cross-functional collaboration and diversity of thought to spark innovation and drive continuous improvement.

Focus on Customer Experience:

Prioritize the delivery of exceptional customer experiences to build loyalty, satisfaction, and long-term relationships with your customers. Invest in understanding your customers' needs, preferences, and pain points, and tailor your products, services, and interactions to meet and exceed their expectations. Solicit feedback from customers regularly and use it to refine and enhance your offerings, processes, and customer service initiatives.

Invest in Talent Development:

Invest in the development and growth of your employees by providing ongoing training, learning opportunities, and career development programs. Support employees in acquiring new skills, advancing their careers, and achieving their professional goals within the organization. By nurturing talent from within and promoting a culture of continuous learning and development, you can attract, retain, and empower top performers who drive your LLC's success.

Embrace Technology and Digital Transformation:

Leverage technology and digital tools to streamline operations, enhance efficiency, and drive innovation across your organization. Embrace digital transformation initiatives such as cloud computing, data analytics, automation, and artificial intelligence to optimize processes, gain actionable insights, and stay competitive in the digital age. Embrace emerging technologies that have the potential to disrupt your industry and explore opportunities to leverage them to your advantage.

Tips for Staying Adaptable and Innovative

Stay Informed and Agile:

Stay informed about industry trends, market developments, and emerging technologies that may impact your business. Keep a pulse on your competitors' activities, customer preferences, and regulatory changes to identify opportunities and threats early. Stay agile and responsive in your decision-making, and be willing to adapt your strategies and tactics based on changing circumstances and market dynamics.

Foster a Culture of Continuous Improvement:

Encourage a mindset of continuous improvement and learning within your organization. Encourage employees to seek out opportunities for growth and development, and provide them with the resources and support they need to succeed. Foster a culture of experimentation, feedback, and iteration, where failure is viewed as an opportunity to learn and grow. Encourage employees to challenge the status quo and explore new ideas and approaches to problem-solving.

Foster Collaboration and Diversity:

Promote collaboration and diversity within your organization to foster creativity, innovation, and resilience. Encourage cross-functional teams to work together on projects and initiatives, leveraging their diverse perspectives and expertise to generate novel ideas and solutions. Embrace diversity in all its forms, including gender, ethnicity, age, and background, and create an inclusive environment where everyone feels valued, respected, and empowered to contribute their unique talents and insights.

Adapt to Changing Customer Needs:

Stay attuned to evolving customer needs, preferences, and behaviors, and be willing to adapt your products, services, and business model accordingly. Solicit feedback from customers regularly through surveys, focus groups, and customer interviews, and use their insights to inform product development, marketing strategies, and service enhancements. Anticipate future trends and shifts in consumer behavior, and proactively adjust your offerings to meet emerging demands.

Foster External Partnerships and Collaborations:

Forge strategic partnerships and collaborations with external stakeholders, including customers, suppliers, industry peers, and research institutions. Collaborate with partners to co-create value, share resources, and access new markets and opportunities. Leverage external expertise, networks, and resources to accelerate innovation, drive growth, and enhance your competitive position in the marketplace.

> *"By implementing these strategies and adopting a proactive and adaptive mindset, you can position your LLC for long-term success in a rapidly changing business landscape. Embracing a holistic approach that combines organizational excellence, innovation, and strategic foresight will enable your LLC to navigate uncertainties, capitalize on opportunities, and thrive in the long run."*

Dear Reader,

As the author of this book, I truly value your thoughts and opinions. Before we dive into the 9-step system for creating an LLC, I would like to kindly request your feedback. Your review is incredibly valuable and helps me improve future editions. If you find the information useful, clear, and actionable, please consider leaving a review to share your thoughts with other potential readers.

Thank you for your support!

The Simple 9 Step Guide to Launching Your LLC

Chapter 1
Research and Planning

Identify Your Business Idea and Market Niche

Launching a successful LLC starts with a solid foundation: identifying a business idea and finding the right market niche. This process requires creativity, research, and strategic thinking. By following a structured approach, you can refine your ideas and choose a niche that maximizes your chances of success.

Brainstorming and Refining Business Ideas

The first step in identifying your business idea is brainstorming. Start by considering your passions, skills, and experiences. Reflect on what you enjoy doing and what you are good at. These personal insights can help you generate business ideas that are not only profitable but also fulfilling.

Next, look for problems that need solving. Many successful businesses are built on the premise of addressing a pain point or need in the market. Think about the challenges you face in your daily life or observe in your community. These can be valuable sources of inspiration for your business idea.

It's also helpful to keep an eye on industry trends. Read industry publications, attend trade shows, and follow thought leaders in your field. This can give you a sense of where the market is heading and help you identify opportunities for innovation.

Once you have a list of potential ideas, start refining them. Evaluate each idea based on its feasibility, market potential, and alignment with your interests and skills. Consider the resources you have available and the amount of time and money you are willing to invest. This will help you narrow down your list to a few promising ideas.

To further refine your ideas, seek feedback from others. Discuss your ideas with friends, family, and mentors. They can provide valuable insights and help you see things from different perspectives. Additionally, consider conducting surveys or focus groups to get feedback from potential customers.

As you refine your ideas, think about how you can differentiate yourself from the competition. What unique value can you offer? How can you do things better or differently than others in your industry? This will be crucial in developing a successful business.

Importance of Identifying a Specific Market Niche

Once you have refined your business ideas, it's time to identify your market niche. A market niche is a specific segment of the market that you will target with your products or services. Identifying a niche is crucial for several reasons.

Firstly, a well-defined niche allows you to focus your efforts and resources. Instead of trying to appeal to everyone, you can tailor your marketing, product development, and customer service to meet the specific needs of your niche. This can result in a more efficient and effective business.

Secondly, targeting a niche can help you stand out in a crowded market. By focusing on a specific segment, you can develop a unique value proposition that sets you apart from the competition. This can make it easier to attract and retain customers.

Thirdly, a niche can provide a more loyal customer base. When you meet the specific needs of a niche, customers are more likely to be satisfied and return for repeat business. This can result in higher customer lifetime value and more stable revenue.

To identify your market niche, start by segmenting the market. Consider factors such as demographics, psychographics, and behaviors. For example, you could segment the market based on age, gender, income, interests, or buying habits. Look for segments that are large enough to be profitable but not so large that they are highly competitive.

Next, assess the needs and preferences of each segment. What are their pain points and desires? How can your products or services address these needs? This will help you identify which segments are most attractive and feasible for your business.

It's also important to evaluate the competition in each segment. Who are the major players? What are their strengths and weaknesses? Are there any gaps in the market that you can fill? This can help you identify opportunities for differentiation and competitive advantage.

Once you have identified a potential niche, test your assumptions. Conduct market research to validate your ideas and ensure there is sufficient demand. This can involve surveys, interviews, or analyzing existing data. The goal is to gather enough information to make an informed decision about your niche.

Developing Your Niche Strategy

After identifying your niche, the next step is to develop a strategy for targeting it. This involves defining your unique value proposition (UVP), developing a marketing plan, and creating products or services that meet the specific needs of your niche.

Your UVP is a clear statement of what makes your business unique and why customers should choose you over the competition. It should be based on your strengths and the specific needs of your niche. Your UVP should be concise, compelling, and easy to understand.

To develop your UVP, start by identifying the key benefits of your products or services. What value do you provide to customers? Next, identify what sets you apart from the competition. This could be your unique features, superior quality, exceptional customer service, or lower prices. Finally, combine these elements into a clear and concise statement that communicates your unique value.

With your UVP in place, develop a marketing plan to reach your target audience. Consider which marketing channels and tactics will be most effective for your niche. This could include social media, content marketing, email marketing, or paid advertising. The goal is to reach your audience where they are and communicate your unique value in a way that resonates with them.

In addition to marketing, focus on developing products or services that meet the specific needs of your niche. This involves understanding their pain points and desires and creating solutions that address them. Consider conducting customer interviews or surveys to gather insights and feedback. This can help you refine your offerings and ensure they meet the needs of your niche.

It's also important to consider your pricing strategy. Your pricing should reflect the value you provide and be competitive within your niche. Consider factors such as your costs, the prices of competitors, and the willingness of customers to pay. This can help you determine a pricing strategy that maximizes profitability while remaining attractive to your target audience.

Building and Maintaining Your Niche

Once you have identified your niche and developed a strategy for targeting it, focus on building and maintaining your presence in the market. This involves consistently delivering value to your customers and staying attuned to their needs and preferences.

One key aspect of building your niche is establishing your brand. Your brand should reflect your unique value proposition and resonate with your target audience. This includes your brand name, logo, messaging, and overall brand identity. Consistent branding can help you build recognition and trust with your audience.

In addition to branding, focus on delivering exceptional customer service. Meeting the needs of your niche requires understanding their preferences and exceeding their expectations. This can involve personalized service, prompt responses to inquiries, and going above and beyond to resolve issues. Exceptional customer service can lead to customer loyalty and positive word-of-mouth, which can be crucial for building your niche.

Another important aspect of maintaining your niche is staying attuned to market trends and changes. The needs and preferences of your niche can evolve over time, and it's important to stay ahead of these changes. This can involve regularly gathering feedback from customers, monitoring industry trends, and being open to innovation. Staying adaptable and responsive can help you maintain your relevance and competitiveness in the market.

Finally, focus on building relationships within your niche. This can involve engaging with your audience through social media, attending industry events, and collaborating with influencers or other businesses in your niche. Building relationships can help you build trust and credibility and create opportunities for growth and collaboration.

Case Studies and Examples

To further illustrate the process of identifying a business idea and finding a market niche, consider the following case studies and examples.

Case Study 1: Dollar Shave Club

Dollar Shave Club is a prime example of a company that identified a specific market niche and developed a unique value proposition to target it. The founders recognized that many men were frustrated with the high cost and inconvenience of purchasing razors. They developed a subscription-based model that delivered affordable razors directly to customers' doors.

By targeting a specific pain point and offering a convenient and cost-effective solution, Dollar Shave Club was able to quickly build a loyal customer base and disrupt the shaving industry. Their unique value proposition, combined with clever marketing and branding, helped them stand out in a crowded market and achieve significant growth.

Case Study 2: Warby Parker

Warby Parker is another example of a company that identified a market niche and developed a successful business around it. The founders recognized that many people were dissatisfied with the high cost and limited selection of eyeglasses. They developed an online business model that offered affordable and stylish eyeglasses with a try-before-you-buy option.

By targeting a specific pain point and offering a unique solution, Warby Parker was able to quickly gain traction and build a loyal customer base. Their focus on customer service, innovative business model, and strong branding helped them stand out in a competitive market and achieve significant growth.

Example: The Gluten-Free Bakery

Consider the example of a gluten-free bakery. The founders recognized a growing demand for gluten-free products among individuals with celiac disease and gluten sensitivities. They developed a bakery that specialized in gluten-free baked goods, targeting a specific market niche.

By focusing on the specific needs of their niche, the gluten-free bakery was able to differentiate itself from traditional bakeries and build a loyal customer base. Their commitment to quality and customer service, combined with effective marketing and branding, helped them achieve success in a competitive market.

Conduct Market Research and Competitive Analysis

Conducting thorough market research and competitive analysis is crucial for any LLC aiming for long-term success. Understanding the market landscape, identifying customer needs, and analyzing competitors help you make informed decisions and develop effective strategies. This part will guide you through the process of conducting market research and competitive analysis, ensuring you have the necessary insights to build a strong foundation for your business.

Conducting Thorough Market Research

Market research is the systematic process of gathering, analyzing, and interpreting information about a market, including information about the target market, competitors, and the industry as a whole. The goal of market research is to understand the market environment, identify opportunities and threats, and make informed business decisions.

Start by defining your objectives. Clearly articulate what you want to achieve with your market research. This could be understanding customer needs, evaluating market size, identifying trends, or assessing competition. Having clear objectives will guide your research and ensure you focus on gathering relevant information.

Next, choose the research methods that best suit your objectives. Market research can be divided into primary and secondary research. Primary research involves collecting original data directly from the source, such as through surveys, interviews, or focus groups. Secondary research involves gathering existing data from external sources, such as industry reports, government publications, or academic studies.

For primary research, develop a research plan that outlines your methods, sample size, and data collection process. For surveys, design questions that are clear, concise, and relevant to your objectives. Use a mix of open-ended and closed-ended questions to gather both quantitative and qualitative data. Ensure your sample size is large enough to be representative of your target market.

Conducting interviews and focus groups can provide deeper insights into customer needs and preferences. Prepare a set of guiding questions but be flexible to allow for in-depth discussions. Choose participants who represent your target market and create a comfortable environment for open and honest communication.

Secondary research involves collecting and analyzing existing data from various sources. Start by identifying credible sources such as industry reports, market research firms, trade associations, and government publications. Look for data on market size, growth trends, customer demographics, buying behavior, and industry forecasts. Analyzing this data can provide a broad understanding of the market landscape and help validate findings from your primary research.

Once you have collected your data, analyze it to identify patterns, trends, and insights. Look for common themes and draw connections between different data points. Use statistical analysis to quantify your findings and identify significant trends. Visualize your data using charts, graphs, and tables to make it easier to interpret and communicate your findings.

Tips on Analyzing Competitors

Analyzing competitors is a critical component of market research. Understanding your competition helps you identify their strengths and weaknesses, uncover market gaps, and develop strategies to differentiate your business. Here are some tips for conducting a comprehensive competitive analysis:

Start by identifying your direct and indirect competitors. Direct competitors are businesses that offer similar products or services and target the same customer segments. Indirect competitors offer different products or services but address similar customer needs or problems. Create a list of your main competitors to focus your analysis.

Gather information about your competitors using various sources. Visit their websites, follow their social media accounts, and subscribe to their newsletters. Review their marketing materials, product descriptions, and customer reviews. Analyze their pricing strategies, product features, and value propositions. Look for press releases, news articles, and industry reports that provide insights into their activities and performance.

Evaluate your competitors' strengths and weaknesses. Identify what they do well and where they fall short. Look for areas where they excel, such as product quality, customer service, or brand reputation. Also, identify their weaknesses, such as gaps in their product offerings, negative customer feedback, or inefficiencies in their operations. Understanding their strengths and weaknesses helps you identify opportunities to differentiate your business.

Analyze your competitors' market positioning and strategies. Determine how they position themselves in the market, what messaging they use, and what channels they leverage. Identify their target customer segments and how they appeal to them. Look for patterns in their marketing tactics, such as promotions, partnerships, or advertising campaigns. Understanding their strategies helps you develop your own positioning and marketing plan.

Examine your competitors' financial performance. While this information may not always be publicly available, you can gather insights from financial reports, industry publications, or market research firms. Look for information on their revenue, profit margins, market share, and growth trends. Analyzing their financial performance helps you assess their market strength and stability.

Evaluate your competitors' customer base and loyalty. Analyze customer reviews, testimonials, and social media comments to understand their customers' satisfaction and loyalty. Look for patterns in the

247

feedback and identify common praises or complaints. Understanding their customer base helps you identify gaps in their offerings and areas where you can provide better value.

Identifying Market Gaps

Identifying market gaps is essential for developing a unique value proposition and differentiating your business from competitors. A market gap is an unmet need or underserved segment in the market that presents an opportunity for your business to fill. Here are some strategies for identifying market gaps:

Start by analyzing your market research and competitive analysis findings. Look for areas where customer needs are not fully met or where competitors have weaknesses. Identify any underserved customer segments or emerging trends that competitors have not yet addressed. These gaps can represent opportunities for your business to provide unique solutions.

Consider the customer journey and identify pain points or challenges that customers face. Look for areas where customers are dissatisfied or where their needs are not adequately addressed. For example, this could be a lack of convenient payment options, poor customer service, or limited product variety. Addressing these pain points can help you create a unique value proposition.

Look for trends and shifts in the market that present new opportunities. This could be changes in customer preferences, technological advancements, or regulatory changes. For example, the growing demand for sustainable products or the increasing adoption of digital technologies can present market gaps that your business can address.

Evaluate your competitors' product offerings and identify any gaps or limitations. Look for areas where competitors have limited product variety, outdated features, or lack of innovation. These gaps can represent opportunities for your business to introduce new products or improve existing ones to better meet customer needs.

Consider conducting a SWOT analysis (Strengths, Weaknesses, Opportunities, Threats) for your business and your competitors. This helps you identify your own strengths and weaknesses, as well as external opportunities and threats. By comparing your SWOT analysis with that of your competitors, you can identify areas where you have a competitive advantage or where the market is underserved.

Engage with your customers and gather feedback on their needs and preferences. Conduct surveys, interviews, or focus groups to understand their pain points, desires, and unmet needs. Analyzing customer feedback helps you identify gaps in the market and develop solutions that better meet their needs.

Case Studies and Examples

To further illustrate the process of conducting market research and competitive analysis, consider the following case studies and examples:

Case Study 1: Airbnb

Airbnb is a prime example of a company that successfully identified a market gap and built a thriving business around it. The founders recognized that traditional hotels were not meeting the needs of travelers looking for unique and affordable accommodation options. They conducted market research to understand travelers' preferences and identified a gap in the market for short-term rentals offered by local hosts.

By analyzing the competition and understanding customer needs, Airbnb developed a unique value proposition that connected travelers with local hosts, offering a more personalized and authentic travel experience. Their market research and competitive analysis helped them identify the right market niche and develop a successful business model that disrupted the traditional hospitality industry.

Case Study 2: Tesla

Tesla is another example of a company that identified market gaps and leveraged them to achieve significant success. The founders recognized the growing demand for sustainable transportation solutions and the limitations of traditional gasoline-powered vehicles. They conducted market research to understand customer preferences and identified a gap in the market for high-performance electric vehicles.

By analyzing competitors and identifying their weaknesses, Tesla developed a unique value proposition that combined sustainability, performance, and innovation. Their competitive analysis helped them identify opportunities to differentiate their vehicles through advanced technology, superior design, and a strong brand. This enabled Tesla to capture a significant share of the electric vehicle market and establish itself as a leader in the industry.

Example: The Organic Skincare Brand

Consider the example of an organic skincare brand. The founders conducted market research to understand the growing demand for natural and organic skincare products. They identified a market gap where many traditional skincare products contained harmful chemicals and lacked transparency in their ingredient sourcing.

By analyzing competitors, they found that while some brands offered natural products, they often lacked quality or transparency. The founders developed a unique value proposition focused on high-quality, organic ingredients, transparent sourcing, and sustainable practices. Their market research and competitive analysis helped them identify the right market niche and develop a successful brand that resonated with health-conscious consumers.

Develop a Business Plan and Define Your Unique Value Proposition

Creating a solid business plan is an essential step in launching and growing your LLC. A well-crafted business plan serves as a roadmap, guiding your business through its initial stages and beyond. It outlines your business goals, strategies, and the steps necessary to achieve them. Additionally, a clear Unique Value Proposition (UVP) differentiates your business from competitors and communicates the unique benefits you offer to customers. This section will provide detailed guidance on developing a comprehensive business plan and defining a compelling UVP.

Key Components of a Business Plan

A business plan typically consists of several key components, each addressing different aspects of your business. Together, these components provide a holistic view of your business, its goals, and the strategies to achieve them. The main sections of a business plan include:

Executive Summary:

The executive summary is a concise overview of your business plan. It should include your business's mission statement, a brief description of your products or services, your target market, and your business objectives. Although it appears first in the document, it is often written last, after all other sections are completed.

Company Description:

This section provides detailed information about your business. Include the legal structure of your LLC, the nature of your business, the industry in which you operate, and the needs you aim to fulfill. Highlight what sets your business apart from others in the industry.

Market Analysis:

Conducting thorough market research and competitive analysis, as previously discussed, is crucial for this section. Provide insights into your target market, including market size, growth trends, and customer demographics. Analyze your competitors, their strengths and weaknesses, and identify market gaps that your business can exploit.

Organization and Management:

Describe your business's organizational structure. Include information about the ownership of your LLC, the management team, and their roles and responsibilities. Highlight the skills and experience of your team members and how they contribute to your business's success.

Products or Services:

Provide detailed information about the products or services you offer. Explain the benefits and features of your offerings, how they meet the needs of your target market, and any competitive advantages they possess. Include information about your product development process, intellectual property, and any future products or services you plan to introduce.

Marketing and Sales Strategy:

Outline your marketing and sales strategies. Describe how you plan to attract and retain customers, including your pricing strategy, advertising and promotion plans, sales tactics, and distribution channels. Highlight any partnerships or collaborations that will help you reach your target market.

Funding Request:

If you are seeking financing, include a section detailing your funding requirements. Specify how much funding you need, how you plan to use the funds, and the potential return on investment for investors. Provide information about your current financial situation and any previous funding you have received.

Financial Projections:

Provide financial forecasts for your business, including income statements, cash flow statements, and balance sheets. Include projections for at least the next three to five years. Use historical data, market research, and industry benchmarks to support your projections. This section demonstrates your business's potential for profitability and financial stability.

Appendix:

The appendix includes supplementary information that supports the main sections of your business plan. This can include resumes of your management team, product photos, patents, legal documents, and any other relevant materials.

Each section of your business plan should be well-researched, clearly written, and logically structured. A comprehensive business plan not only helps you manage your business more effectively but also serves as a valuable tool when seeking financing or partnerships.

Importance of a Clear Unique Value Proposition (UVP)

A Unique Value Proposition (UVP) is a statement that clearly articulates the unique benefits your business offers to customers and how you differentiate from competitors. It is a crucial component of your business strategy, as it helps you attract and retain customers by addressing their specific needs and preferences. A strong UVP communicates the value of your products or services and why customers should choose your business over others.

A clear UVP is essential for several reasons:

Differentiation:

In a competitive market, a UVP helps you stand out by highlighting what makes your business unique. It differentiates your products or services from those of your competitors, making it easier for customers to see the value you offer.

Customer Focus:

A UVP is centered around the needs and desires of your target market. It demonstrates that you understand your customers' pain points and have designed your offerings to address them. This customer-centric approach builds trust and loyalty.

Marketing Effectiveness:

A well-defined UVP provides a clear and compelling message that can be used across all marketing channels. It helps you communicate the benefits of your products or services in a way that resonates with your target audience, improving the effectiveness of your marketing efforts.

Value Perception:

A strong UVP enhances the perceived value of your offerings. It explains why your products or services are worth the price and how they provide better value than competing options. This perception of value can influence purchasing decisions and increase sales.

Internal Alignment:

A clear UVP aligns your team around a common understanding of your business's unique value. It guides decision-making, product development, and customer service, ensuring that all aspects of your business are focused on delivering the promised value.

To develop a compelling UVP, follow these steps:

Understand Your Target Market:

Conduct thorough market research to understand the needs, preferences, and pain points of your target market. Identify the specific problems your customers face and how your products or services can solve them. Gather insights from surveys, interviews, focus groups, and customer feedback.

Identify Your Unique Strengths:

Assess your business's strengths and competitive advantages. Identify what sets you apart from competitors and how these strengths translate into unique benefits for your customers. Consider aspects such as product quality, innovation, customer service, brand reputation, and any proprietary technologies or processes.

Articulate Your Benefits:

Clearly articulate the key benefits your products or services offer to customers. Focus on the outcomes and value your offerings provide, rather than just the features. Explain how your products or services solve your customers' problems, improve their lives, or fulfill their desires.

Differentiate From Competitors:

Analyze your competitors' value propositions and identify gaps or weaknesses in their offerings. Highlight how your UVP addresses these gaps and offers superior value. Emphasize what makes your business unique and why customers should choose you over competitors.

Create a Clear and Compelling Statement:

Craft a concise and compelling UVP statement that communicates your unique value in a way that resonates with your target audience. Use clear and straightforward language, avoiding jargon or complex terms. Your UVP should be easily understood and memorable.

Test and Refine:

Test your UVP with your target audience to ensure it resonates and effectively communicates your value. Gather feedback and make necessary adjustments to refine your UVP. Continuously evaluate and update your UVP to reflect changes in the market, customer preferences, and your business's offerings.

Case Studies and Examples

To further illustrate the process of developing a business plan and defining a UVP, consider the following case studies and examples:

Case Study 1: Warby Parker

Warby Parker is a direct-to-consumer eyewear brand that successfully developed a strong UVP and business plan. The founders identified a market gap where traditional eyewear retailers were charging high prices for glasses. They conducted market research to understand customer needs and preferences, revealing that consumers wanted affordable, stylish eyewear and a convenient shopping experience.

Warby Parker's UVP is centered around offering high-quality, affordable glasses with a convenient online shopping experience. They differentiate by cutting out the middleman and selling directly to consumers, allowing them to offer lower prices. Additionally, they provide a home try-on program, where customers can select five frames to try on at home before making a purchase. This unique value proposition addresses the pain points of high prices and inconvenience, resonating with their target market.

Warby Parker's business plan includes a detailed market analysis, identifying the target market, and understanding their needs. Their marketing and sales strategy focuses on online sales, social media marketing, and word-of-mouth referrals. They also emphasize their commitment to social responsibility, with a "Buy a Pair, Give a Pair" program that donates a pair of glasses for every pair sold. This comprehensive business plan and strong UVP have contributed to Warby Parker's success and growth.

Case Study 2: Dollar Shave Club

Dollar Shave Club is another example of a company that developed a compelling UVP and business plan. The founders recognized that traditional razors were expensive and inconvenient to purchase. They conducted market research to understand the needs of male consumers and identified a desire for affordable, high-quality razors with a convenient delivery service.

Dollar Shave Club's UVP is centered around offering high-quality razors at an affordable price, delivered directly to customers' doors. They differentiate by providing a subscription model that eliminates the need for customers to go to the store to purchase razors. Their marketing emphasizes humor and relatability, creating a strong brand identity that resonates with their target market.

Dollar Shave Club's business plan includes a comprehensive market analysis, identifying their target market of price-sensitive and convenience-seeking consumers. Their marketing strategy leverages online advertising, viral videos, and social media to reach their audience. They also focus on customer retention by providing a seamless subscription experience and excellent customer service. This well-defined business plan and unique UVP have driven Dollar Shave Club's rapid growth and market success.

Example: The Eco-Friendly Cleaning Products Brand

Consider the example of an eco-friendly cleaning products brand. The founders conducted market research to understand the growing demand for sustainable and non-toxic cleaning products. They identified a market gap where many traditional cleaning products contained harmful chemicals and were not environmentally friendly.

The brand's UVP is centered around offering high-quality, eco-friendly cleaning products that are safe for both consumers and the environment. They differentiate by using natural ingredients, sustainable packaging, and transparent sourcing. Their UVP communicates the benefits of a healthier home and a cleaner planet, resonating with health-conscious and environmentally aware consumers.

The business plan includes a detailed market analysis, identifying the target market of health-conscious and environmentally aware consumers. Their marketing strategy focuses on online sales, influencer partnerships, and educational content about the benefits of eco-friendly cleaning products. They also emphasize their commitment to sustainability, with initiatives such as reducing plastic waste and supporting environmental causes. This comprehensive business plan and strong UVP position the brand for success in the growing market for sustainable products.

Chapter 2
Legal and Regulatory Compliance

Choose a Name for Your LLC and Check Availability

Selecting a unique and memorable name for your LLC is a crucial step in establishing your business identity. The right name not only reflects your brand's values and mission but also distinguishes your business from competitors. It is essential to choose a name that is easy to remember, pronounce, and spell, while also ensuring that it is available and compliant with legal requirements. This section will guide you through the process of selecting a business name and checking its availability.

Tips on Selecting a Unique and Memorable Business Name

Choosing a business name is a creative process that requires careful consideration and strategic thinking. Here are some tips to help you select a unique and memorable name for your LLC:

Reflect Your Brand Identity:

Your business name should align with your brand identity, mission, and values. Think about the message you want to convey to your target audience and how your name can communicate that effectively. For example, if your business focuses on sustainability, you might choose a name that reflects eco-friendliness and environmental responsibility.

Keep It Simple and Clear:

A simple and clear name is easier for customers to remember, pronounce, and spell. Avoid using complex words, jargon, or acronyms that might confuse your audience. A straightforward name enhances brand recognition and recall, making it easier for customers to find and recommend your business.

Be Descriptive but Not Restrictive:

While it's important for your name to convey what your business does, avoid being too specific or restrictive. A name that is too narrow may limit your ability to expand your product or service offerings in the future. For example, instead of naming your business "John's Tire Repair," you might choose "John's Auto Services," which allows for growth into other areas of automotive care.

Consider Your Target Audience:

Think about the preferences and cultural context of your target audience. Choose a name that resonates with them and reflects their values and lifestyle. Consider how your name will be perceived by different demographic groups and ensure it appeals to your intended customers.

Ensure Uniqueness:

Your business name should be distinct and not easily confused with existing businesses. Conduct a thorough search to ensure that your chosen name is unique and not already in use by another company. A unique name helps avoid legal issues and protects your brand identity.

Think About SEO and Online Presence:

In today's digital age, it's essential to consider search engine optimization (SEO) when choosing a business name. A name that includes relevant keywords can improve your search engine rankings and make it easier for customers to find you online. Additionally, check the availability of domain names and social media handles that match your business name.

Test for Usability and Appeal:

Before finalizing your business name, test it with potential customers, friends, and family. Gather feedback on how the name is perceived, whether it is easy to remember and pronounce, and whether it effectively communicates your brand's message. Use this feedback to refine and improve your name choice.

Check for Trademark Issues:

Conduct a trademark search to ensure that your chosen name does not infringe on any existing trademarks. Using a name that is already trademarked can lead to legal disputes and require you to rebrand your business. You can perform a trademark search through the United States Patent and Trademark Office (USPTO) or a similar authority in your country.

Consider Long-Term Viability:

Choose a name that will stand the test of time and remain relevant as your business grows and evolves. Avoid trendy or faddish names that may quickly become outdated. Think about how your name will fit with your business's future vision and goals.

By following these tips, you can choose a business name that effectively represents your brand, resonates with your target audience, and sets you up for long-term success.

How to Check the Availability of Your Chosen Name

Once you have brainstormed and refined your business name ideas, the next step is to check the availability of your chosen name. This involves ensuring that the name is not already in use by another business and that it complies with legal requirements. Here are the steps to check the availability of your business name:

Conduct a Business Name Search:

Start by conducting a business name search through your state's Secretary of State website or business registration office. This search will help you determine whether your chosen name is already in use by another registered business in your state. Most states have an online database where you can perform this search for free.

Check Domain Name Availability:

In addition to checking the business name availability, it's important to check the availability of domain names for your website. Use domain registration websites like GoDaddy, Namecheap, or Bluehost to search for available domain names that match your business name. Securing a matching domain name is crucial for establishing a strong online presence.

Search Trademark Databases:

Conduct a trademark search to ensure that your chosen name does not infringe on any existing trademarks. You can search the United States Patent and Trademark Office (USPTO) database for trademarks registered in the U.S. If you plan to operate internationally, consider searching trademark databases in other countries as well. This step helps you avoid potential legal issues and protects your brand.

Check Social Media Handles:

Consistent branding across social media platforms is important for building your online presence. Check the availability of social media handles that match your business name on platforms like Facebook, Twitter, Instagram, LinkedIn, and others. Securing matching handles helps create a cohesive and recognizable brand.

Verify Compliance With Naming Rules:

Ensure that your chosen name complies with your state's naming rules for LLCs. Most states have specific requirements for business names, including the use of certain words or phrases (e.g., "LLC" or "Limited Liability Company") and restrictions on using certain terms (e.g., "bank" or "insurance" without proper authorization). Review your state's naming guidelines to ensure compliance.

Reserve Your Business Name:

If your chosen name is available and complies with legal requirements, consider reserving it with your state's business registration office. Reserving your name ensures that it is held for your use while you complete the process of forming your LLC. The reservation period varies by state, but it typically ranges from 30 to 120 days.

Consult Legal Counsel:

If you have any doubts or concerns about the availability or compliance of your chosen business name, consider consulting with a legal professional. An attorney with experience in business law can provide valuable guidance and help you navigate the complexities of naming your LLC.

By following these steps, you can ensure that your chosen business name is available, legally compliant, and ready for use. This process helps protect your brand identity and sets the foundation for a successful LLC.

Case Study and Example

To further illustrate the process of choosing a business name and checking its availability, consider the following case study and example:

Case Study: GreenLeaf Eco-Friendly Products

Jane, an entrepreneur passionate about sustainability, decided to launch an LLC that sells eco-friendly household products. She wanted a name that reflected her commitment to the environment and resonated with health-conscious consumers. After brainstorming several ideas, she chose the name "GreenLeaf Eco-Friendly Products."

To ensure the name was unique and available, Jane followed these steps:

Conducting a Business Name Search:

Jane visited her state's Secretary of State website and conducted a business name search for "GreenLeaf Eco-Friendly Products." The search results showed no existing businesses with that name in her state, indicating that the name was available for registration.

Checking Domain Name Availability:

Jane used a domain registration website to search for available domain names. She found that "greenleafecoproducts.com" was available and promptly registered the domain to secure her online presence.

Searching Trademark Databases:

Jane conducted a trademark search using the USPTO database to ensure that "GreenLeaf Eco-Friendly Products" did not infringe on any existing trademarks. The search confirmed that no similar trademarks were registered, allowing her to proceed with confidence.

Checking Social Media Handles:

Jane checked the availability of social media handles for "GreenLeaf-Eco" on platforms like Facebook, Twitter, and Instagram. She found that the handles were available and created accounts to maintain consistent branding across social media.

Verifying Compliance With Naming Rules:

Jane reviewed her state's naming guidelines for LLCs and confirmed that "GreenLeaf Eco-Friendly Products, LLC" complied with the requirements. She included "LLC" in her business name to meet the legal requirements.

Reserving the Business Name:

To secure the name while completing the LLC formation process, Jane reserved "GreenLeaf Eco-Friendly Products, LLC" with her state's business registration office. This reservation ensured that no other business could register the name during the reservation period.

Consulting Legal Counsel:

Jane consulted with a business attorney to review her chosen name and ensure compliance with all legal requirements. The attorney confirmed that the name was available and compliant, allowing Jane to proceed with confidence.

By following these steps, Jane successfully chose a unique and memorable name for her LLC and ensured its availability and compliance with legal requirements.

Example: TechNova Innovations

Consider the example of a tech startup focused on developing innovative software solutions. The founders wanted a name that conveyed cutting-edge technology and forward-thinking innovation. After brainstorming, they chose the name "TechNova Innovations."

To ensure the name was available and legally compliant, the founders took the following steps:

Conducting a Business Name Search:

The founders conducted a business name search on their state's Secretary of State website and found that "TechNova Innovations" was not already in use, indicating its availability for registration.

Checking Domain Name Availability:

They searched for available domain names and found that "technovainnovations.com" was available. They promptly registered the domain to secure their online presence.

Searching Trademark Databases:

They performed a trademark search using the USPTO database and confirmed that "TechNova Innovations" did not infringe on any existing trademarks.

Checking Social Media Handles:

The founders checked the availability of social media handles for "TechNova" on platforms like LinkedIn, Twitter, and Instagram. They found that the handles were available and created accounts to maintain consistent branding.

Verifying Compliance With Naming Rules:

They reviewed their state's naming guidelines for LLCs and confirmed that "TechNova Innovations, LLC" complied with the requirements, including the use of "LLC" in the business name.

Reserving the Business Name:

To secure the name while completing the LLC formation process, the founders reserved "TechNova Innovations, LLC" with their state's business registration office.

Consulting Legal Counsel:

The founders consulted with a business attorney to review their chosen name and ensure compliance with all legal requirements. The attorney confirmed that the name was available and compliant.

By following these steps, the founders of TechNova Innovations successfully chose a unique and memorable name for their LLC and ensured its availability and compliance with legal requirements.

Select Your Registered Agent and Office Location

When forming an LLC, two critical decisions you'll need to make involve selecting a registered agent and choosing an office location. Both decisions have significant implications for your business operations and compliance with state regulations. This section will explore the role of a registered agent, how to choose one, and provide tips on selecting an appropriate office location.

The Role of a Registered Agent

A registered agent is an individual or a business entity designated to receive legal documents and official communications on behalf of your LLC. These documents include service of process (such as lawsuits), government correspondence, and compliance-related notifications. The registered agent plays a crucial role in ensuring that your LLC remains in good standing with state regulations and is promptly informed of any legal or administrative actions.

The importance of having a registered agent cannot be overstated. Here are the key functions and benefits of having a registered agent for your LLC:

Ensuring Legal Compliance:

One of the primary roles of a registered agent is to ensure that your LLC complies with state requirements. Most states mandate that an LLC must have a registered agent with a physical address in the state where the LLC is registered. This requirement ensures that there is a reliable point of contact for the LLC within the state.

Receiving Legal Documents:

The registered agent is responsible for receiving and forwarding legal documents to your LLC. These documents include summons, subpoenas, and other legal notices. Having a registered agent ensures that you do not miss any critical legal deadlines or court appearances, which could result in default judgments or other legal consequences.

Maintaining Privacy:

Using a registered agent can help maintain your privacy. Instead of having your personal address listed on public records, the registered agent's address is used. This arrangement helps protect your personal privacy and reduces the risk of unsolicited mail or visitors.

Providing a Reliable Point of Contact:

A registered agent provides a consistent and reliable point of contact for your LLC. This reliability is especially important if your LLC operates in multiple states or if you do not have a physical office location in the state where your LLC is registered.

Managing Compliance Notifications:

The registered agent also receives compliance-related notifications from the state, such as annual report reminders, tax notices, and renewal deadlines. This service helps ensure that your LLC stays compliant with state requirements and avoids penalties or administrative dissolution.

How to Choose a Registered Agent

Choosing the right registered agent for your LLC is an important decision that can impact your business operations and legal compliance. Here are some considerations to keep in mind when selecting a registered agent:

Eligibility Requirements:

The first step in choosing a registered agent is to understand the eligibility requirements in your state. Generally, a registered agent can be an individual who is at least 18 years old and has a physical address in the state where the LLC is registered. Alternatively, a registered agent can be a business entity that is authorized to conduct business in the state.

Availability and Reliability:

The registered agent must be available during regular business hours to receive legal documents and official communications. Ensure that the registered agent you choose has a reliable presence and can consistently meet this requirement. Some states require the registered agent to be available during specific hours, so confirm these requirements with your state's regulations.

Professional Registered Agent Services:

Many businesses choose to hire a professional registered agent service. These services specialize in handling legal documents and compliance notifications for LLCs. Professional registered agents offer several advantages, including expertise in managing legal documents, ensuring timely delivery, and providing additional compliance support. Research reputable registered agent services and consider their track record, customer reviews, and pricing.

Experience and Expertise:

Consider the experience and expertise of the registered agent. A registered agent with experience in handling legal and compliance matters for LLCs can provide valuable support and guidance. They can help ensure that your LLC meets all legal requirements and can assist with navigating any compliance challenges that arise.

Physical Address Requirement:

Ensure that the registered agent has a physical address (not a P.O. Box) in the state where your LLC is registered. This address requirement is crucial for receiving legal documents and official communications. Verify that the registered agent's address meets the state's requirements and is regularly monitored for incoming documents.

Customer Support and Communication:

Evaluate the customer support and communication offered by the registered agent. Prompt and effective communication is essential for managing legal and compliance matters. Choose a registered agent that provides responsive customer support and keeps you informed about important documents and deadlines.

Cost Considerations:

The cost of registered agent services can vary widely. Compare the pricing of different registered agent services and consider the value they provide. While it's important to choose a registered agent that fits within your budget, prioritize quality and reliability over cost alone. Some services offer additional features, such as compliance reminders and document storage, which can be valuable for your LLC.

Flexibility and Scalability:

If your LLC plans to expand to multiple states, consider a registered agent service that offers flexibility and scalability. Some registered agent services operate nationwide and can serve as your registered agent in multiple states. This scalability can simplify the management of your registered agent needs as your LLC grows.

Tips on Selecting an Appropriate Office Location

Choosing the right office location is a critical decision that can impact your business's success and operational efficiency. The location of your office affects your brand image, customer accessibility, employee satisfaction, and overall business operations. Here are some tips to help you select an appropriate office location for your LLC:

Understand Your Business Needs:

Start by understanding the specific needs of your business. Consider factors such as the type of business you operate, the nature of your products or services, and your target market. For example, a retail business may prioritize high foot traffic and visibility, while a tech startup may prioritize access to talent and proximity to industry hubs.

Consider Your Target Market:

Your office location should be convenient and accessible for your target market. Analyze the demographics, preferences, and behaviors of your target customers to determine the best location. Consider factors such as proximity to your customers, ease of access, and the availability of parking or public transportation.

Evaluate the Competition:

Assess the presence of competitors in potential locations. Being close to competitors can have both advantages and disadvantages. On one hand, it can indicate a thriving market with demand for your products or services. On the other hand, it may also mean intense competition. Evaluate the competitive landscape and choose a location that offers strategic advantages.

Accessibility and Convenience:

Ensure that your office location is easily accessible for both customers and employees. Consider factors such as transportation options, traffic patterns, and parking availability. A convenient location can enhance customer satisfaction and employee productivity.

Assess the Local Business Environment:

Research the local business environment and community. Consider factors such as the availability of business support services, networking opportunities, and the overall business climate. A supportive business environment can contribute to your LLC's growth and success.

Analyze Costs and Budget:

Consider the costs associated with different office locations, including rent, utilities, maintenance, and taxes. Evaluate these costs in relation to your budget and financial projections. While it's important to choose a location that fits within your budget, also consider the potential return on investment and long-term benefits.

Evaluate the Space and Amenities:

Assess the physical space and amenities offered by potential office locations. Consider factors such as the size and layout of the space, the availability of meeting rooms, and the quality of facilities. Ensure that the office space meets your business needs and can accommodate future growth.

Consider Zoning and Legal Requirements:

Verify that the potential office location complies with zoning and legal requirements for your type of business. Check local zoning regulations to ensure that your business activities are permitted in the chosen location. Compliance with zoning laws is essential to avoid legal issues and operational disruptions.

Assess the Workforce Availability:

Consider the availability of talent and workforce in the potential office location. If your business relies on skilled employees, choose a location with access to a pool of qualified candidates. Proximity to universities, training centers, and industry hubs can be advantageous.

Think About Brand Image and Perception:

Your office location can influence your brand image and perception. Choose a location that aligns with your brand identity and values. For example, a prestigious address in a business district can enhance your brand's credibility and reputation.

Plan for Future Growth:

Consider the potential for future growth and expansion when selecting an office location. Choose a location that can accommodate your business's growth and evolving needs. This foresight can save you the hassle and costs of relocating in the future.

Negotiate Lease Terms:

When finalizing an office location, negotiate favorable lease terms that align with your business goals. Consider factors such as lease duration, renewal options, rent escalation clauses, and maintenance responsibilities. A well-negotiated lease can provide stability and flexibility for your business.

Case Study and Example

To illustrate the process of selecting a registered agent and office location, consider the following case study and example:

Case Study: HealthWave Wellness Center

Emily, the founder of HealthWave Wellness Center, needed to select a registered agent and an office location for her LLC. HealthWave Wellness Center offers holistic wellness services, including yoga classes, massage therapy, and nutrition counseling. Emily wanted a name and location that reflected her business's focus on health and wellness.

Choosing a Registered Agent:

Emily researched professional registered agent services and selected a reputable company with experience in managing compliance for health and wellness businesses. The registered agent service provided a reliable address for receiving legal documents and compliance notifications, ensuring that HealthWave Wellness Center remained in good standing with state regulations.

Selecting an Office Location:

Emily prioritized finding an office location that was accessible to her target market, which included health-conscious individuals and professionals seeking wellness services. She chose a location in a vibrant neighborhood known for its health and wellness community. The location was easily accessible by public transportation and had ample parking, making it convenient for clients.

Emily also considered the physical space and amenities of potential locations. She selected an office space with a calming and welcoming atmosphere, which aligned with her brand's focus on holistic wellness. The space included yoga studios, therapy rooms, and a nutrition counseling area, providing a comprehensive wellness experience for clients.

By carefully selecting a registered agent and office location, Emily positioned HealthWave Wellness Center for success. The registered agent ensured legal compliance, while the strategic office location attracted clients and supported the business's growth.

File Articles of Organization With the State

Filing the Articles of Organization is a critical step in forming your LLC. This legal document officially registers your LLC with the state, providing it with recognition and the ability to operate within the state's legal framework. Properly filing your Articles of Organization ensures that your business meets state requirements and can legally conduct business activities. In this section, we will explain the process of filing Articles of Organization and provide tips on ensuring accuracy and compliance.

Understanding the Articles of Organization

The Articles of Organization, also known as a Certificate of Formation or Certificate of Organization in some states, is a foundational document that outlines basic information about your LLC. This document includes essential details such as the name of the LLC, the registered agent, the business address, and the purpose of the LLC. Filing this document with the state is necessary to legally establish your LLC.

Steps to File Articles of Organization

Filing Articles of Organization involves several steps, each of which requires careful attention to detail. Here's a comprehensive guide to help you through the process:

Obtain the Form

The first step is to obtain the Articles of Organization form from the Secretary of State's office or the relevant state agency that handles business registrations. Most states provide the form online, which you can download and complete electronically or print out and complete by hand. Visit the official website of your state's Secretary of State or business services division to find the correct form.

Gather Required Information

Before you start filling out the form, gather all the necessary information. This preparation will help ensure that you have everything you need to complete the form accurately. The information typically required includes:

- **LLC Name**: The name of your LLC must be unique and comply with state naming requirements. Ensure that the name is distinguishable from other registered entities in the state.
- **Registered Agent Information**: Provide the name and address of your registered agent, who will receive legal documents on behalf of your LLC.
- **Business Address**: Include the physical address of your LLC's principal place of business. Some states may also require the mailing address if it is different from the physical address.
- **Management Structure**: Indicate whether your LLC will be member-managed or manager-managed. This designation determines who will have authority to make decisions for the LLC.
- **Purpose of the LLC**: Some states require you to state the purpose of your LLC, which can be a general purpose or a specific business activity.

Complete the Form

Carefully complete the Articles of Organization form, providing accurate and complete information for each required section. Pay attention to any specific instructions provided by the state, as requirements may vary. Here are some key sections to focus on:

- **LLC Name**: Ensure that the name you provide matches the name you reserved during the name availability check. Double-check the spelling and format to avoid any discrepancies.
- **Registered Agent**: Confirm that the registered agent's name and address are correct. This information is crucial for legal and compliance purposes.
- **Business Address**: Verify that the address provided is accurate and complete. Include suite numbers or other address details as needed.
- **Management Structure**: Clearly indicate whether the LLC is member-managed or manager-managed. This designation impacts the governance and decision-making process of your LLC.
- **Signature**: Most states require the Articles of Organization to be signed by an organizer or authorized person. Ensure that the signature is provided as required.

File the Form With the State

Once you have completed the Articles of Organization form, you need to file it with the state. There are typically two ways to file:

- **Online Filing**: Many states offer online filing through their official websites. Online filing is often faster and more convenient, allowing you to complete the process electronically and receive confirmation more quickly.
- **Mail or In-Person Filing**: If you prefer, you can also file the form by mail or in person. Mail the completed form to the address provided by the state, along with any required filing fee. If filing in person, visit the Secretary of State's office or the relevant state agency to submit the form.

Pay the Filing Fee

Filing the Articles of Organization typically requires a filing fee, which varies by state. Ensure that you include the correct payment with your submission. Accepted payment methods may include checks, money orders, or credit/debit cards for online filings. Verify the amount and payment instructions provided by the state to avoid any delays.

Receive Confirmation

After filing the Articles of Organization and paying the filing fee, you will receive confirmation from the state. The confirmation may come in the form of an acknowledgment receipt, a stamped copy of the filed Articles of Organization, or a Certificate of Organization. This confirmation serves as official proof that your LLC has been legally formed and is recognized by the state.

Tips for Ensuring Accuracy and Compliance

Filing the Articles of Organization accurately and ensuring compliance with state requirements are essential for the successful formation of your LLC. Here are some tips to help you achieve accuracy and compliance:

Double-Check Information:

Carefully review all the information provided in the Articles of Organization form before filing. Double-check the spelling, addresses, and other details to ensure accuracy. Mistakes or omissions can lead to delays or rejection of your filing.

Follow State-Specific Instructions:

Each state has its own requirements and instructions for filing Articles of Organization. Follow the state-specific guidelines provided with the form. Pay attention to any unique requirements or additional documentation needed for your state.

Consult Legal Advice if Needed:

If you are unsure about any aspect of the Articles of Organization or the filing process, consider consulting legal advice. An attorney or legal professional with experience in business formation can provide valuable guidance and ensure that your filing is compliant with state regulations.

Use Professional Filing Services:

If you prefer a hands-off approach, you can use professional filing services that specialize in business formation. These services can handle the filing process on your behalf, ensuring accuracy and compliance. While there is a cost associated with these services, they can save you time and reduce the risk of errors.

Keep Copies of Filed Documents:

After filing the Articles of Organization, keep copies of all filed documents and confirmation receipts. These records are important for your business records and may be required for future reference or compliance purposes.

Stay Informed About State Requirements:

Stay informed about any changes or updates to state requirements for LLC formation. State regulations may change over time, and staying up-to-date ensures that your LLC remains compliant with current laws.

Monitor Filing Status:

After submitting the Articles of Organization, monitor the filing status with the state. Some states provide online portals where you can check the status of your filing. Monitoring the status helps you stay informed about any issues or delays that may arise.

Prepare for Ongoing Compliance:

Filing the Articles of Organization is just the first step in ensuring legal compliance for your LLC. Be prepared for ongoing compliance requirements, such as filing annual reports, paying state fees, and maintaining a registered agent. Staying proactive about compliance helps avoid penalties and keeps your LLC in good standing.

Common Mistakes to Avoid

When filing the Articles of Organization, it's important to avoid common mistakes that can lead to delays or complications. Here are some common mistakes to watch out for:

Incomplete or Incorrect Information:

One of the most common mistakes is providing incomplete or incorrect information on the Articles of Organization form. Ensure that all required fields are filled out accurately and completely. Double-check the information to avoid errors.

Failure to Follow State Guidelines:

Each state has specific guidelines and requirements for filing Articles of Organization. Failing to follow these guidelines can result in rejection of your filing. Review the state's instructions carefully and ensure that you meet all requirements.

Using a Non-Compliant LLC Name:

Your LLC name must comply with state naming requirements and be distinguishable from other registered entities. Using a name that is too similar to an existing business or does not meet naming criteria can lead to rejection. Verify the availability and compliance of your chosen name before filing.

Incorrect Filing Fee Payment:

Filing the Articles of Organization requires a filing fee, and incorrect payment can delay the process. Ensure that you pay the correct amount and use an accepted payment method. Verify the fee amount and payment instructions provided by the state.

Neglecting to Include Required Signatures:

Most states require the Articles of Organization to be signed by an organizer or authorized person. Neglecting to include the required signature(s) can result in rejection. Ensure that the form is signed as required before filing.

Not Keeping Copies of Filed Documents:

After filing, it's important to keep copies of all filed documents and confirmation receipts. Failing to keep these records can lead to difficulties in the future if you need to reference the filed documents. Maintain organized records of all filed documents for your LLC.

Example of Filing Articles of Organization

To illustrate the process, let's consider the example of filing Articles of Organization for a hypothetical LLC named "EcoFriendly Solutions LLC."

Step 1: Obtain the Form

John, the founder of EcoFriendly Solutions LLC, visits the official website of the Secretary of State's office in his state. He downloads the

Articles of Organization form and reviews the state-specific instructions.

Step 2: Gather Required Information

John gathers the necessary information for the Articles of Organization:

- LLC Name: EcoFriendly Solutions LLC
- Registered Agent: Sarah Johnson, 123 Green St, Springfield, IL
- Business Address: 456 Elm St, Springfield, IL
- Management Structure: Member-Managed
- Purpose of LLC: To provide eco-friendly products and consulting services

Step 3: Complete the Form

John carefully completes the Articles of Organization form, providing accurate information for each section. He ensures that the LLC name matches the name he reserved during the name availability check.

Step 4: File the Form With the State

John decides to file the Articles of Organization online for convenience. He uploads the completed form through the state's online filing portal and pays the filing fee using his credit card.

Step 5: Pay the Filing Fee

John ensures that he pays the correct filing fee as specified by the state. The online portal provides a secure payment method, and he receives an acknowledgment receipt for the payment.

Step 6: Receive Confirmation

A few days later, John receives an email confirmation from the state, including a stamped copy of the filed Articles of Organization and a Certificate of Organization. EcoFriendly Solutions LLC is now officially registered and recognized by the state.

Obtain Necessary Licenses and Permits

Obtaining the necessary licenses and permits is a crucial step in the process of launching your LLC. These documents grant you the legal authority to conduct specific business activities within your jurisdiction. Failing to obtain the required licenses and permits can result in fines, penalties, or even the closure of your business. In this section, we will discuss the importance of obtaining these documents and provide steps for identifying and applying for them.

Importance of Obtaining Licenses and Permits

Obtaining the required licenses and permits is essential for several reasons:

Legal Compliance:

Operating without the necessary licenses and permits can lead to legal consequences. Regulatory agencies enforce compliance with licensing requirements to protect consumers, ensure public safety, and maintain fairness in the marketplace.

Professional Credibility:

Holding the appropriate licenses and permits demonstrates your commitment to professionalism and compliance with industry standards. It instills confidence in customers, suppliers, and partners, enhancing your reputation in the business community.

Risk Mitigation:

Proper licensing helps mitigate risks associated with your business activities. It ensures that you adhere to industry regulations and standards, reducing the likelihood of lawsuits, disputes, or regulatory actions.

Access to Opportunities:

Many contracts, partnerships, and financing opportunities require proof of licensing and permits. Holding the necessary documents opens doors to potential collaborations, contracts, and funding opportunities for your LLC.

Business Continuity:

Maintaining current licenses and permits is essential for the ongoing operation of your LLC. Renewing licenses and permits on time helps avoid disruptions to your business operations and ensures continuity.

Steps for Obtaining Licenses and Permits

Obtaining licenses and permits involves several steps, each of which requires thorough research and attention to detail. Here's a guide to help you navigate the process:

1. Identify Required Licenses and Permits

The first step is to identify the specific licenses and permits required for your business activities. The types of licenses and permits you need depend on factors such as your industry, location, and the nature of your business operations. Common types of licenses and permits include:

- **Business License**: A general license required to operate a business within a specific jurisdiction.

- **Professional License**: A license required for individuals in certain professions, such as doctors, lawyers, or real estate agents.
- **Zoning Permit**: A permit required for businesses to operate in compliance with local zoning regulations.
- **Health Permit**: A permit required for businesses involved in food service, healthcare, or other activities that impact public health.
- **Building Permit**: A permit required for construction, renovation, or alteration of commercial buildings.
- **Environmental Permit**: A permit required for businesses that may impact the environment, such as manufacturing or waste management.

Research the licensing requirements applicable to your industry and location. You can contact local government agencies, industry associations, or online resources to identify the specific licenses and permits you need.

2. Understand Application Requirements

Once you have identified the required licenses and permits, research the application process and requirements for each document. Each licensing authority may have its own application forms, fees, documentation requirements, and review processes. Understand the specific requirements for each license or permit to ensure a smooth application process.

3. Gather Necessary Documentation

Gather all the documentation required for each license or permit application. Common documents may include:

- **Business Information**: Provide details about your LLC, such as its legal name, address, ownership structure, and contact information.

- **Personal Information**: Include personal information for the LLC's owners, officers, or managers, such as names, addresses, Social Security numbers, and government-issued identification.
- **Proof of Business Ownership**: Provide documentation proving your ownership or authority to operate the business, such as Articles of Organization, operating agreements, or corporate resolutions.
- **Financial Statements**: Depending on the license or permit, you may need to submit financial statements, business plans, or projections to demonstrate financial stability and viability.
- **Certificates and Qualifications**: If applicable, provide copies of professional licenses, certifications, or qualifications required for your industry.

Ensure that you have all the required documentation prepared and organized before starting the application process.

4. Complete Application Forms

Complete the application forms for each license or permit accurately and completely. Pay attention to instructions and guidelines provided by the licensing authority. Provide all requested information, double-checking for accuracy and consistency.

5. Submit Applications and Fees

Once you have completed the application forms and gathered the necessary documentation, submit your applications to the appropriate licensing authorities. Include any required fees or payments with your applications. Accepted payment methods may include checks, money orders, or electronic payments, depending on the licensing authority's preferences.

6. Monitor Application Progress

After submitting your applications, monitor the progress of each application closely. Some licensing authorities provide online portals or tracking systems where you can check the status of your applications. Follow up with the licensing authority if you have not received confirmation or updates within the expected timeframe.

7. Address Any Requests for Additional Information

During the application review process, the licensing authority may request additional information or documentation to complete the review. Respond promptly to any requests for clarification or supplementary materials. Provide the requested information accurately and comprehensively to expedite the application process.

8. Obtain Approvals and Permits

Once your applications have been reviewed and approved, you will receive the necessary licenses and permits from the licensing authority. Review the documents carefully to ensure accuracy and compliance with the terms and conditions specified. Keep copies of all licenses and permits in a secure and easily accessible location.

9. Renew Licenses and Permits as Needed

Many licenses and permits have expiration dates and require renewal at regular intervals. Monitor the expiration dates of your licenses and permits and initiate the renewal process well in advance to avoid lapses in compliance. Follow any renewal instructions provided by the licensing authority and pay any required renewal fees on time.

Tips for Obtaining Licenses and Permits

Start Early:

Begin the process of obtaining licenses and permits as soon as possible, as the application and review process may take time. Starting early allows you to address any challenges or delays that may arise during the process.

Seek Professional Assistance:

If you are unsure about the licensing requirements or application process, consider seeking assistance from legal or business professionals with experience in your industry. They can provide guidance and support to ensure that you meet all regulatory requirements.

Stay Organized:

Keep detailed records of all communication, documentation, and interactions related to the licensing and permitting process. Organize your paperwork in a systematic manner to facilitate easy access and retrieval when needed.

Double-Check Requirements:

Review the requirements for each license and permit carefully to ensure that you have met all criteria before submitting your applications. Missing or incomplete information can lead to delays or denials.

Maintain Compliance:

Once you have obtained the necessary licenses and permits, ensure ongoing compliance with all applicable regulations and requirements. Stay informed about any updates or changes to licensing laws and regulations that may affect your business.

Plan for Expansion:

If you anticipate expanding your business operations or entering new markets, research and understand the licensing requirements for those areas in advance. Planning ahead can help streamline the expansion process and avoid compliance issues down the road.

Seek Feedback:

If possible, seek feedback from other business owners or industry peers who have gone through the process of obtaining licenses and permits. Their insights and experiences can provide valuable guidance and help you navigate the process more effectively.

Chapter 3
Financial Setup and Tax Planning

Open a Business Bank Account

Opening a business bank account is a crucial step in establishing the financial foundation of your LLC. It offers numerous benefits and is essential for managing your business finances separately from your personal funds. Here's why having a separate business bank account is important and how you can go about opening one.

Benefits of Having a Separate Business Bank Account

Legal Separation:

One of the primary reasons to open a business bank account is to establish a clear separation between your personal finances and your business finances. This separation is essential for legal and liability purposes, ensuring that your personal assets are protected in the event of legal action against your business.

Professionalism:

Having a dedicated business bank account conveys professionalism and credibility to your customers, suppliers, and investors. It demonstrates that you are running a legitimate business entity with organized financial management practices.

Tracking Business Expenses:

With a separate business bank account, you can easily track your business income and expenses. This simplifies accounting processes, making it easier to prepare financial statements, file taxes, and monitor your business's financial health.

Facilitates Tax Reporting:

Keeping your business finances separate makes tax reporting much more straightforward. You can easily identify and categorize business transactions, making it easier to claim deductions and comply with tax regulations.

Access to Business Banking Services:

Business bank accounts often come with additional features and services tailored to the needs of business owners, such as merchant services, business credit cards, and lines of credit. These services can help you manage cash flow, access financing, and streamline financial operations.

Steps for Opening a Business Bank Account

Choose the Right Bank:

Research and compare different banks to find one that offers the features and services that best suit your business needs. Consider factors such as fees, account features, online banking capabilities, and branch locations.

Gather Required Documentation:

Before visiting the bank, gather the necessary documentation to open a business bank account. This typically includes your LLC's formation documents (such as the Articles of Organization), your Employer Identification Number (EIN), and identification documents for the LLC's authorized signatories.

Schedule an Appointment:

Contact the bank to schedule an appointment to open a business bank account. This allows you to meet with a representative who can guide you through the process and answer any questions you may have.

Visit the Bank:

Bring all required documentation to your appointment at the bank. The bank representative will review your documents, verify your identity, and assist you in completing the necessary paperwork to open the account.

Deposit Funds:

To activate your business bank account, you will need to make an initial deposit. The amount required may vary depending on the bank and the type of account you are opening.

Select Account Features:

Choose the type of business bank account that best suits your needs, whether it's a checking account, savings account, or a combination of both. Consider features such as online banking, mobile banking, overdraft protection, and account management tools.

Set Up Online Banking:

Once your account is opened, take advantage of online banking services to manage your account conveniently from anywhere. Set up online bill pay, account alerts, and other features to streamline your financial management processes.

Review Account Terms and Fees:

Take the time to review the terms and conditions of your business bank account, including any associated fees and charges. Understand the bank's policies regarding minimum balances, transaction limits, and overdraft fees.

Maintain Accurate Records:

Keep detailed records of all transactions conducted through your business bank account. Regularly reconcile your account to ensure that your records match the bank's records and to identify any discrepancies or errors promptly.

By following these steps, you can establish a separate business bank account efficiently and effectively. This foundational step sets the stage for proper financial management and compliance with legal and regulatory requirements, ultimately supporting the success and growth of your LLC.

Obtain an Employer Identification Number (EIN)

Obtaining an Employer Identification Number (EIN) is a critical step in the process of establishing your LLC. An EIN, also known as a Federal Tax Identification Number, is a unique nine-digit number assigned by the Internal Revenue Service (IRS) to identify your business entity for tax purposes. Here, we will discuss the importance of an EIN for your LLC and provide detailed steps for obtaining one from the IRS.

Importance of an EIN for Your LLC

Obtaining an Employer Identification Number (EIN) is a pivotal step in establishing your LLC and laying the groundwork for its success. Let's delve deeper into the significance of an EIN for your LLC, exploring each aspect in detail:

Tax Identification:

As you embark on your journey as an entrepreneur, understanding the importance of an EIN as your LLC's tax identification number is paramount. This nine-digit identifier serves as a unique identifier for your business entity in the eyes of the Internal Revenue Service (IRS). With an EIN, you are equipped to fulfill your tax obligations effectively, from filing tax returns to paying taxes accurately and on time. Whether it's income tax, employment tax, or other tax-related matters, having an EIN streamlines the process and ensures compliance with federal tax regulations.

Employer Requirements:

If your LLC has aspirations of growth and expansion that involve hiring employees, an EIN becomes indispensable. As an employer, you are responsible for withholding and remitting various employment taxes on behalf of your employees. These include federal income tax withholding, Social Security, and Medicare taxes. An EIN is essential for reporting these taxes to the IRS and ensuring that your business remains compliant with employment tax regulations. By obtaining an EIN early on, you set the stage for seamless payroll tax management as your workforce grows.

Business Banking:

Establishing a separate business bank account is not only a best practice but often a requirement for LLCs. Many financial institutions mandate the use of an EIN to open a business bank account. This separation of personal and business finances is crucial for financial management and legal compliance. With a dedicated business bank account linked to your EIN, you can track income and expenses more effectively, simplify tax preparation, and demonstrate the legitimacy of your business operations to financial institutions and potential investors.

Legal Compliance:

Operating your LLC without an EIN is akin to navigating uncharted waters without a compass. An EIN not only facilitates tax compliance but also plays a vital role in establishing your LLC as a distinct legal entity. By obtaining an EIN, you formalize your LLC's existence in the eyes of the law, separating it from the personal assets and liabilities of its owners. This legal distinction shields your personal finances from business debts and liabilities, providing a layer of protection and peace of mind. Moreover, an EIN is a prerequisite for filing various tax returns, including income tax returns and employment tax returns, ensuring that your LLC remains in good standing with the IRS.

Business Relationships:

In the dynamic landscape of entrepreneurship, building strong business relationships is key to success. An EIN serves as more than just a tax identifier; it is a symbol of legitimacy and professionalism that can open doors to valuable opportunities. When seeking business loans, establishing credit lines, or entering into agreements with vendors or suppliers, having an EIN adds credibility to your LLC and instills confidence in potential partners and stakeholders. It streamlines administrative processes, facilitates financial transactions, and fosters trust in your business dealings.

Steps for Obtaining an EIN From the IRS

Obtaining an Employer Identification Number (EIN) from the IRS is a straightforward process, but it requires careful attention to detail to ensure accuracy and efficiency. Here are the step-by-step instructions to guide you through the process of obtaining an EIN for your LLC:

Determine Eligibility:

Before diving into the application process, it's essential to confirm that your LLC is eligible to obtain an EIN. While most businesses structured as LLCs are eligible, there may be exceptions based on certain criteria. To verify eligibility, consult the IRS website or seek guidance from a tax professional who can provide tailored advice based on your specific circumstances.

Prepare Required Information:

Gather all the necessary information needed to complete the EIN application. This includes details about your LLC, such as its legal name, mailing address, business structure, and the names and Social Security Numbers (SSNs) of the LLC's owners. Having this information on hand will streamline the application process and ensure that you provide accurate details.

Choose Application Method:

The IRS offers multiple methods for applying for an EIN, allowing you to choose the option that best suits your preferences and needs. The most convenient and efficient method is to apply online through the IRS website using the EIN Assistant tool. Alternatively, you can opt to apply by mail or fax using Form SS-4, or by phone. Consider factors such as accessibility, convenience, and turnaround time when selecting your preferred application method.

Complete the Application:

If you've chosen to apply online, navigate to the IRS website and access the EIN Assistant tool. Follow the prompts to complete the online application, providing accurate information about your LLC and its owners. Take your time to ensure that all entries are correct and consistent with your LLC's legal documentation. Double-checking the application for accuracy can help prevent delays and avoid potential issues down the line.

Submit the Application:

Once you've completed the application, review it carefully to verify the accuracy of the information provided. If applying online, submit the application electronically through the IRS website. For applications submitted by mail or fax, print and sign the completed Form SS-4 and follow the instructions provided for submission. Prompt and accurate submission of the application will expedite the processing of your EIN.

Receive Your EIN:

Upon successful submission of your application, the IRS will assign an EIN to your LLC. If you applied online, you will receive your EIN immediately upon completion of the application process. In contrast, applications submitted by mail or fax may take a few weeks to process. Upon receiving your EIN, make a note of it and store it securely for future reference.

Update Business Records:

With your newly acquired EIN in hand, it's crucial to update your LLC's records to reflect the change. Provide your EIN to banks, financial institutions, business partners, and other relevant parties as needed for tax and business purposes. Ensuring that your business records are up to date and accurate will help streamline administrative processes and maintain compliance with regulatory requirements.

Obtaining an EIN is a straightforward process that is essential for the proper functioning and compliance of your LLC. By following these steps and obtaining your EIN promptly, you can ensure that your business is equipped to fulfill its tax obligations and operate smoothly.

Set Up Accounting Systems and Software

Setting up accounting systems and software is a critical aspect of managing your LLC's finances effectively. Accurate accounting is essential for making informed business decisions, maintaining compliance with tax regulations, and ensuring the financial health and stability of your company. In this section, we will explore the importance of accurate accounting and provide tips on selecting and setting up accounting software tailored to the needs of your LLC.

Importance of Accurate Accounting

Accurate accounting is the foundation of financial management for any business, regardless of its size or industry. Here are some key reasons why accurate accounting is essential for the success of your LLC:

Financial Decision-Making:

Accurate financial records provide valuable insights into your LLC's performance, allowing you to make informed decisions about budgeting, investments, pricing strategies, and resource allocation. By having a clear understanding of your financial position, you can identify areas of strength and opportunities for improvement, guiding your business towards sustainable growth and profitability.

Tax Compliance:

Proper accounting ensures that your LLC remains compliant with tax regulations and reporting requirements. Accurate financial records are necessary for preparing and filing tax returns, calculating tax liabilities, and claiming deductions and credits. Failing to maintain accurate accounting records can result in penalties, fines, and legal consequences, potentially jeopardizing the financial health and reputation of your business.

Financial Planning:

Effective financial planning is essential for setting goals, forecasting future performance, and mitigating financial risks. Accurate accounting allows you to track revenue, expenses, cash flow, and other key financial metrics, providing the data needed to develop realistic budgets and forecasts. By monitoring your LLC's financial performance over time, you can identify trends, anticipate challenges, and implement proactive strategies to achieve your business objectives.

Investor Confidence:

For LLCs seeking external financing or investment, accurate accounting instills confidence in investors and lenders by demonstrating transparency, accountability, and financial stability. Well-maintained financial records enable stakeholders to assess the viability and potential return on investment of your business, facilitating capital raising efforts and fostering trust and credibility within the investment community.

Business Growth:

As your LLC grows and expands, accurate accounting becomes even more critical for managing increased complexity and scale. Robust accounting systems and processes provide the foundation for scalability, allowing you to efficiently manage larger volumes of transactions, streamline operations, and adapt to evolving business needs. By investing in accurate accounting from the outset, you can position your LLC for long-term success and sustainable growth.

Tips on Selecting and Setting Up Accounting Software

Choosing the right accounting software is essential for streamlining financial management processes, improving efficiency, and maintaining accurate and up-to-date financial records. Here are some tips to help you select and set up accounting software that meets the needs of your LLC:

Assess Your Needs:

Before selecting accounting software, assess your LLC's specific accounting requirements, including the volume of transactions, complexity of financial reporting, integration with other business systems, and user accessibility. Identify key features and functionalities that are essential for your business, such as invoicing, expense tracking, budgeting, payroll management, and inventory management.

Consider Scalability:

Choose accounting software that can grow with your business and accommodate future expansion and increased transaction volumes. Scalable software solutions offer flexibility and customization options, allowing you to adapt to changing business needs without the need for costly upgrades or migration to a new system.

Ease of Use:

Look for accounting software that is user-friendly and intuitive, with a well-designed interface and navigation system. Ease of use is crucial for ensuring that you and your team can quickly learn how to use the software effectively and efficiently. Consider conducting a demo or trial of the software to evaluate its usability and suitability for your LLC's needs.

Integration Capabilities:

Ensure that the accounting software you choose integrates seamlessly with other essential business systems and tools, such as CRM software, payment processors, e-commerce platforms, and banking services. Integration allows for automated data transfer and synchronization, eliminating manual data entry and reducing the risk of errors and discrepancies.

Data Security:

Protecting sensitive financial data is paramount for any business. Choose accounting software that employs robust security measures, such as encryption, user authentication, data backup, and access controls. Verify that the software provider complies with industry standards and regulations for data protection and privacy, such as GDPR or HIPAA, if applicable to your business.

Customer Support and Training:

Select a software provider that offers comprehensive customer support, including technical assistance, training resources, and ongoing maintenance and updates. Reliable customer support ensures that you can quickly resolve any issues or questions that arise during the implementation and use of the software, minimizing disruptions to your business operations.

Cost and Pricing:

Consider the cost and pricing structure of accounting software, including upfront fees, subscription plans, and additional charges for advanced features or support services. Evaluate the total cost of ownership over time, taking into account factors such as scalability, customization, and potential savings in time and resources. Choose a software solution that offers value for money and aligns with your budgetary constraints and long-term financial goals.

By following these tips and best practices, you can select and set up accounting software that empowers your LLC to manage its finances effectively, make informed business decisions, and achieve sustainable growth and success.

Consult With Tax Professionals to Develop a Tax Strategy

Consulting with tax professionals is a crucial step in ensuring the financial health and compliance of your LLC. Tax professionals, such as certified public accountants (CPAs) and tax advisors, possess the expertise and knowledge needed to navigate the complexities of tax regulations, maximize tax savings opportunities, and develop effective tax strategies tailored to your business objectives. In this section, we will discuss the benefits of working with tax professionals and provide tips on developing an effective tax strategy for your LLC.

Benefits of Working With Tax Professionals

Expertise and Knowledge:

Tax professionals have in-depth knowledge of tax laws, regulations, and compliance requirements at the federal, state, and local levels. They stay updated on changes in tax legislation and rulings, allowing them to provide accurate and timely advice on tax matters relevant to your LLC. By leveraging their expertise, you can ensure compliance with tax laws while minimizing your tax liabilities.

Customized Advice:

Tax professionals understand that every business is unique, with its own set of financial circumstances, goals, and challenges. They take the time to assess your LLC's financial situation, industry-specific considerations, and long-term objectives to provide personalized tax advice and recommendations. Whether you are a sole proprietor, partnership, or corporation, tax professionals can tailor their services to meet your specific needs and priorities.

Tax Planning Strategies:

Tax professionals can help you develop proactive tax planning strategies designed to optimize your LLC's tax position and minimize tax liabilities. They analyze your income, expenses, deductions, credits, and other tax-related factors to identify opportunities for tax savings and efficiency. By strategically timing income and expenses, maximizing deductions and credits, and utilizing tax-advantaged investment strategies, tax professionals can help you retain more of your hard-earned income and reinvest it back into your business.

Risk Mitigation:

Tax professionals play a vital role in identifying and mitigating tax-related risks and exposures that could potentially impact your LLC's financial stability and reputation. They conduct thorough tax risk assessments, review your tax returns for accuracy and compliance, and implement safeguards and controls to prevent errors, omissions, or discrepancies that could trigger audits, penalties, or legal issues. By proactively addressing tax risks, tax professionals help safeguard your business and protect your interests.

Representation and Advocacy:

In the event of an IRS audit, tax dispute, or tax-related issue, having a tax professional on your side can provide invaluable support and representation. Tax professionals act as advocates for your LLC, communicating with tax authorities on your behalf, providing documentation and evidence to support your position, and negotiating settlements or resolutions when necessary. Their expertise and experience in dealing with tax authorities can help resolve disputes efficiently and minimize the potential impact on your business operations.

Tips on Developing an Effective Tax Strategy

Start Early:

Developing a tax strategy should be an ongoing process that starts early in your LLC's lifecycle. Work with tax professionals to establish tax planning goals and objectives, assess your current tax situation, and identify opportunities for tax optimization and savings. By starting early, you can implement proactive tax planning strategies that yield long-term benefits and minimize surprises come tax time.

Understand Your Tax Obligations:

Familiarize yourself with the tax obligations and requirements applicable to your LLC based on its business structure, industry, and location. Understand the different types of taxes you are subject to, such as income tax, self-employment tax, payroll tax, sales tax, and excise tax. Be aware of filing deadlines, reporting requirements, and compliance obligations to avoid penalties and fines.

Maximize Deductions and Credits:

Take advantage of available deductions and credits to reduce your LLC's taxable income and lower your overall tax liability. Work with tax professionals to identify eligible expenses, investments, and activities that qualify for tax deductions and credits, such as business expenses, depreciation, research and development credits, and retirement contributions. Maximize deductions and credits wherever possible to retain more of your earnings and reinvest them back into your business.

Optimize Entity Structure:

Evaluate your LLC's entity structure to ensure it aligns with your tax planning goals and objectives. Depending on your business activities, income levels, and growth plans, you may benefit from electing a different tax classification, such as S corporation or C corporation, to optimize your tax position and minimize taxes. Consult with tax professionals to assess the tax implications of different entity structures and determine the most advantageous option for your LLC.

Plan for Estimated Taxes:

If your LLC expects to owe $1,000 or more in taxes for the year, you are generally required to make estimated tax payments to the IRS and state tax authorities throughout the year. Develop a strategy for estimating and paying quarterly taxes based on your LLC's projected income, deductions, and tax liabilities. Work with tax professionals to calculate estimated tax payments accurately, avoid underpayment penalties, and optimize cash flow management.

Stay Compliant:

Compliance with tax laws and regulations is essential for avoiding penalties, fines, and legal consequences that could harm your LLC's financial health and reputation. Stay informed about changes in tax legislation, reporting requirements , and filing deadlines relevant to your LLC's business activities and industry. Maintain accurate and organized financial records, including income statements, balance sheets, expense reports, and supporting documentation, to facilitate tax preparation and reporting. Keep abreast of any updates or amendments to tax laws that may impact your LLC's tax obligations, and consult with tax professionals to ensure compliance with all applicable tax regulations.

Monitor Tax Efficiency:

Regularly review and monitor the tax efficiency of your LLC's operations, investments, and financial decisions. Assess the tax implications of major business transactions, such as acquisitions, divestitures, mergers, and capital investments, to identify potential tax risks and opportunities. Conduct tax planning scenarios and sensitivity analyses to evaluate the impact of different tax strategies on your LLC's financial performance and cash flow. Adjust your tax strategy as needed to adapt to changing market conditions, business goals, and regulatory developments.

Document Tax Positions:

Maintain comprehensive documentation of your LLC's tax positions, decisions, and strategies to support compliance, audit defense, and risk management efforts. Document the rationale behind tax planning decisions, including legal opinions, tax memos, correspondence with tax authorities, and relevant financial data and analyses. Retain copies of tax returns, schedules, and supporting documentation for the applicable statutory retention periods to demonstrate compliance with tax laws and regulations.

Review and Update Regularly:

Tax planning is not a one-time exercise but an ongoing process that requires regular review and updates to reflect changes in your LLC's business environment, tax laws, and financial objectives. Schedule periodic meetings with tax professionals to review your tax strategy, assess its effectiveness, and identify areas for improvement or optimization. Stay proactive and responsive to changes in tax legislation, economic conditions, and industry trends that may impact your LLC's tax position and profitability.

By working closely with tax professionals and following these tips, you can develop an effective tax strategy that minimizes tax liabilities, maximizes tax savings, and enhances the financial performance and sustainability of your LLC. Remember that tax planning is an essential aspect of business management and requires careful consideration, diligence, and expertise to achieve optimal results.

Chapter 4
Branding and Marketing

Design Your Brand Logo and Visual Identity

Creating a compelling visual identity is essential for establishing brand recognition and attracting customers to your LLC. Your brand's visual elements, including your logo, color palette, typography, and imagery, play a crucial role in conveying your brand's personality, values, and identity. In this section, we'll discuss the importance of a strong visual identity and provide tips on designing a memorable logo and other brand materials.

Importance of a Strong Visual Identity

Your visual identity acts as the face of your LLC, serving as the first point of contact for potential customers and leaving a lasting impression. It encompasses various elements such as your logo, color scheme, typography, and imagery, all of which work together to communicate your brand's essence and values. Establishing a strong visual identity is crucial for several reasons, each of which plays a vital role in shaping how your brand is perceived and experienced by your audience.

Brand Recognition:

Consistency in your visual identity helps customers recognize and remember your brand amidst a sea of competitors. A distinctive logo and consistent use of visual elements make it easier for customers to identify your products or services, even in a crowded marketplace. When customers can easily recognize your brand, they are more likely to choose your products or services over others.

Professionalism and Credibility:

A well-designed visual identity conveys professionalism and credibility, instilling confidence in your brand among customers. High-quality branding materials, including a polished logo and cohesive brand imagery, signal to customers that your LLC is trustworthy and reputable. This perception of professionalism can positively impact customers' willingness to engage with your business and make purchases.

Emotional Connection:

Visual elements have the power to evoke emotions and perceptions that influence how customers feel about your brand. A visually appealing and cohesive brand identity can evoke positive emotions, such as trust, excitement, or joy, and create a strong emotional connection with your target audience. By tapping into your audience's emotions, you can foster loyalty and advocacy, turning customers into brand ambassadors.

Brand Consistency:

Consistency is key to building a strong and memorable brand identity. When your visual branding is consistent across all channels and touchpoints, it reinforces your brand's message and values, creating a unified brand experience for customers. Whether they interact with your website, social media profiles, or physical storefront, customers should encounter a consistent visual identity that reinforces your brand's identity and resonates with them.

Maintaining consistency in your visual identity helps to establish brand recognition, build trust and credibility, create emotional connections with your audience, and reinforce your brand's message and values. By investing in a strong visual identity, you can differentiate your brand from competitors, leave a lasting impression on customers, and lay the foundation for long-term success.

Tips for Designing a Memorable Logo and Brand Materials

Understand Your Brand:

Before designing your logo and brand materials, take the time to understand your brand's identity, values, and target audience. Consider the emotions and associations you want to evoke and how you want your brand to be perceived.

Simplicity is Key:

Keep your logo and brand materials simple and easy to recognize. Avoid clutter and unnecessary elements that can dilute your brand message. A clean and minimalist design will make your brand more memorable and versatile across different platforms and applications.

Reflect Your Brand Personality:

Your logo and visual identity should reflect the personality and essence of your brand. Whether your brand is playful and whimsical or professional and sophisticated, ensure that your visual elements align with your brand's tone and voice.

Choose Colors Wisely:

Colors play a significant role in brand perception and can evoke specific emotions and associations. Select a color palette that resonates with your brand's personality and values. Consider the psychological effects of different colors and how they influence customer perceptions.

Typography Matters:

Choose typography that complements your brand's visual identity and conveys the right tone and personality. Select fonts that are legible and appropriate for your brand's message and audience. Experiment with different font pairings to create visual interest while maintaining readability.

Versatility and Scalability:

Ensure that your logo and brand materials are versatile and scalable across different mediums and sizes. Your logo should look equally impressive on a business card, website, or billboard. Test your design in various formats and sizes to ensure readability and visual impact.

Seek Professional Help:

If you're not confident in your design skills, consider hiring a professional graphic designer or branding agency to create your logo and visual identity. Experienced designers can bring your vision to life and ensure that your branding materials are polished, professional, and aligned with your brand's objectives.

Gather Feedback:

Once you've created initial designs, gather feedback from trusted colleagues, friends, or target customers. Solicit constructive criticism and incorporate valuable insights to refine your designs further. Iteration is key to creating a memorable and effective visual identity.

By understanding your brand, keeping your designs simple and memorable, and seeking professional help when needed, you can create a visual identity that resonates with your target audience and sets your LLC apart from the competition.

Develop a Website and Establish Online Presence

In today's digital age, having a strong online presence is essential for the success of your LLC. Your website serves as the digital storefront for your business, allowing potential customers to learn more about your products or services, engage with your brand, and make purchases. Establishing an online presence not only expands your reach to a broader audience but also enhances your credibility and competitiveness in the marketplace. Here's why having an online presence is crucial and steps for creating a professional website:

Importance of an Online Presence

Having a robust online presence is paramount for the success and growth of your LLC in today's digital age. Let's delve into the importance of establishing and maintaining an online presence:

Accessibility and Convenience:

With an online presence, your business becomes accessible to customers 24/7, regardless of their location or time zone. Through your website, customers can effortlessly access information about your products or services, browse your offerings, and make purchases at their convenience. This accessibility enhances the overall customer experience, making it easier for potential customers to engage with your brand and increasing the likelihood of conversion. By removing barriers to access, you can cater to a broader audience and capitalize on opportunities for growth.

Brand Visibility and Awareness:

An online presence significantly enhances your brand's visibility and awareness in the digital landscape. By leveraging search engine optimization (SEO) techniques and social media platforms, you can increase your online visibility and reach a broader audience. Appearing in search engine results and engaging with users on social media platforms allows you to connect with potential customers who may not have otherwise discovered your business. A well-optimized website improves your search engine rankings, making it easier for customers to find you online and boosting brand recognition and recall.

Credibility and Trustworthiness:

In today's digitally-driven marketplace, consumers rely heavily on online research to inform their purchasing decisions. A professional-looking website instills confidence in your brand and enhances your credibility and trustworthiness. When customers encounter a well-designed website with relevant content and positive customer reviews, they are more likely to perceive your business as legitimate and trustworthy. Establishing a strong online presence not only reassures customers about the reliability of your products or services but also fosters long-term trust and loyalty.

Competitive Advantage:

An online presence provides you with a competitive edge in the market by allowing you to stay visible and accessible to customers who prefer to shop and engage online. In an increasingly digital world, businesses that lack an online presence risk falling behind competitors who are readily available and visible to customers online. By investing in a professional website and implementing digital marketing strategies, you can differentiate your brand, attract new customers, and retain existing ones. Moreover, an online presence allows you to monitor and adapt to changes in consumer behavior and market trends, giving you a strategic advantage in a competitive landscape.

Steps for Creating a Professional Website

Creating a professional website for your LLC is a crucial step in establishing a strong online presence and attracting customers. Here's an in-depth look at the steps involved in creating a professional website:

Define Your Goals and Audience:

Before diving into website development, take the time to define your goals and target audience. Consider what you want to achieve with your website and who your ideal customers are. Understanding your audience's needs, preferences, and pain points will guide your website's design, content, and functionality. Whether your goal is to generate leads, sell products, or provide valuable information, aligning your website with your business objectives is essential for success.

Choose a Domain Name and Hosting Provider:

Selecting a domain name that reflects your brand and is easy to remember and spell is crucial for establishing your online identity. Choose a reliable hosting provider that offers the features and resources you need to support your website. Factors such as uptime, security, scalability, and customer support should be considered when choosing a hosting provider. Opt for a hosting plan that aligns with your budget and technical requirements to ensure optimal performance and reliability.

Design Your Website:

Designing a visually appealing and user-friendly website is essential for creating a positive first impression and engaging visitors. Choose a responsive website design that adapts seamlessly to different devices and screen sizes, ensuring a consistent user experience across desktops, tablets, and smartphones. Focus on creating a clean and intuitive layout, with clear navigation and high-quality visuals that reflect your brand identity. Incorporate whitespace, contrast, and hierarchy to guide users' attention and facilitate easy navigation.

Create Compelling Content:

Develop informative and engaging content that resonates with your target audience and communicates your brand's value proposition. Clearly articulate your products or services, unique selling points, and benefits to your customers. Use compelling visuals, such as images, videos, and infographics, to enhance the presentation of your content and captivate your audience's attention. Incorporate relevant keywords strategically to improve your website's search engine visibility and attract organic traffic.

Optimize for Search Engines:

Implementing search engine optimization (SEO) best practices is essential for improving your website's visibility and ranking in search engine results. Optimize your website's meta tags, headings, and content with relevant keywords to enhance its relevance and authority in the eyes of search engines. Create descriptive and keyword-rich page titles and meta descriptions to improve click-through rates and drive organic traffic to your website. Regularly monitor your website's performance using analytics tools and make data-driven optimizations to improve its SEO performance over time.

Integrate Calls to Action (CTAs):

Include clear and compelling calls to action (CTAs) throughout your website to guide visitors toward desired actions, such as signing up for a newsletter, requesting a quote, or making a purchase. Design CTAs that stand out visually and use persuasive language to encourage engagement and conversions. Place CTAs strategically on relevant pages and sections of your website to maximize their effectiveness and drive user interaction.

Test and Iterate:

Testing your website across different devices, browsers, and screen sizes is essential to ensure compatibility and functionality. Conduct usability tests with real users to identify any usability issues or pain points and make necessary adjustments to improve the user experience. Solicit feedback from friends, family, or colleagues and incorporate their input into your website's design and content. Regularly monitor your website's performance using analytics tools to track key metrics such as traffic, engagement, and conversion rates. Use this data to make informed decisions and iterative improvements to enhance your website's effectiveness over time.

By following these steps and investing in a professional website, you can establish a strong online presence for your LLC, attract more customers, and position your business for success in the digital marketplace.

Create Marketing Collateral and Content

- Discuss the role of marketing collateral in brand promotion.
- Provide tips on creating effective marketing content.

Implement Social-Media and Digital Marketing Campaigns

Implementing social media and digital marketing campaigns is essential for promoting your LLC and reaching your target audience in today's digital landscape. By leveraging the power of social media platforms and digital marketing channels, you can increase brand visibility, engage with customers, and drive traffic to your website. Here's an in-depth look at the benefits of social media and digital marketing, along with steps for planning and executing effective campaigns:

Benefits of Social Media and Digital Marketing

Social media and digital marketing offer a plethora of benefits for businesses looking to establish a strong online presence and connect with their target audience. Let's delve into the various advantages of leveraging these channels to promote your LLC:

Increased Brand Visibility:

Social media and digital marketing provide powerful platforms for enhancing your brand's visibility and expanding your reach to a wider audience. Through strategic content distribution and targeted advertising campaigns, you can ensure that your brand is prominently featured in front of potential customers as they navigate the digital landscape. By establishing a presence on popular social media platforms like Facebook, Instagram, Twitter, and LinkedIn, and leveraging digital marketing channels such as search engine optimization (SEO) and display advertising, you can significantly enhance your brand's visibility and attract more attention to your products or services.

Engagement and Interaction:

One of the most significant benefits of social media is its ability to foster direct interaction and engagement with your audience. Through likes, comments, shares, and direct messages, you can build meaningful relationships with your customers, address their inquiries or concerns in real-time, and gather valuable feedback about your products or services. Moreover, digital marketing campaigns, such as email marketing and content marketing, enable you to engage with your audience by delivering relevant and personalized content that resonates with their interests and needs. By fostering a culture of engagement and interaction, you can strengthen customer relationships, increase brand loyalty, and drive long-term business success.

Targeted Advertising:

Digital marketing offers unparalleled precision when it comes to targeting specific demographics, interests, and behaviors. Social media platforms and digital advertising networks provide robust targeting options that allow you to reach the right audience with your marketing messages. By leveraging advanced targeting parameters such as age, gender, location, interests, and online behaviors, you can ensure that your ads are served to individuals who are most likely to be interested in your products or services. This targeted approach not only maximizes the impact of your marketing campaigns but also helps you achieve higher conversion rates and return on investment (ROI).

Cost-Effectiveness:

Compared to traditional advertising channels such as television, radio, and print media, social media and digital marketing offer a more cost-effective means of reaching your target audience. Many digital marketing platforms, including social media advertising platforms like Facebook Ads and Google Ads, offer flexible pricing models that allow you to set your budget and optimize your spending based on performance metrics such as cost per click (CPC) or cost per acquisition (CPA). Additionally, digital marketing campaigns often have lower barriers to entry and can generate a higher ROI compared to traditional advertising methods, making them an attractive option for businesses with limited budgets or resources.

Measurable Results:

One of the most significant advantages of digital marketing is its ability to provide access to comprehensive analytics and performance metrics that enable you to track the effectiveness of your campaigns in real-time. From website traffic and click-through rates to conversion rates and customer acquisition costs, you can measure various key performance indicators (KPIs) to evaluate the success of your marketing efforts. This data-driven approach allows you to make informed decisions and optimize your campaigns for better results, ultimately driving greater ROI and business growth.

Social media and digital marketing offer numerous benefits for businesses seeking to enhance their online presence, engage with their audience, and drive business results. By leveraging these channels effectively, you can increase brand visibility, foster meaningful interactions with your audience, target specific demographics with precision, optimize your marketing spend, and track the performance of your campaigns in real-time.

Steps for Planning and Executing Digital Marketing Campaigns

Planning and executing digital marketing campaigns require careful strategizing and meticulous implementation to achieve your desired outcomes. Here are the steps you can follow to effectively plan and execute your digital marketing initiatives:

Define Your Objectives:

The first step in planning any digital marketing campaign is to define your objectives and goals. Ask yourself what you want to achieve with your campaign. Are you looking to increase brand awareness, drive website traffic, generate leads, or boost sales? Clearly defining your objectives will help you shape your campaign strategy and determine the metrics you'll use to measure success.

Know Your Audience:

Understanding your target audience is crucial for the success of your digital marketing campaigns. Take the time to research and analyze your audience's demographics, interests, preferences, and online behavior. Create detailed buyer personas to identify who your ideal customers are and where they spend their time online. This knowledge will inform your content strategy, messaging, and channel selection.

Choose the Right Platforms:

Once you've identified your target audience, choose the social media platforms and digital marketing channels that align with your audience and objectives. Consider factors such as platform demographics, user engagement, and ad targeting options when making your selection. Focus your efforts on the platforms where your audience is most active and where you can achieve the best results for your campaign.

Create Compelling Content:

Develop high-quality content that resonates with your target audience and aligns with your brand message and values. Whether it's blog posts, social media posts, videos, or infographics, focus on creating content that educates, entertains, or inspires your audience. Tailor your content to address the needs and pain points of your target audience and encourage them to engage with your brand.

Develop a Content Calendar:

Plan your content distribution schedule in advance by creating a content calendar. This calendar should outline the types of content you'll publish, the platforms you'll use, and the dates and times of publication. Consistency is key to maintaining engagement and building brand awareness. By planning your content in advance, you can ensure that your messaging is cohesive and aligned with your campaign objectives.

Implement Targeted Advertising:

Leverage the targeting capabilities of social media advertising platforms and digital advertising networks to reach your ideal audience with precision. Define your audience demographics, interests, and behaviors, and tailor your ad creative and messaging accordingly. Experiment with different ad formats, targeting options, and messaging to identify what resonates best with your audience and drives the desired action.

Monitor and Measure Performance:

Once your digital marketing campaigns are live, it's essential to monitor their performance using analytics tools and performance metrics. Track key metrics such as website traffic, engagement, conversion rates, and ROI to evaluate the effectiveness of your campaigns. Use this data to identify areas for improvement and make adjustments to optimize your campaign performance.

Optimize and Iterate:

Continuously optimize your digital marketing campaigns based on performance data and insights. Experiment with different ad creatives, targeting options, and messaging to identify what resonates best with your audience. Iterate on your campaign strategy based on what works and what doesn't to improve results over time. By continuously testing and refining your approach, you can maximize the impact of your digital marketing efforts and achieve your business objectives.

By following these steps and leveraging the benefits of social media and digital marketing, you can effectively promote your LLC, engage with your audience, and achieve your marketing objectives in today's digital age.

Chapter 5
Technology Integration

Choose and Implement Digital Tools for LLC Management

When managing your LLC, leveraging digital tools can streamline operations, improve efficiency, and enhance productivity. However, with the abundance of options available, selecting the right digital tools can be overwhelming. Here, we'll discuss essential digital tools for managing your LLC and provide tips on selecting and implementing these tools effectively.

Accounting Software

Accounting software plays a crucial role in managing the financial aspects of your LLC, providing you with the tools and capabilities needed to keep track of your expenses, invoices, budgets, and financial reports. It streamlines your accounting processes, saves time, reduces errors, and helps you make more informed financial decisions. Here's why accounting software is indispensable for your LLC:

Firstly, accounting software automates many manual accounting tasks, such as data entry and reconciliation, allowing you to streamline your financial processes and improve efficiency. Instead of spending hours manually entering data into spreadsheets or ledgers, you can automate these tasks with accounting software, freeing up valuable time to focus on other aspects of your business.

Secondly, accounting software provides real-time visibility into your financial performance, allowing you to monitor your income, expenses, and cash flow at a glance. With up-to-date financial data readily available, you can make informed decisions about your business's finances and identify potential issues or opportunities before they become significant problems.

Thirdly, accounting software helps you stay organized and compliant with tax regulations by accurately tracking your expenses, income, and tax obligations. Many accounting software solutions offer features such as tax preparation tools, automatic tax calculations, and electronic filing options, making it easier to file your taxes accurately and on time.

Moreover, accounting software enables you to generate detailed financial reports with just a few clicks, providing valuable insights into your LLC's financial health and performance. Whether you need a balance sheet, profit and loss statement, cash flow statement, or customized financial report, accounting software makes it easy to create professional-looking reports that you can share with stakeholders, investors, or lenders.

When selecting accounting software for your LLC, consider factors such as ease of use, scalability, and integration with other business tools. Look for software that offers a user-friendly interface and intuitive navigation, as well as robust features that can grow with your business as it scales. Additionally, choose software that integrates seamlessly with other tools and systems you use, such as banking platforms, invoicing software, and payroll solutions, to streamline your financial workflows and ensure data consistency across your organization.

Popular accounting software options for LLCs include QuickBooks, Xero, and FreshBooks, each offering a range of features and pricing plans to suit different business needs. Evaluate your requirements carefully and choose the software that best aligns with your budget, functionality, and long-term growth goals.

Project Management Tools

Project management tools are indispensable for efficiently organizing tasks, collaborating with team members, and tracking project progress within your LLC. These tools provide a centralized platform where you can plan, execute, and monitor projects, ensuring that everyone stays aligned and on track toward achieving your business objectives.

One of the key features offered by project management tools is task lists or to-do lists, which allow you to break down projects into manageable tasks and assign them to team members. This helps ensure clarity and accountability, as each team member knows exactly what they need to do and by when. Task lists also enable you to prioritize tasks, set deadlines, and track progress, helping you stay organized and focused on key deliverables.

Another valuable feature of project management tools is kanban boards, which provide a visual representation of tasks and workflows. Kanban boards allow you to move tasks through different stages of completion, such as "To Do," "In Progress," and "Completed," providing a clear overview of project status and helping you identify bottlenecks or areas that require attention. This visual approach to project management enhances transparency and facilitates collaboration among team members.

Gantt charts are another essential feature offered by many project management tools, particularly for projects with complex timelines or dependencies. Gantt charts visually represent project schedules, showing task dependencies, milestones, and deadlines in a timeline format. This allows you to visualize project timelines, identify critical paths, and adjust schedules as needed to ensure timely project delivery. Gantt charts also facilitate communication and alignment among team members by providing a shared understanding of project timelines and milestones.

Furthermore, project management tools often include collaboration features such as file sharing, commenting, and real-time updates, allowing team members to communicate and collaborate effectively. These collaboration tools facilitate seamless communication, eliminate the need for lengthy email chains or meetings, and ensure that everyone is on the same page regarding project status and updates.

Popular project management tools for LLCs include Trello, Asana, and Monday.com, each offering a range of features and functionalities to support different project management needs. When selecting a project management tool for your LLC, consider factors such as ease of use, scalability, integration with other tools, and pricing. Choose a tool that aligns with your team's workflow and project management preferences, ensuring that it enhances productivity and efficiency rather than adding unnecessary complexity.

Customer Relationship Management (CRM) Software

Customer Relationship Management (CRM) software is instrumental in helping you effectively manage customer relationships, track interactions, and streamline your sales and marketing processes within your LLC. By centralizing customer data and providing valuable insights, CRM software empowers you to deliver personalized experiences, nurture leads, and drive revenue growth.

One of the key features of CRM software is contact management, which allows you to organize and store customer information in a centralized database. This includes details such as contact information, communication history, purchase history, and preferences. By maintaining a comprehensive record of customer interactions, you can better understand your customers' needs and preferences, anticipate their future requirements, and tailor your marketing and sales efforts accordingly.

Lead tracking is another critical feature offered by CRM software, enabling you to capture and manage leads throughout the sales process. CRM systems allow you to track lead sources, assign leads to sales representatives, and monitor lead status and progression through the sales pipeline. This ensures that leads are effectively nurtured and followed up on, increasing the likelihood of conversion and driving sales revenue.

CRM software also facilitates seamless integration with email platforms, enabling you to send personalized emails, track email interactions, and automate email marketing campaigns. By integrating CRM with your email system, you can maintain a complete record of email communications with customers and prospects, track email open rates and click-through rates, and segment your email lists based on customer behavior and preferences.

Sales pipeline management is another key feature of CRM software, providing visibility into the sales process and helping sales teams track opportunities from initial contact to closure. CRM systems allow you to visualize the sales pipeline, track deal stages, forecast revenue, and identify potential bottlenecks or areas for improvement. This enables sales teams to prioritize opportunities, allocate resources effectively, and close deals more efficiently.

Popular CRM software options for LLCs include Salesforce, HubSpot CRM, and Zoho CRM, each offering a range of features and functionalities to support different sales and marketing needs. When selecting a CRM system for your LLC, consider factors such as ease of use, scalability, customization options, and integration capabilities. Choose a CRM solution that aligns with your sales and marketing objectives and integrates seamlessly with other business tools, ensuring that it enhances productivity and efficiency across your organization.

Communication and Collaboration Tools

Communication and collaboration tools play a pivotal role in fostering effective communication and collaboration among team members, particularly in today's increasingly remote or distributed work environments. These tools facilitate real-time communication, file sharing, and project collaboration, enabling teams to stay connected, aligned, and productive regardless of their physical location.

One of the key features offered by communication and collaboration tools is video conferencing, which allows teams to conduct face-to-face meetings and discussions virtually. Video conferencing platforms such as Zoom, Microsoft Teams, and Google Meet enable teams to hold virtual meetings, share screens, and collaborate in real-time, fostering a sense of presence and connection even when team members are geographically dispersed.

Instant messaging is another essential feature provided by communication and collaboration tools, allowing team members to communicate quickly and efficiently in real-time. Platforms like Slack, Microsoft Teams, and Discord offer instant messaging capabilities, enabling teams to send messages, share files, and collaborate on projects seamlessly. Instant messaging helps teams stay connected and informed, facilitating quick decision-making and problem-solving.

File sharing and document collaboration are integral components of communication and collaboration tools, allowing teams to share files, documents, and resources effortlessly. Platforms like Google Drive, Microsoft OneDrive, and Dropbox provide secure cloud storage and file-sharing capabilities, enabling teams to access files from anywhere, collaborate on documents in real-time, and track version history. This promotes transparency, enhances workflow efficiency, and ensures that team members have access to the latest information and resources.

Document collaboration features offered by communication and collaboration tools enable multiple users to work on documents simultaneously, make edits in real-time, and track changes. Platforms such as Google Docs, Microsoft Office Online, and Notion allow teams to collaborate on documents, spreadsheets, and presentations, facilitating seamless collaboration and ensuring that everyone is working from the same version of the document.

When selecting communication and collaboration tools for your LLC, consider factors such as user-friendliness, reliability, security, and integration capabilities. Choose tools that are intuitive and easy to use, ensuring that your team can adopt them quickly and effectively. Additionally, prioritize tools that offer robust security features to protect sensitive information and ensure data privacy.

Integration capabilities are also crucial when choosing communication and collaboration tools, as they allow for seamless integration with other business tools and applications. Look for tools that integrate with your existing software ecosystem, such as project management tools, CRM systems, and productivity suites, to streamline workflows and enhance productivity across your organization.

Document Management Systems

Document management systems are indispensable tools for any business looking to streamline document organization, storage, and management processes. These systems provide a centralized platform for storing and managing documents securely, ensuring that your team can access the information they need quickly and efficiently.

One of the key features offered by document management systems is version control, which allows you to track changes to documents over time and maintain a clear record of revisions. With version control, you can easily revert to previous versions of documents if needed, preventing data loss and ensuring accuracy and integrity of information.

Access controls are another essential feature provided by document management systems, allowing you to control who can access, view, edit, and share documents within your organization. By implementing access controls, you can restrict access to sensitive information and ensure that only authorized users have permissions to view or modify documents, enhancing data security and compliance with regulatory requirements.

Document sharing capabilities offered by document management systems enable seamless collaboration among team members, regardless of their location. Platforms like Google Drive, Dropbox Business, and Microsoft OneDrive allow teams to share documents securely, collaborate on projects in real-time, and track changes made by multiple users. This promotes transparency, enhances communication, and improves workflow efficiency within your organization.

File syncing is another valuable feature provided by document management systems, allowing users to access and synchronize documents across multiple devices and platforms. With file syncing, your team can access documents from anywhere, whether they're working in the office, at home, or on the go, ensuring that everyone has access to the latest information and resources.

When selecting a document management system for your LLC, consider factors such as storage capacity, collaboration features, security, and ease of use. Choose a system that offers sufficient storage capacity to accommodate your organization's document storage needs, while also providing robust collaboration features to facilitate seamless teamwork and communication.

Security is paramount when it comes to document management systems, so be sure to choose a platform that offers advanced security features such as encryption, data loss prevention, and two-factor authentication. Additionally, ensure that the system complies with industry regulations and standards to protect sensitive information and ensure regulatory compliance.

Finally, prioritize ease of use when selecting a document management system, as user-friendly interfaces and intuitive features will facilitate adoption and usage among your team members. Choose a system that offers a simple and intuitive user interface, along with comprehensive training and support resources to help your team get up to speed quickly.

Email Marketing Software

Email marketing software plays a crucial role in your LLC's marketing strategy, enabling you to communicate with your audience effectively and drive engagement and conversions. These platforms offer a range of features designed to streamline the process of creating, sending, and tracking email campaigns, allowing you to deliver targeted and personalized messages to your subscribers.

One of the key features offered by email marketing software is customizable email templates, which allow you to create professional-looking emails without the need for coding or design expertise. These templates typically come with pre-designed layouts and themes that you can customize with your brand colors, logos, and messaging, ensuring consistency with your brand identity.

List segmentation is another essential feature provided by email marketing software, allowing you to divide your email subscribers into smaller, more targeted segments based on criteria such as demographics, interests, or purchase history. By segmenting your email list, you can send more relevant and personalized content to each group, increasing the effectiveness of your campaigns and driving higher engagement and conversions.

Automation capabilities offered by email marketing software enable you to set up automated email sequences or workflows that trigger based on certain actions or events, such as new subscriber sign-ups, website visits, or purchase behavior. These automated workflows allow you to nurture leads, welcome new subscribers, or re-engage inactive subscribers without requiring manual intervention, saving you time and effort while maintaining consistent communication with your audience.

Analytics and reporting features provided by email marketing software allow you to track the performance of your email campaigns in real-time and measure key metrics such as open rates, click-through rates, and conversion rates. By analyzing these metrics, you can gain valuable insights into the effectiveness of your campaigns, identify areas for improvement, and optimize your email marketing strategy for better results.

When selecting email marketing software for your LLC, consider factors such as ease of use, scalability, pricing, and integration with other tools and platforms. Choose a platform that offers an intuitive interface and user-friendly features, making it easy for you to create and manage email campaigns without requiring technical expertise.

Scalability is important, especially if your email list is expected to grow over time. Ensure that the platform can accommodate your growing subscriber base and provide advanced features and functionality as your needs evolve.

Pricing is another consideration, so choose a platform that offers pricing plans and features that align with your budget and requirements. Many email marketing platforms offer tiered pricing plans based on the number of subscribers or emails sent per month, so evaluate your needs and choose a plan that offers the best value for your investment.

Integration with your CRM system is crucial for seamless lead management and tracking. Choose an email marketing platform that integrates seamlessly with your CRM system, allowing you to sync contacts, track interactions, and manage leads effectively across both platforms.

Time Tracking and Employee Management Tools

Time tracking and employee management tools play a crucial role in ensuring the efficient operation of your LLC by helping you monitor employee productivity, track hours worked, and manage schedules effectively. These tools offer a range of features designed to streamline time tracking, scheduling, payroll management, and performance evaluation, empowering you to optimize workforce management and improve overall productivity.

One of the key features offered by time tracking and employee management tools is time tracking functionality, which allows you to accurately track the hours worked by your employees on various projects or tasks. By implementing time tracking software, you can gain insights into how employees allocate their time, identify potential inefficiencies or bottlenecks, and make data-driven decisions to improve productivity and resource allocation.

Scheduling features provided by these tools enable you to create and manage employee schedules efficiently, ensuring adequate coverage and optimal resource utilization. You can create shift schedules, assign tasks or projects to specific employees, and track attendance and time off requests seamlessly. This helps you avoid scheduling conflicts, reduce overtime costs, and optimize workforce allocation based on business needs.

Integration with payroll systems is another important feature offered by time tracking and employee management tools, allowing you to streamline payroll processing and ensure accurate and timely payment to employees. These tools can automatically sync time tracking data with your payroll software, calculate wages or salaries based on hours worked, and generate payroll reports for easy processing.

Performance analytics features provided by time tracking and employee management tools enable you to assess employee productivity, identify top performers, and address areas for improvement. You can generate performance reports, track key metrics such as billable hours or project completion rates, and evaluate employee performance objectively. This helps you recognize and reward top performers, provide targeted training or support to employees who may be struggling, and optimize workforce performance overall.

When selecting time tracking and employee management tools for your LLC, consider factors such as ease of use, scalability, integration capabilities, and pricing. Choose tools that offer an intuitive interface and user-friendly features, making it easy for you and your team to adopt and use the software effectively.

Scalability is important, especially if your LLC is growing or if you have plans to expand your workforce in the future. Ensure that the tools you choose can accommodate your evolving needs and provide advanced features and functionality as your business grows.

Integration capabilities are crucial for seamless workflow integration and data synchronization. Choose tools that integrate seamlessly with other business systems and software, such as payroll, accounting, or project management software, allowing you to streamline processes and improve efficiency across your organization.

Pricing is another consideration, so choose tools that offer pricing plans and features that align with your budget and requirements. Many time tracking and employee management tools offer tiered pricing plans based on the number of users or features included, so evaluate your needs and choose a plan that offers the best value for your investment.

When selecting and implementing digital tools for your LLC, consider your business needs, budget, and scalability. Take the time to research and evaluate different options, and choose tools that align with your goals and objectives. Once you've selected the right tools, ensure proper training and support for your team to maximize their effectiveness and adoption.

Set Up Cloud Storage and Data Security Measures

Data security is paramount for any business, including your LLC. With the increasing digitization of business operations and the prevalence of cyber threats, safeguarding your company's data is crucial to protect sensitive information, maintain customer trust, and comply with regulatory requirements. In this section, we'll highlight the importance of data security and provide steps for setting up cloud storage and implementing security measures to protect your LLC's valuable data.

Importance of Data Security

Data security is a critical aspect of running any business, including your LLC. In today's digital age, where sensitive information is stored and transmitted electronically, protecting your data is paramount to safeguarding your business, maintaining customer trust, and ensuring regulatory compliance. Let's delve into the importance of data security and why it should be a top priority for your LLC.

Protection of Sensitive Information:

Your LLC likely collects and stores various types of sensitive information, ranging from customer data and financial records to proprietary business information. This information is invaluable to your business operations but is also highly susceptible to security threats. Without adequate data security measures in place, this sensitive information could be vulnerable to unauthorized access, disclosure, or alteration, potentially leading to data breaches or cyberattacks. By implementing robust data security measures, you can protect your sensitive information from falling into the wrong hands and mitigate the risk of security incidents.

Maintaining Customer Trust:

In today's digital economy, customer trust is paramount to the success of your business. Customers expect businesses to handle their personal information with care and respect their privacy. A data breach or security incident can severely damage your LLC's reputation and erode customer trust, leading to loss of business and revenue. By prioritizing data security and implementing stringent security measures, you demonstrate your commitment to protecting customer data and maintaining confidentiality. This fosters trust and confidence among your customers, enhancing your brand reputation and credibility in the marketplace.

Compliance With Regulations:

Many industries are subject to stringent data protection regulations and compliance requirements aimed at safeguarding customer data and ensuring privacy rights. For example, the General Data Protection Regulation (GDPR) in the European Union and the Health Insurance Portability and Accountability Act (HIPAA) in the United States impose strict obligations on businesses regarding the collection, storage, and processing of personal data. Failure to comply with these regulations can result in severe penalties, fines, or legal consequences for your LLC. Implementing data security measures helps ensure compliance with regulatory requirements, mitigating the risk of non-compliance and protecting your business from potential legal liabilities.

Prevention of Financial Loss:

Data breaches and security incidents can have significant financial implications for your LLC. The costs associated with data breaches can be substantial, including expenses related to data recovery, forensic investigations, legal fees, regulatory fines, and loss of business opportunities. Moreover, the long-term financial impact of a data breach, such as damage to brand reputation and loss of customer trust, can far outweigh the immediate costs. By investing in data security measures upfront, you can mitigate the risk of financial loss associated with security incidents and protect the financial stability of your LLC.

Business Continuity:

Data security is essential for ensuring the continuity of your LLC's operations, particularly in the face of security incidents or cyberattacks. A security breach can disrupt your business operations, causing downtime, loss of productivity, and damage to critical systems or infrastructure. By implementing robust data security measures, you reduce the risk of disruptions and ensure that your business can continue operating smoothly and efficiently, even in the event of a security incident. This promotes business continuity and resilience, allowing your LLC to withstand unforeseen challenges and maintain operational stability.

Data security is a fundamental aspect of running a successful business in today's digital landscape. By prioritizing data security and implementing robust security measures, you can protect sensitive information, maintain customer trust, ensure regulatory compliance, mitigate financial risks, and promote business continuity. Make data security a top priority for your LLC to safeguard your business, your customers, and your reputation in an increasingly interconnected world.

Steps for Setting Up Cloud Storage and Implementing Security Measures

Assess Your Data Security Needs:

Begin by assessing your LLC's data security needs and identifying the types of data you need to protect. Consider factors such as the sensitivity of the data, regulatory requirements, and potential security risks. This assessment will help you determine the appropriate level of security measures needed to protect your data effectively.

Choose a Secure Cloud Storage Provider:

Select a reputable and secure cloud storage provider that meets your business requirements and compliance needs. Look for providers that offer robust security features, such as data encryption, access controls, audit trails, and regular security updates. Popular cloud storage providers include Google Drive, Dropbox Business, Microsoft OneDrive, and Amazon Web Services (AWS).

Implement Strong Access Controls:

Implement strong access controls to restrict access to sensitive data and ensure that only authorized users can access it. Use role-based access

337

controls (RBAC) to assign permissions based on job roles and responsibilities, limiting access to data on a need-to-know basis. Regularly review and update access permissions to reflect changes in personnel or job roles.

Encrypt Your Data:

Encrypt your data both in transit and at rest to protect it from unauthorized access or interception. Use strong encryption algorithms to encrypt data before it is transmitted over the internet or stored in the cloud. Many cloud storage providers offer built-in encryption features to encrypt data automatically, but you can also use third-party encryption tools for added security.

Enable Multi-Factor Authentication (MFA):

Enable multi-factor authentication (MFA) for an additional layer of security when accessing cloud storage accounts. MFA requires users to provide multiple forms of verification, such as a password and a one-time code sent to their mobile device, before granting access to the account. This helps prevent unauthorized access, even if login credentials are compromised.

Regularly Backup Your Data:

Regularly backup your data to ensure that you have copies available in case of data loss or corruption. Use automated backup solutions to schedule regular backups of your critical business data to the cloud. This ensures that your data is protected against accidental deletion, hardware failure, or cyberattacks, allowing you to restore it quickly and minimize downtime.

Monitor and Audit Activity:

Implement monitoring and auditing tools to track user activity and detect any suspicious or unauthorized behavior. Monitor access logs, file activity, and system events to identify potential security incidents or anomalies. Regularly review audit logs and conduct security audits to ensure compliance with security policies and regulatory requirements.

Provide Employee Training:

Provide comprehensive training to your employees on data security best practices, including how to securely store and access data, recognize phishing attempts, and report security incidents. Educate employees about the importance of data security and their role in protecting sensitive information, fostering a culture of security awareness within your organization.

By following these steps and implementing robust data security measures, you can protect your LLC's valuable data and mitigate the risk of security breaches or data loss. Prioritize data security as an essential aspect of your business operations, and regularly review and update your security measures to address evolving

Train Staff on Using Technology Platforms Effectively

Training your staff to effectively use technology platforms is crucial for maximizing the efficiency and productivity of your LLC. In today's digital age, technology plays a central role in virtually every aspect of business operations, from communication and collaboration to project management and customer service. By investing in staff training, you empower your team to leverage technology tools and platforms effectively, enabling them to perform their roles more efficiently and contribute to the overall success of your business. Let's explore the importance of staff training and provide valuable tips for ensuring that your team is equipped to utilize technology platforms to their full potential.

Importance of Staff Training

Staff training is a critical component of ensuring the success and efficiency of your LLC in today's digital age. It is essential for equipping your team with the necessary skills and knowledge to leverage technology platforms effectively, optimize workflows, foster collaboration, make informed decisions, and adapt to evolving business landscapes. Let's delve deeper into the importance of staff training in optimizing efficiency, enhancing collaboration, improving decision-making, and adapting to change within your organization.

Optimizing Efficiency:

Effective use of technology platforms can significantly streamline workflows and automate repetitive tasks, leading to increased efficiency and productivity within your LLC. However, without proper training, your team may struggle to fully utilize these tools or may resort to inefficient workarounds. Comprehensive training programs ensure that your staff are equipped with the skills and knowledge needed to leverage technology platforms to their fullest extent, maximizing efficiency across your organization.

By providing training on how to effectively use software applications, project management tools, communication platforms, and other digital resources, you enable your team to work more efficiently and effectively. They can automate routine tasks, organize and prioritize their work more efficiently, and leverage advanced features of technology platforms to optimize their workflows. This not only saves time and effort but also allows your team to focus on higher-value tasks that drive business growth and innovation.

Enhancing Collaboration:

Collaboration is essential for driving innovation, creativity, and productivity within your LLC. Many technology platforms facilitate collaboration among team members by allowing them to communicate, share documents, and collaborate on projects in real-time, regardless of their location or time zone. However, effective collaboration requires more than just access to these tools—it also requires the ability to use them proficiently.

Through targeted training, you can empower your team to leverage collaboration tools effectively, fostering seamless communication and collaboration among team members. Training programs can cover topics such as effective communication practices, document sharing and version control, project management techniques, and virtual meeting etiquette. By providing your team with the skills and knowledge needed to collaborate effectively, you can break down silos, promote cross-functional teamwork, and drive better outcomes for your LLC.

Improving Decision-Making:

Data-driven decision-making is essential for driving strategic initiatives and achieving business objectives. Technology platforms often provide valuable insights and data that can inform decision-making processes. However, interpreting and analyzing this data requires a certain level of technological proficiency.

Investing in staff training ensures that your team members have the skills and knowledge needed to access, analyze, and interpret data effectively. Training programs can cover topics such as data analysis techniques, data visualization tools, and best practices for interpreting and presenting data. By equipping your team with the skills needed to make informed decisions based on data-driven insights, you can drive business growth, identify new opportunities, and optimize performance across your organization.

Adapting to Change:

The business landscape is constantly evolving, with new technologies and tools emerging at a rapid pace. To remain competitive, your team must be adaptable and willing to embrace change. Through ongoing training and professional development, you can ensure that your staff have the skills and knowledge needed to adapt to new technologies and platforms as they are introduced.

Training programs can cover topics such as emerging technologies, software updates, and industry trends, keeping your team informed and up-to-date on the latest advancements in their field. By fostering a culture of continuous learning and professional development, you can empower your team to stay ahead of the curve, respond effectively to changes in the business environment, and drive innovation within your LLC.

Staff training is essential for optimizing efficiency, enhancing collaboration, improving decision-making, and adapting to change within your LLC. By investing in comprehensive training programs, you can empower your team to leverage technology platforms effectively, drive better business outcomes, and position your organization for long-term success in today's dynamic and competitive business landscape.

Tips for Training Your Team

Assess Training Needs:

Before implementing a training program, take the time to assess the specific technology skills and knowledge gaps within your team. Identify which platforms and tools are used most frequently in your LLC and where additional training may be needed to enhance proficiency.

Tailor Training Programs:

Design training programs that are tailored to the specific needs and skill levels of your team members. Consider offering different levels of training based on existing proficiency levels, ranging from basic introductory courses to advanced certification programs.

Provide Hands-On Training:

Hands-on training is often the most effective way for staff to learn how to use technology platforms. Offer interactive workshops, demonstrations, and simulations that allow team members to practice using the tools in a controlled environment and receive immediate feedback and support from trainers.

Offer Ongoing Support:

Training should not be a one-time event but rather an ongoing process that evolves as technology and business needs change. Provide ongoing support and resources to help staff reinforce their learning, troubleshoot issues, and stay up-to-date on the latest updates and features of technology platforms.

Encourage Peer Learning:

Encourage collaboration and peer learning among team members by creating opportunities for knowledge sharing and skill exchange. Establish mentorship programs or peer-to-peer learning groups where more experienced staff can mentor and support newer team members in developing their technology skills.

Monitor Progress and Provide Feedback:

Monitor the progress of staff training programs and provide regular feedback to team members on their performance and proficiency levels. Recognize and celebrate milestones and achievements to encourage continued learning and motivation among staff.

Stay Flexible and Adapt:

Recognize that different team members may have varying learning styles and preferences. Be flexible in your approach to training and adapt your methods as needed to accommodate the diverse needs of your team. Consider offering a mix of in-person and online training options to accommodate different schedules and preferences.

By prioritizing staff training and equipping your team with the skills and knowledge needed to effectively use technology platforms, you can enhance efficiency, collaboration, decision-making, and adaptability within your LLC. Invest in comprehensive training programs that are tailored to the specific needs of your team, provide hands-on learning opportunities, and offer ongoing support and resources to ensure long-term success and proficiency.

Chapter 6
Social Responsibility and Sustainability Initiatives

Define Your Corporate Social Responsibility (CSR) Goals

Corporate Social Responsibility (CSR) is a concept that involves integrating social and environmental concerns into business operations and interactions with stakeholders. It encompasses a company's efforts to contribute positively to society while also striving to minimize any negative impacts associated with its operations. Embracing CSR goes beyond the traditional focus on profit maximization and emphasizes the importance of ethical, sustainable, and socially responsible business practices.

The concept of CSR is based on the idea that businesses have a responsibility to not only generate profits for shareholders but also to consider the well-being of other stakeholders, including employees, customers, suppliers, communities, and the environment. By aligning business goals with broader social and environmental objectives, companies can create value for society while also enhancing their long-term sustainability and reputation.

Benefits Associated With Embracing CSR

Enhanced Reputation and Brand Image:

Demonstrating a commitment to CSR can enhance your company's reputation and brand image, positioning you as a socially responsible and ethical business. Consumers are increasingly conscious of the social and environmental impact of the companies they support, and businesses that prioritize CSR are more likely to attract and retain customers who share these values.

Improved Stakeholder Relations:

CSR initiatives can help build stronger relationships with stakeholders, including employees, customers, investors, suppliers, and local communities. By engaging with these stakeholders and addressing their concerns, companies can foster trust, loyalty, and goodwill, which can lead to long-term business success.

Competitive Advantage:

Embracing CSR can provide a competitive advantage by differentiating your company from competitors and attracting socially conscious consumers and investors. Companies that demonstrate a commitment to CSR may be preferred over those that prioritize profits at the expense of social and environmental considerations.

Employee Engagement and Satisfaction:

CSR initiatives can boost employee morale, engagement, and satisfaction by providing opportunities for employees to contribute to meaningful causes and make a positive impact in their communities. Engaged and motivated employees are more likely to be productive, loyal, and committed to the company's success.

Risk Mitigation:

Addressing social and environmental issues proactively through CSR initiatives can help mitigate potential risks to your business, including regulatory compliance issues, reputational damage, and supply chain disruptions. By identifying and addressing these risks early, companies can avoid costly consequences and maintain business continuity.

Defining and Setting CSR Goals for Your Company

Conduct a Stakeholder Analysis:

Start by identifying and prioritizing your company's key stakeholders, including employees, customers, suppliers, investors, and local communities. Understand their needs, expectations, and concerns related to social and environmental issues, and consider how your business activities impact these stakeholders.

Identify Material Issues:

Conduct a materiality assessment to identify the social and environmental issues that are most relevant and significant to your business and stakeholders. Consider factors such as industry trends, stakeholder expectations, regulatory requirements, and potential risks and opportunities. Focus on issues that have the greatest impact on your company's operations, reputation, and long-term sustainability.

Set SMART Goals:

Once you have identified material issues, develop specific, measurable, achievable, relevant, and time-bound (SMART) goals to address these issues. For example, you may set goals related to reducing greenhouse gas emissions, increasing energy efficiency, improving workplace diversity and inclusion, or supporting local community development initiatives. Ensure that your goals are aligned with your company's overall mission, values, and strategic objectives.

Establish Key Performance Indicators (KPIs):

Define KPIs to measure progress towards your CSR goals and track performance over time. Identify quantitative and qualitative metrics that are relevant to each goal and establish baseline measurements to benchmark progress. Regularly monitor and evaluate your performance against these KPIs to ensure that you are making meaningful progress towards your CSR objectives.

Engage Stakeholders:

Involve stakeholders in the process of defining and setting CSR goals to ensure buy-in and support for your initiatives. Seek input and feedback from employees, customers, investors, and other relevant stakeholders to ensure that your goals are aligned with their expectations and priorities. Establish channels for ongoing communication and engagement to keep stakeholders informed and involved throughout the implementation process.

Integrate CSR Into Business Strategy:

Integrate CSR goals and objectives into your company's overall business strategy and decision-making processes. Ensure that CSR considerations are taken into account when developing business plans, allocating resources, and evaluating performance. Embedding CSR into the fabric of your organization will help drive meaningful change and create lasting value for both your company and society.

By following these steps, you can effectively define and set CSR goals that align with your company's values, priorities, and aspirations, and contribute to positive social and environmental impact while also enhancing your business success.

Identify Opportunities for Sustainable Practices

Sustainability has become an increasingly important consideration for businesses across the globe. It involves meeting the needs of the present without compromising the ability of future generations to meet their own needs. In the context of business, sustainability encompasses environmental, social, and economic dimensions, often referred to as the triple bottom line. Embracing sustainable practices is not only essential for addressing pressing global challenges such as climate change, resource depletion, and social inequality but also for ensuring long-term business success and resilience.

The importance of sustainability in business cannot be overstated. Here are some key reasons why businesses should prioritize sustainability:

Environmental Conservation:

Sustainable practices help minimize environmental impact by reducing resource consumption, waste generation, and greenhouse gas emissions. By conserving natural resources, protecting biodiversity, and mitigating pollution, businesses can contribute to the preservation of ecosystems and the health of the planet.

Risk Mitigation:

Embracing sustainability can help businesses mitigate various risks associated with environmental and social issues. For example, adopting energy-efficient technologies and renewable energy sources can reduce exposure to volatile energy prices and regulatory changes. Similarly, implementing sustainable supply chain practices can mitigate risks related to resource scarcity, supply chain disruptions, and reputational damage.

Cost Savings:

Sustainable practices often lead to cost savings through increased efficiency, reduced waste, and lower operating expenses. For example, investing in energy-efficient equipment and processes can lower energy bills, while implementing waste reduction and recycling programs can minimize disposal costs. By optimizing resource use and minimizing waste, businesses can improve their bottom line while also benefiting the environment.

Enhancing Brand Reputation:

Consumers are increasingly demanding products and services from companies that demonstrate a commitment to sustainability and social responsibility. Embracing sustainable practices can enhance your brand reputation, attract environmentally conscious consumers, and differentiate your business from competitors. By communicating your sustainability efforts transparently and authentically, you can build trust and loyalty among customers, employees, and other stakeholders.

Regulatory Compliance:

Governments around the world are implementing regulations and policies aimed at promoting sustainability and addressing environmental and social issues. By proactively adopting sustainable practices, businesses can ensure compliance with existing and future regulations, avoid fines and penalties, and maintain a positive relationship with regulators.

Now, let's discuss how you can identify and implement sustainable practices in your business:

Conduct a Sustainability Assessment:

Start by conducting a comprehensive assessment of your business operations to identify areas where sustainability improvements can be made. Consider environmental impact, social responsibility, and economic viability when evaluating your current practices and identifying opportunities for improvement. Engage employees, suppliers, customers, and other stakeholders in the assessment process to gain diverse perspectives and insights.

Set Sustainability Goals:

Based on the findings of your sustainability assessment, set clear and measurable sustainability goals aligned with your business objectives and values. Consider establishing goals related to energy and resource efficiency, waste reduction, carbon footprint reduction, social equity, and community engagement. Ensure that your goals are specific, achievable, and time-bound, and communicate them to all stakeholders to foster accountability and alignment.

Invest in Sustainable Technologies and Practices:

Invest in technologies and practices that promote sustainability across your business operations. This may include upgrading to energy-efficient equipment, adopting renewable energy sources, implementing water conservation measures, optimizing transportation and logistics, and minimizing packaging waste. Consider conducting a cost-benefit analysis to evaluate the potential return on investment and prioritize initiatives that offer the greatest environmental and economic benefits.

Engage Employees and Stakeholders:

Engage employees and stakeholders in sustainability initiatives by raising awareness, providing training and education, and encouraging participation and feedback. Empower employees to contribute ideas and suggestions for improving sustainability in their respective areas of expertise and influence. Foster a culture of sustainability throughout your organization by integrating sustainability principles into policies, procedures, and decision-making processes.

Collaborate with Suppliers and Partners:

Collaborate with suppliers and business partners to promote sustainability throughout your supply chain. Encourage suppliers to adopt sustainable practices, such as ethical sourcing, fair labor practices, and environmental stewardship. Establish sustainability criteria for supplier selection and evaluation and work with partners who share your commitment to sustainability. By working together, you can leverage collective influence and drive positive change across your supply chain.

Measure and Monitor Progress:

Implement robust monitoring and measurement systems to track progress towards your sustainability goals and objectives. Collect and analyze relevant data, metrics, and key performance indicators (KPIs) to evaluate the effectiveness of your sustainability initiatives and identify areas for improvement. Regularly review and report on your sustainability performance to stakeholders, and use feedback and insights to refine and enhance your sustainability strategy over time.

By following these tips, you can identify and implement sustainable practices that align with your business goals, values, and aspirations, and contribute to positive environmental, social, and economic impact. Sustainable businesses not only benefit the planet and society but also create value for stakeholders and position themselves for long-term success and resilience in a rapidly changing world.

Engage With Local Communities and Stakeholders

Engaging with local communities and stakeholders is essential for building strong relationships, fostering trust, and creating mutual value for your business and the community. Community engagement goes beyond traditional corporate social responsibility (CSR) initiatives by involving stakeholders in meaningful dialogue, collaboration, and partnership to address shared challenges and opportunities. Here are some key benefits of community engagement and strategies for building strong relationships with local communities and stakeholders:

Benefits of Community Engagement:

Community engagement offers numerous benefits for businesses of all sizes, from enhancing reputation to accessing valuable resources and mitigating risks. Here's a detailed exploration of the benefits of community engagement:

Enhanced Reputation and Brand Image:

Engaging with local communities and stakeholders is a tangible demonstration of your commitment to corporate citizenship and social responsibility. By actively participating in community initiatives, such as volunteering, sponsoring local events, or supporting charitable causes, you showcase your business's values and commitment to making a positive impact beyond profit margins. This proactive involvement helps to differentiate your brand from competitors and build a reputation as a socially conscious and trustworthy organization. Customers, employees, and other stakeholders are more likely to support businesses that demonstrate genuine care for the communities they serve, leading to enhanced brand loyalty and positive word-of-mouth recommendations.

Increased Customer Loyalty and Satisfaction:

Community engagement fosters deeper connections between businesses and their customers by aligning corporate values with community interests and priorities. By supporting local events, charities, and organizations that resonate with your target audience, you demonstrate shared values and a commitment to the well-being of the community. This authentic engagement strengthens customer loyalty and satisfaction, as customers feel a sense of pride and affiliation with businesses that contribute positively to their local area. Moreover, customers are more likely to choose businesses that they perceive as socially responsible, leading to increased customer retention and long-term profitability.

Access to Talent and Resources:

Building relationships with local communities and stakeholders opens doors to a diverse pool of talent, expertise, and resources that can benefit your business. Engaging with educational institutions, nonprofit organizations, and community groups provides opportunities to identify potential partners, collaborators, and employees with unique skills and perspectives. By fostering connections with local talent, businesses can recruit skilled workers, interns, or volunteers who are familiar with the community and share a passion for its well-being. Additionally, tapping into local networks and ecosystems enables businesses to access resources such as funding, infrastructure, and market insights that can support innovation and growth initiatives.

Risk Mitigation and Resilience:

Community engagement plays a crucial role in mitigating various risks that businesses may face, including reputational risks, regulatory risks, and social risks. By actively engaging with local communities and stakeholders, businesses can identify and address community concerns, anticipate potential issues, and proactively manage conflicts and challenges. Building strong relationships with local stakeholders creates a foundation of trust and mutual respect, which can help businesses navigate crises and disruptions more effectively. In times of adversity, businesses with robust community relationships are better positioned to mobilize support, rally resources, and maintain stakeholder trust, ensuring business continuity and resilience in the face of uncertainty.

Strategies for Building Strong Relationships With Local Communities and Stakeholders

Building strong relationships with local communities and stakeholders is essential for businesses committed to corporate social responsibility and sustainability. Here are strategies you can implement to foster meaningful connections and collaboration:

Listen and Learn:

Begin by actively listening to the needs, priorities, and concerns of local communities and stakeholders. Conduct stakeholder interviews, surveys, and focus groups to gather feedback and insights. Engage with community leaders, elected officials, and representatives of local organizations to understand the dynamics and aspirations of the community. By demonstrating a genuine interest in listening and learning from local stakeholders, you can build trust, credibility, and empathy.

Be Transparent and Authentic:

Transparency and authenticity are paramount for building trust and credibility with local communities and stakeholders. Communicate openly and honestly about your business activities, goals, and impact on the community. Share information about your corporate values, policies, and practices, including environmental, social, and governance (ESG) initiatives. Be transparent about your successes, challenges, and areas for improvement, demonstrating a genuine commitment to responsible business practices.

Identify Shared Goals and Priorities:

Identify shared goals and priorities that align with the needs and aspirations of local communities and stakeholders. Collaborate with stakeholders to identify key issues and opportunities that require collective action and partnership. Focus on areas where your business can make a meaningful and positive impact, such as education, health, environmental conservation, or economic development. By working together towards common goals, you can create shared value and drive sustainable change.

Engage in Meaningful Partnerships:

Foster meaningful partnerships with local organizations, nonprofits, government agencies, and community groups to address community needs and advance shared goals. Collaborate on community projects, initiatives, and events that benefit the community and align with your business objectives. Consider forming advisory boards, task forces, or community councils to facilitate ongoing dialogue and collaboration with local stakeholders. By engaging in meaningful partnerships, you can leverage collective expertise, resources, and influence to achieve greater impact and sustainability.

Empower and Invest in the Community:

Empower local communities by investing in education, workforce development, and economic opportunities. Support initiatives that promote skills training, job creation, entrepreneurship, and economic empowerment, particularly in underserved and marginalized communities. Provide scholarships, internships, and mentorship programs to support local talent development and retention. By investing in the community, you can create pathways to prosperity and social mobility while building goodwill and loyalty among local stakeholders.

Measure and Communicate Impact:

Measure and communicate the impact of your community engagement initiatives to stakeholders. Collect data and metrics to assess the effectiveness and outcomes of your programs and initiatives. Share success stories, case studies, and testimonials that highlight the positive impact of your efforts on the community. Be transparent about your progress towards achieving shared goals and commitments, and solicit feedback from stakeholders to inform continuous improvement and innovation.

Community engagement is essential for building strong relationships, fostering trust, and creating shared value for businesses and local communities. By actively engaging with local stakeholders, businesses can enhance their reputation, build customer loyalty, access talent and resources, mitigate risks, and contribute to the well-being and resilience of the communities they serve.

Chapter 7
Personal Development and Growth Strategies

Set Personal and Professional Goals

Setting personal and professional goals is crucial for guiding your growth and development, both in your personal life and your career. By establishing clear objectives, you provide yourself with direction and motivation to work towards achieving your aspirations. Here's why goal setting is essential and some tips on how to set and achieve your goals effectively.

Importance of Goal Setting for Personal and Professional Growth

Clarity and Focus:

Setting goals helps you gain clarity about what you want to achieve and where you want to go in life. It provides you with a clear direction and focus, allowing you to channel your time, energy, and resources towards activities that align with your objectives.

Motivation and Inspiration:

Goals act as powerful motivators, inspiring you to take action and pursue your dreams. When you have well-defined goals, you're more likely to stay committed and persistent in the face of challenges or setbacks, as you're driven by the desire to achieve your desired outcomes.

Measurable Progress:

By setting specific, measurable, achievable, relevant, and time-bound (SMART) goals, you can track your progress and measure your success along the way. Regularly monitoring your achievements against your goals enables you to stay accountable and make necessary adjustments to stay on track.

Personal Growth and Development:

Goal setting encourages personal growth and development by pushing you out of your comfort zone and challenging you to learn new skills, acquire knowledge, and develop competencies. As you work towards achieving your goals, you gain valuable experience and insights that contribute to your overall growth and development.

Career Advancement:

In a professional context, setting career goals is essential for advancing your career and achieving success. Whether it's aiming for a promotion, expanding your skill set, or launching your own business, having clear career goals helps you navigate your career path and make strategic decisions that align with your aspirations.

Tips on Setting and Achieving Goals

Reflect on Your Values and Priorities:

Begin by reflecting on your values, passions, and priorities in life. Identify what matters most to you and what you aspire to achieve personally and professionally. Use this self-awareness to set goals that are meaningful and aligned with your values.

Be Specific and Concrete:

When setting goals, make sure they are specific, measurable, achievable, relevant, and time-bound (SMART). Clearly define what you want to accomplish, how you will measure success, and by when you intend to achieve your goals.

Break Down Goals Into Smaller Steps:

Break down larger goals into smaller, manageable tasks or milestones. This makes your goals less overwhelming and allows you to focus on making progress one step at a time. Celebrate your achievements as you reach each milestone, which can boost your motivation and confidence.

Write Down Your Goals:

Document your goals by writing them down in a journal, planner, or digital app. This helps solidify your commitment to your goals and serves as a visual reminder of what you're working towards. Review your goals regularly and make any necessary adjustments as you progress.

Create an Action Plan:

Develop a clear action plan outlining the specific steps you need to take to achieve each of your goals. Break down your goals into actionable tasks with deadlines and prioritize them based on their importance and urgency. Having a roadmap to follow makes it easier to stay organized and focused on your objectives.

Stay Flexible and Adapt:

While it's important to set ambitious goals, it's also essential to remain flexible and adaptable in the face of changing circumstances. Be open to adjusting your goals or action plan as needed, especially if unexpected challenges arise or if you receive new information that warrants a change in direction.

Seek Support and Accountability:

Share your goals with trusted friends, family members, or mentors who can provide support, encouragement, and accountability. Consider joining a mastermind group, accountability partnership, or online community where you can connect with like-minded individuals who share similar goals and aspirations.

Celebrate Your Achievements:

Celebrate your successes and milestones along the way, no matter how small they may seem. Recognize your progress and give yourself credit for your hard work and dedication. Celebrating your achievements boosts your morale and reinforces your commitment to pursuing your goals.

By setting personal and professional goals that are aligned with your values and aspirations, and by following these tips for effective goal setting and achievement, you can empower yourself to live a fulfilling and purposeful life while continuously striving for growth and success.

Practice Self-Care and Stress Management Techniques

Practicing self-care and stress management techniques is vital for entrepreneurs to maintain their well-being and optimize their performance in both their personal and professional lives. As an entrepreneur, you likely face numerous challenges and responsibilities on a daily basis, which can lead to high levels of stress and burnout if not managed effectively. Here, we'll explore the importance of self-care for entrepreneurs and provide strategies for managing stress and maintaining well-being.

Importance of Self-Care for Entrepreneurs

Enhanced Productivity and Performance:

Taking care of yourself is essential for maintaining high levels of productivity and performance in your entrepreneurial endeavors. When you prioritize self-care, you're better equipped to manage stress, stay focused, and make sound decisions, leading to improved efficiency and effectiveness in your work.

Better Physical Health:

Neglecting self-care can take a toll on your physical health, leading to various health issues such as fatigue, insomnia, and weakened immune function. By incorporating self-care practices into your routine, such as exercise, proper nutrition, and adequate sleep, you can boost your overall health and energy levels, enabling you to tackle the demands of entrepreneurship with vitality and resilience.

Improved Mental Well-Being:

Entrepreneurship can be mentally taxing, often leading to feelings of anxiety, overwhelm, and burnout. Engaging in self-care activities such as mindfulness meditation, relaxation techniques, and hobbies can help alleviate stress, promote mental clarity, and enhance emotional well-being. Prioritizing mental health is crucial for sustaining long-term success and satisfaction as an entrepreneur.

Balanced Work-Life Integration:

Maintaining a healthy work-life balance is essential for preventing burnout and maintaining overall life satisfaction. By practicing self-care, you can create boundaries between work and personal life, allowing yourself time to recharge, spend quality time with loved ones, and pursue interests outside of work. Achieving a harmonious work-life integration promotes greater happiness and fulfillment in both domains.

Strategies for Managing Stress and Maintaining Well-being

Establish Daily Self-Care Rituals:

Incorporate daily self-care rituals into your routine to nurture your physical, mental, and emotional well-being. This may include activities such as exercise, meditation, journaling, or spending time in nature. Consistency is key, so commit to prioritizing self-care practices each day, even amidst busy schedules.

Set Boundaries:

Establish clear boundaries between work and personal life to prevent burnout and maintain balance. Set designated work hours, limit work-related activities outside of those hours, and create dedicated time for relaxation, leisure, and social connections. Communicate your boundaries to clients, colleagues, and employees to ensure they respect your personal time.

Practice Stress Management Techniques:

Learn and practice stress management techniques to cope with the inevitable challenges and pressures of entrepreneurship. Deep breathing exercises, progressive muscle relaxation, and visualization are effective techniques for reducing stress and promoting relaxation. Experiment with different strategies to identify what works best for you.

Delegate and Prioritize Tasks:

Delegate tasks that are not essential to your role as an entrepreneur and prioritize activities that align with your core objectives and values. Avoid overcommitting yourself and learn to say no to tasks or opportunities that do not serve your well-being or contribute to your goals. Focus on activities that have the greatest impact on your business and delegate or outsource non-essential tasks whenever possible.

Cultivate Supportive Relationships:

Surround yourself with supportive friends, family members, mentors, and peers who understand the demands of entrepreneurship and can offer encouragement, guidance, and perspective. Lean on your support network during times of stress or uncertainty, and don't hesitate to seek professional help if you're struggling with mental health issues.

Practice Mindfulness and Gratitude:

Cultivate mindfulness and gratitude practices to cultivate a positive mindset and reduce stress. Mindfulness meditation, gratitude journaling, and reflective practices can help you stay grounded, present, and appreciative of the present moment. By focusing on the here and now and expressing gratitude for your blessings, you can enhance your overall well-being and resilience.

Maintain Healthy Habits:

Prioritize your physical health by adopting healthy lifestyle habits such as regular exercise, nutritious eating, and adequate sleep. Physical activity releases endorphins, reduces stress hormones, and boosts mood and energy levels. Aim to eat a balanced diet rich in fruits, vegetables, lean proteins, and whole grains, and prioritize quality sleep to support optimal health and well-being.

Seek Professional Support:

If you're struggling to manage stress or maintain your well-being, don't hesitate to seek support from mental health professionals, counselors, or coaches. Professional support can provide you with the tools, strategies, and insights needed to navigate challenges effectively and enhance your overall resilience and well-being.

Practicing self-care and stress management techniques is essential for entrepreneurs to thrive personally and professionally. By prioritizing self-care, setting boundaries, practicing stress management techniques, and cultivating supportive relationships, you can maintain your well-being, enhance your resilience, and sustain long-term success and fulfillment in your entrepreneurial journey.

Seek Mentorship and Professional Development Opportunities

Seeking mentorship and professional development opportunities can significantly contribute to your growth and success as an entrepreneur. Mentors offer valuable guidance, wisdom, and support based on their own experiences, while professional development opportunities help you acquire new skills, expand your knowledge, and stay abreast of industry trends. In this section, we'll discuss the benefits of mentorship and professional development and provide tips on finding and working with mentors effectively.

Benefits of Mentorship and Professional Development

Access to Guidance and Expertise:

One of the primary benefits of mentorship is gaining access to the guidance and expertise of experienced professionals who have navigated similar challenges and achieved success in their respective fields. Mentors can offer valuable insights, advice, and perspective based on their own experiences, helping you make informed decisions, avoid common pitfalls, and accelerate your learning curve as an entrepreneur.

Networking Opportunities:

Mentorship often provides access to valuable networking opportunities, allowing you to connect with industry leaders, experts, and other professionals within your field. Through your mentor's network, you may gain introductions to potential collaborators, clients, investors, or partners, expanding your professional connections and opportunities for growth and collaboration.

Personalized Support and Accountability:

A mentor provides personalized support and accountability tailored to your individual needs, goals, and aspirations. Whether you're facing specific challenges, seeking advice on strategic decisions, or looking for encouragement and motivation, a mentor can offer guidance, feedback, and support to help you stay focused, motivated, and accountable to your goals.

Skill Development and Growth:

Engaging in professional development opportunities allows you to acquire new skills, deepen your expertise, and stay relevant in a rapidly evolving business landscape. Whether through workshops, seminars, online courses, or conferences, investing in your professional development enables you to expand your knowledge, enhance your capabilities, and adapt to changing industry trends and technologies.

Increased Confidence and Self-Efficacy:

Mentorship and professional development can boost your confidence and self-efficacy as an entrepreneur by providing validation, encouragement, and recognition of your abilities and potential. Working with a mentor who believes in your capabilities and invests in your growth can instill greater confidence and resilience, empowering you to overcome challenges and pursue ambitious goals with conviction and determination.

Tips for Finding and Working With Mentors

Clarify Your Goals and Needs:

Before seeking a mentor, take the time to clarify your goals, needs, and expectations for the mentoring relationship. Identify specific areas where you could benefit from guidance and support, such as business strategy, leadership development, or industry insights. Having a clear understanding of what you hope to achieve will help you find a mentor whose expertise aligns with your needs.

Research Potential Mentors:

Conduct research to identify potential mentors who possess the knowledge, experience, and qualities you're seeking. Look for individuals who have achieved success in your industry or field, demonstrate leadership and integrity, and are willing to invest in mentoring others. Consider reaching out to your professional network, industry associations, or alumni networks to identify potential mentors.

Initiate Contact:

Once you've identified potential mentors, reach out to them with a personalized and respectful message expressing your interest in establishing a mentoring relationship. Clearly articulate why you admire their work, explain how you believe their expertise could benefit you, and express your willingness to learn and grow under their guidance. Be concise, genuine, and respectful of their time and commitments.

Be Open to Feedback and Learning:

Approach the mentoring relationship with an open mind and a willingness to receive feedback, guidance, and constructive criticism. Be receptive to your mentor's insights and perspectives, even if they challenge your assumptions or comfort zone. Remember that mentorship is a reciprocal relationship based on mutual respect, trust, and learning.

Establish Clear Expectations:

Clarify expectations and boundaries upfront to ensure a productive and mutually beneficial mentoring relationship. Discuss the frequency and format of your interactions, the topics you'd like to focus on, and any specific goals or milestones you hope to achieve. Establish clear communication channels and mechanisms for providing feedback and assessing progress.

Show Gratitude and Appreciation:

Express gratitude and appreciation to your mentor for their time, guidance, and support throughout the mentoring relationship. Acknowledge their contributions and celebrate your achievements and milestones together. Consider expressing your appreciation through handwritten notes, small gestures of kindness, or testimonials highlighting the impact of their mentorship on your growth and success.

Seeking mentorship and professional development opportunities can significantly enhance your growth and success as an entrepreneur. By leveraging the guidance, expertise, and support of mentors and investing in your ongoing learning and skill development, you can accelerate your personal and professional growth, overcome challenges, and achieve greater fulfillment and success in your entrepreneurial journey.

Chapter 8
Global Expansion and Future Planning

Research International Markets and Expansion Opportunities

International expansion can offer numerous benefits for your business, including access to new markets, increased revenue potential, and diversification of risk. However, it also presents a unique set of challenges, ranging from cultural differences to regulatory complexities. In this section, we'll discuss the benefits and challenges of international expansion and provide steps for researching and evaluating international markets effectively.

Benefits of International Expansion

Access to New Markets:

Expanding internationally allows you to access new markets and customer segments that may not be available in your domestic market. By diversifying your customer base geographically, you can reduce dependency on any single market and mitigate the impact of fluctuations or downturns in specific regions.

Increased Revenue Potential:

International expansion opens up opportunities for revenue growth beyond the limitations of your domestic market. By tapping into larger or faster-growing markets abroad, you can unlock new sources of revenue and scale your business more rapidly than would be possible domestically.

Diversification of Risk:

Operating in multiple markets diversifies your business risk and reduces exposure to country-specific economic, political, or regulatory risks. By spreading your operations across different regions, you can buffer the impact of adverse events or market conditions in any single market.

Access to Talent and Resources:

International expansion can provide access to a broader talent pool, specialized expertise, and resources that may not be readily available in your domestic market. By establishing a presence in strategic locations, you can tap into local talent, knowledge, and infrastructure to support your business growth and innovation initiatives.

Brand Globalization:

Expanding internationally can enhance your brand's global presence and reputation, positioning your business as a credible and competitive player on the world stage. A successful international expansion can strengthen brand recognition and perception, attracting customers, partners, and investors worldwide.

Challenges of International Expansion

Cultural Differences:

Cultural differences can pose significant challenges when expanding internationally, affecting communication, marketing strategies, and business practices. Differences in language, customs, values, and business etiquette require careful consideration and adaptation to ensure effective cross-cultural communication and relationship-building.

Regulatory and Legal Complexities:

Navigating foreign regulatory and legal requirements can be complex and time-consuming, requiring a thorough understanding of local laws, regulations, and compliance standards. Failure to comply with local regulations can result in legal and financial consequences, including fines, penalties, and reputational damage.

Logistical and Operational Challenges:

International expansion involves logistical and operational challenges, including supply chain management, distribution, and infrastructure constraints. Managing global logistics, customs clearance, and transportation networks requires careful planning and coordination to ensure timely and cost-effective delivery of goods and services.

Market Entry Barriers:

Entering new international markets often involves overcoming various market entry barriers, such as trade barriers, tariffs, licensing requirements, and competitive dynamics. Understanding market entry barriers and developing effective market entry strategies are essential for successfully penetrating new markets and gaining a competitive foothold.

Currency and Exchange Rate Risks:

Operating in multiple currencies exposes businesses to currency exchange rate risks, which can impact profitability, cash flow, and financial performance. Fluctuations in exchange rates can affect the cost of goods, pricing strategies, and revenue repatriation, requiring effective risk management strategies to mitigate exposure.

Steps for Researching and Evaluating International Markets

Market Analysis:

Begin by conducting a comprehensive analysis of potential international markets to assess their attractiveness and suitability for expansion. Evaluate market size, growth potential, competitive landscape, consumer demographics, purchasing power, and regulatory environment to identify promising opportunities.

Market Research:

Conduct market research to gather insights into consumer preferences, behavior, and trends in target markets. Use surveys, focus groups, interviews, and secondary research sources to collect data and analyze market dynamics, competitive positioning, and market entry barriers.

Risk Assessment:

Evaluate the political, economic, legal, and cultural risks associated with each target market to assess their impact on your business operations and expansion strategy. Consider factors such as political stability, economic indicators, regulatory environment, intellectual property protection, and cultural nuances to identify potential risks and challenges.

Competitive Analysis:

Analyze the competitive landscape in target markets to understand the strengths, weaknesses, opportunities, and threats posed by existing competitors. Identify key competitors, their market positioning, product offerings, pricing strategies, distribution channels, and market share to inform your competitive strategy and differentiation.

Partner Identification:

Identify potential local partners, distributors, suppliers, and collaborators in target markets to support your market entry and expansion efforts. Evaluate potential partners based on their market knowledge, reputation, network, capabilities, and alignment with your business objectives to establish mutually beneficial partnerships.

Financial Analysis:

Conduct a financial analysis to assess the costs, investment requirements, and potential returns associated with international expansion. Evaluate factors such as market entry costs, operating expenses, revenue projections, and profitability targets to determine the financial viability and feasibility of expansion into target markets.

Legal and Regulatory Due Diligence:

Conduct thorough due diligence on the legal and regulatory requirements applicable to each target market to ensure compliance and mitigate legal risks. Consult with legal experts, regulatory advisors, and industry associations to understand local laws, regulations, permits, licenses, taxes, and customs procedures relevant to your business activities.

Market Entry Strategy:

Develop a market entry strategy tailored to the unique characteristics and dynamics of each target market. Consider factors such as market segmentation, positioning, pricing, distribution channels, promotional tactics, and strategic partnerships to optimize your market entry approach and maximize your chances of success.

Researching and evaluating international markets is essential for successful global expansion. By understanding the benefits and challenges of international expansion, conducting thorough market research and analysis, and developing a strategic approach to market entry, you can identify promising opportunities, mitigate risks, and pave the way for sustainable growth and success in international markets.

Evaluate Legal and Regulatory Requirements for Global Operations

Navigating the legal and regulatory landscape of global operations is a critical aspect of international business expansion. Understanding and complying with international laws and regulations is essential to mitigate legal risks, ensure regulatory compliance, and maintain the integrity of your operations. In this section, we'll highlight key considerations for global compliance and provide tips on navigating international legal and regulatory requirements effectively.

Key Considerations for Global Compliance

Legal System Variations:

One of the primary challenges of operating globally is the diversity of legal systems across different countries and regions. Legal systems can vary significantly in terms of their structure, principles, and procedures, ranging from common law systems to civil law systems and hybrid systems. Understanding the legal framework of each jurisdiction where you operate or plan to expand is essential for compliance.

Regulatory Complexity:

International regulations can be complex and multifaceted, encompassing a wide range of areas such as trade, taxation, employment, intellectual property, data privacy, and consumer protection. Each country may have its own set of regulations governing various aspects of business operations, requiring careful attention to detail and compliance with local laws and regulatory requirements.

Cross-Border Transactions:

Engaging in cross-border transactions involves additional legal and regulatory considerations related to import/export regulations, customs duties, tariffs, trade agreements, and foreign exchange controls. Understanding the legal requirements and documentation involved in international trade is essential to ensure compliance and facilitate smooth cross-border transactions.

Corporate Governance:

Corporate governance standards and practices may vary across different countries, influencing the legal and regulatory framework governing corporate entities. Compliance with corporate governance principles, regulations, and reporting requirements is essential to ensure transparency, accountability, and integrity in corporate operations, particularly for publicly traded companies.

Intellectual Property Protection:

Intellectual property (IP) rights are subject to varying levels of protection and enforcement across different jurisdictions. Understanding the IP laws and regulations in target markets is crucial for protecting your trademarks, patents, copyrights, and trade secrets from infringement, counterfeiting, and unauthorized use. Implementing robust IP protection strategies and enforcement mechanisms is essential to safeguard your valuable intellectual assets.

Data Privacy and Security:

Data privacy and security regulations have become increasingly stringent and complex in the wake of growing concerns about data breaches, identity theft, and privacy violations. Compliance with data protection laws such as the European Union's General Data Protection Regulation (GDPR) and the California Consumer Privacy Act (CCPA) is essential for businesses that collect, process, or store personal data. Implementing data privacy policies, procedures, and safeguards is critical to protect sensitive information and ensure compliance with applicable regulations.

Tips on Navigating International Legal and Regulatory Requirements

Conduct Comprehensive Due Diligence:

Before entering new markets or expanding operations internationally, conduct comprehensive due diligence to assess the legal and regulatory landscape of target countries. Identify relevant laws, regulations, permits, licenses, and compliance requirements applicable to your business activities and industry sector.

Engage Legal Experts:

Seek guidance from legal experts with expertise in international law and cross-border transactions. Work with experienced international attorneys, legal advisors, or law firms familiar with the legal systems and regulatory environments of target markets. Legal professionals can provide valuable insights, guidance, and support to navigate complex legal issues and ensure compliance with international laws and regulations.

Establish Legal Compliance Frameworks:

Develop robust legal compliance frameworks and policies to ensure adherence to international laws and regulations across your global operations. Establish clear guidelines, procedures, and controls to monitor and enforce compliance with legal requirements, mitigate risks, and address potential legal issues proactively.

Stay Informed and Updated:

Stay informed about changes in international laws, regulations, and compliance standards that may impact your business operations. Monitor regulatory developments, legislative updates, and industry trends relevant to your business sector to stay ahead of regulatory changes and adapt your compliance strategies accordingly.

Invest in Training and Education:

Invest in training and education programs to enhance the legal awareness and compliance knowledge of your employees, managers, and key stakeholders. Provide training on relevant legal topics, regulatory requirements, and ethical standards to ensure that all personnel understand their legal obligations and responsibilities.

Establish Compliance Audits and Monitoring:

Implement regular compliance audits and monitoring mechanisms to assess and verify adherence to legal and regulatory requirements across your global operations. Conduct internal audits, reviews, and assessments to identify areas of non-compliance, gaps in compliance controls, and opportunities for improvement. Take corrective actions to address any deficiencies and strengthen your compliance measures.

Seek Regulatory Guidance and Assistance:

Seek regulatory guidance and assistance from government agencies, trade associations, and industry bodies in target markets. Consult with regulatory authorities, compliance experts, or local advisors to clarify regulatory requirements, obtain necessary permits or licenses, and address compliance-related inquiries or issues.

Navigating international legal and regulatory requirements requires careful consideration, diligence, and compliance measures to ensure legal compliance and mitigate associated risks. By understanding key legal considerations, engaging legal experts, establishing robust compliance frameworks, and staying informed about regulatory developments, you can navigate international legal complexities effectively and operate your global business with confidence and integrity.

Develop a Long-Term Growth Strategy and Roadmap

Developing a long-term growth strategy and roadmap is essential for the sustainable success and expansion of your business. Long-term planning provides a clear direction, sets achievable goals, and enables you to anticipate and adapt to changes in the competitive landscape and market dynamics. In this section, we'll discuss the importance of long-term planning and provide steps for developing a comprehensive growth strategy and roadmap tailored to your business objectives and aspirations.

Importance of Long-Term Planning

Strategic Direction:

Long-term planning helps you define your vision, mission, and strategic objectives for the future. It allows you to articulate where you want your business to be in the long term and develop a roadmap for achieving your goals. By establishing a clear strategic direction, you can align your resources, investments, and efforts towards realizing your vision and fulfilling your business's purpose.

Risk Management:

Long-term planning enables you to identify and mitigate potential risks, challenges, and uncertainties that may impact your business's growth and success. By conducting scenario analysis, risk assessments, and strategic foresight exercises, you can anticipate future risks and develop contingency plans to minimize their impact on your business operations. Proactive risk management strategies enhance your resilience and ability to navigate uncertainties effectively.

Resource Allocation:

Long-term planning helps you allocate resources, including financial, human, and technological resources, strategically to support your growth initiatives and strategic priorities. By forecasting future resource requirements and investment needs, you can optimize resource allocation, prioritize initiatives, and allocate resources where they will have the greatest impact on achieving your long-term objectives.

Adaptability and Flexibility:

Long-term planning enables you to build flexibility and adaptability into your business strategy to respond to changing market conditions, emerging trends, and evolving customer preferences. By regularly reviewing and updating your strategic plan, you can incorporate new information, insights, and feedback to ensure your business remains agile and responsive to external dynamics and internal changes.

Stakeholder Alignment:

Long-term planning fosters alignment and buy-in among key stake-holders, including employees, investors, customers, suppliers, and partners. By communicating your long-term vision, goals, and strategies clearly and transparently, you can engage stakeholders in the planning process, build trust, and secure their commitment to supporting your growth journey. Alignment of interests and shared understanding of long-term objectives enhance collaboration and collective efforts towards achieving organizational success.

Steps for Developing a Comprehensive Growth Strategy and Roadmap

Conduct a SWOT Analysis:

Begin by conducting a comprehensive SWOT (Strengths, Weaknesses, Opportunities, Threats) analysis to assess your business's internal strengths and weaknesses, as well as external opportunities and threats. Identify your competitive advantages, core competencies, and areas for improvement to inform your growth strategy and prioritize strategic initiatives.

Define Your Vision and Objectives:

Clearly articulate your long-term vision, mission, and strategic objectives for the future. Define what success looks like for your business and establish measurable goals and key performance indicators (KPIs) to track progress and evaluate performance. Your objectives should be specific, measurable, achievable, relevant, and time-bound (SMART) to provide clarity and focus for your growth efforts.

Identify Growth Drivers and Opportunities:

Identify key growth drivers and opportunities that align with your business's strengths, capabilities, and market potential. Analyze market trends, customer needs, competitor strategies, and industry dynamics to identify emerging opportunities for expansion, diversification, innovation, and market penetration. Prioritize growth initiatives based on their strategic fit, feasibility, and potential impact on long-term growth and profitability.

Develop Strategic Initiatives:

Develop a set of strategic initiatives and action plans to achieve your long-term objectives and capitalize on identified growth opportunities. Define specific initiatives, milestones, and timelines for each strategic priority, and allocate resources and responsibilities accordingly. Consider factors such as market entry strategies, product development, geographic expansion, strategic partnerships, mergers and acquisitions, and digital transformation initiatives as part of your growth roadmap.

Assess Resource Requirements:

Evaluate the resource requirements and investment needs associated with implementing your growth strategy. Determine the financial, human, and technological resources required to support your strategic initiatives and ensure their successful execution. Develop a budgeting and resource allocation plan to allocate resources effectively and optimize return on investment (ROI) for your growth initiatives.

Establish Performance Metrics:

Establish clear performance metrics and KPIs to monitor progress, track performance, and measure the success of your growth strategy. Define quantifiable targets and benchmarks for key areas such as revenue growth, market share, customer acquisition, customer satisfaction, operational efficiency, and financial performance. Regularly review and analyze performance data to assess the effectiveness of your growth initiatives and make informed decisions to drive continuous improvement.

Create a Flexible Implementation Plan:

Develop a flexible implementation plan that allows for adaptation and adjustment based on changing market conditions and business priorities. Anticipate potential challenges, risks, and uncertainties that may arise during the execution of your growth strategy and develop contingency plans to mitigate their impact. Regularly review and reassess your strategic plan, make course corrections as needed, and remain agile in responding to new opportunities and challenges.

Communicate and Engage Stakeholders:

Communicate your growth strategy and roadmap effectively to key stakeholders, including employees, investors, customers, suppliers, and partners. Ensure alignment and buy-in by engaging stakeholders in the planning process, soliciting feedback, and addressing concerns or questions proactively. Foster a culture of transparency, collaboration, and accountability to rally support for your growth initiatives and inspire collective action towards achieving shared goals.

Developing a comprehensive growth strategy and roadmap is essential for achieving sustainable growth and long -term success in today's dynamic and competitive business environment. By following these steps and principles, you can effectively navigate the complexities of long-term planning and chart a course for your business's future growth and prosperity.

Remember that developing a growth strategy and roadmap is an ongoing process that requires continuous monitoring, evaluation, and adaptation. Stay agile, responsive, and proactive in adjusting your plans and strategies as needed to capitalize on emerging opportunities, mitigate risks, and stay ahead of the curve. With a clear vision, strategic focus, and disciplined execution, you can position your business for long-term success and achieve your aspirations for growth and impact.

In conclusion, the development of a comprehensive growth strategy and roadmap is a critical component of long-term business success. By understanding the importance of long-term planning, defining clear objectives, identifying growth opportunities, and engaging stakeholders, you can create a roadmap that guides your business towards sustainable growth and competitive advantage. By following the steps outlined in this section and remaining committed to your vision, you can navigate the complexities of global expansion and future planning with confidence and clarity.

Chapter 9
Review and Adaptation

Regularly Review and Assess Your LLC's Performance

Regular performance reviews are essential for the sustained success and growth of your LLC. These reviews allow you to evaluate your progress, identify areas for improvement, and make informed decisions that drive your business forward. In this section, we will explore the importance of regular performance reviews and provide detailed tips on conducting effective assessments and evaluations.

The Importance of Regular Performance Reviews

Conducting regular performance reviews is crucial for several reasons. First and foremost, it ensures that your business remains aligned with its goals and objectives. Without regular assessments, you risk drifting away from your strategic direction and failing to achieve your long-term vision. Performance reviews help you stay on track by providing a clear picture of where you stand and what needs to be done to reach your targets.

Performance reviews also allow you to measure the effectiveness of your strategies and initiatives. By regularly evaluating your performance, you can determine whether your current approach is delivering the desired results. This enables you to identify what is working well and what is not, allowing you to make necessary adjustments and improvements. Without this critical feedback loop, you may continue to invest time and resources into strategies that are not yielding positive outcomes.

Another key benefit of regular performance reviews is that they help you identify and address issues before they become major problems. By regularly monitoring your performance, you can catch potential issues early and take corrective action before they escalate. This proactive approach can save you significant time, money, and effort in the long run.

Moreover, performance reviews provide an opportunity to celebrate successes and recognize the hard work and achievements of your team. Acknowledging and rewarding accomplishments can boost morale, motivation, and engagement, creating a positive and productive work environment. Regular reviews also foster a culture of accountability and continuous improvement, where everyone is committed to achieving their best and contributing to the success of the business.

Tips on Conducting Effective Assessments and Evaluations

Conducting effective performance reviews requires a structured and systematic approach. Here are some tips to help you carry out thorough and meaningful assessments and evaluations:

Set Clear Objectives and Metrics

Before conducting a performance review, it is essential to establish clear objectives and metrics that align with your business goals. Determine what you want to achieve through the review and what specific aspects of performance you will assess. This could include financial performance, operational efficiency, customer satisfaction, employee engagement, and other relevant areas.

Define key performance indicators (KPIs) and metrics that will allow you to measure progress and evaluate success. These should be specific, measurable, achievable, relevant, and time-bound (SMART). For example, if you are assessing sales performance, your KPIs might include revenue growth, average order value, and conversion rates.

Gather Relevant Data and Information

Collecting accurate and relevant data is critical for an effective performance review. This data will serve as the foundation for your assessment and provide the evidence needed to make informed decisions. Depending on your objectives and metrics, you may need to gather data from various sources, such as financial statements, sales reports, customer feedback, employee surveys, and operational records.

Ensure that the data you collect is comprehensive, up-to-date, and reliable. Use data analytics tools and software to analyze and interpret the information, identifying trends, patterns, and insights. This will help you gain a deeper understanding of your performance and identify areas for improvement.

Involve Key Stakeholders

Engaging key stakeholders in the performance review process is essential for gaining diverse perspectives and insights. This includes involving your management team, employees, customers, and other relevant stakeholders. Each group can provide valuable feedback and contribute to a more holistic assessment of your performance.

Hold meetings and discussions with your management team to review the data and analyze the results. Encourage open and honest communication, where everyone feels comfortable sharing their views and opinions. This collaborative approach can lead to more innovative solutions and strategies for improvement.

Conduct a SWOT Analysis

A SWOT analysis is a valuable tool for assessing your strengths, weaknesses, opportunities, and threats. This structured framework allows you to evaluate your internal capabilities and external environment, providing a comprehensive view of your business performance.

Identify your strengths, such as unique capabilities, resources, and competitive advantages. Recognize your weaknesses, including areas where you may be lacking or underperforming. Explore opportunities for growth and improvement, such as emerging markets, new technologies, and industry trends. Finally, assess potential threats and risks that could impact your business, such as economic downturns, regulatory changes, and competitive pressures.

Evaluate Financial Performance

Financial performance is a critical aspect of your overall business health and success. Regularly reviewing your financial statements and metrics will help you understand your revenue, expenses, profitability, and cash flow. Key financial metrics to assess include gross profit margin, net profit margin, return on investment (ROI), and debt-to-equity ratio.

Analyze your financial performance against your budget and forecast, identifying any variances and their causes. Look for trends and patterns in your financial data, such as seasonal fluctuations or changes in customer behavior. This will help you make informed decisions about resource allocation, cost management, and investment opportunities.

Assess Operational Efficiency

Operational efficiency is another crucial factor that impacts your business performance. Evaluate your processes, workflows, and systems to determine how effectively and efficiently you are delivering your products or services. Key metrics to assess include cycle time, lead time, inventory turnover, and production yield.

Identify bottlenecks, inefficiencies, and areas for improvement in your operations. Consider implementing lean principles and process improvement methodologies, such as Six Sigma or Kaizen, to streamline your operations and eliminate waste. Investing in technology and automation can also enhance your operational efficiency and productivity.

Measure Customer Satisfaction and Loyalty

Customer satisfaction and loyalty are key indicators of your business performance and success. Regularly gathering and analyzing customer feedback will help you understand their needs, preferences, and experiences. Key metrics to assess include Net Promoter Score (NPS), customer satisfaction score (CSAT), and customer retention rate.

Conduct surveys, interviews, and focus groups to gather qualitative and quantitative feedback from your customers. Analyze this feedback to identify trends, patterns, and areas for improvement. Use this information to enhance your products, services, and customer experience, building stronger relationships and loyalty with your customers.

Evaluate Employee Engagement and Performance

Your employees are a critical asset to your business, and their engagement and performance significantly impact your overall success. Regularly assessing employee engagement and performance will help you understand their satisfaction, motivation, and productivity. Key metrics to assess include employee satisfaction score (ESS), employee turnover rate, and productivity metrics.

Conduct employee surveys, performance reviews, and one-on-one meetings to gather feedback and assess their performance. Identify areas where employees may need additional support, training, or development. Recognize and reward high performers, and address any issues or concerns promptly and effectively.

Develop Action Plans for Improvement

Based on the insights and findings from your performance review, develop action plans to address areas for improvement and capitalize on opportunities. Set clear, actionable, and measurable goals that align with your overall business objectives. Assign responsibilities and time-lines to ensure accountability and track progress.

Communicate your action plans to your team and stakeholders, ensuring everyone understands the priorities and their roles in achieving the goals. Monitor the implementation of your action plans regularly, and adjust them as needed based on feedback and changing circumstances.

Implement Continuous Improvement

Performance reviews should not be a one-time event but an ongoing process of continuous improvement. Regularly assess your performance, gather feedback, and make necessary adjustments to your strategies and plans. Foster a culture of continuous improvement, where everyone is committed to learning, growing, and achieving their best.

Encourage innovation and experimentation, where employees feel empowered to suggest and test new ideas and approaches. Celebrate successes and learn from failures, using them as opportunities for growth and improvement. By continuously striving for excellence, you can achieve sustained success and long-term growth for your business.

Regular performance reviews are essential for the sustained success and growth of your LLC. They help you stay aligned with your goals, measure the effectiveness of your strategies, identify and address issues early, and foster a culture of accountability and continuous improvement. By following the tips provided, you can conduct thorough and meaningful assessments and evaluations, driving your business forward and achieving long-term success.

Gather Feedback From Customers, Employees, and Stakeholders

Feedback is a vital component of any successful business strategy. It provides insight into what is working, what isn't, and where there are opportunities for improvement. Gathering feedback from customers, employees, and stakeholders is essential for driving continuous improvement, fostering innovation, and ensuring that your business remains aligned with its goals and objectives. In this section, we will highlight the value of feedback in improving your business and provide detailed strategies for collecting and utilizing feedback effectively.

The Value of Feedback in Improving Your Business

Feedback serves as a critical tool for understanding the needs, expectations, and experiences of those who interact with your business. It provides a wealth of information that can be used to enhance products, services, and processes, ultimately leading to greater customer satisfaction, employee engagement, and stakeholder trust. Here are some key reasons why feedback is invaluable for your business:

Identifying Strengths and Weaknesses

Feedback helps you identify both your strengths and areas where you need improvement. By understanding what you are doing well, you can continue to build on these strengths and differentiate your business from competitors. Conversely, recognizing your weaknesses allows you to address issues before they become significant problems, ensuring that you can maintain high standards of quality and service.

Enhancing Customer Satisfaction

Customer feedback provides direct insights into their experiences and perceptions of your products and services. By listening to your customers, you can identify areas where you can improve their experience, leading to increased satisfaction and loyalty. Happy customers are more likely to return and recommend your business to others, driving growth and profitability.

Improving Employee Engagement

Employee feedback is crucial for understanding their level of engagement, satisfaction, and motivation. Engaged employees are more productive, provide better customer service, and are less likely to leave the company. By acting on employee feedback, you can create a positive work environment that fosters collaboration, innovation, and retention.

Building Stronger Stakeholder Relationships

Feedback from stakeholders, including investors, suppliers, and community members, helps you understand their expectations and concerns. By addressing their feedback, you can build stronger, more trusting relationships that support your business objectives and enhance your reputation.

Driving Innovation and Continuous Improvement

Feedback is a source of new ideas and perspectives that can drive innovation and continuous improvement. By actively seeking and incorporating feedback, you can stay ahead of industry trends, respond to changing market conditions, and continuously improve your products, services, and processes.

Strategies for Collecting Feedback

Collecting feedback effectively requires a strategic approach that ensures you gather relevant, accurate, and actionable information. Here are some strategies to help you collect feedback from customers, employees, and stakeholders:

Customer Feedback

Customers are the lifeblood of your business, and their feedback is essential for understanding their needs and improving their experience. Here are some ways to collect customer feedback:

Surveys and Questionnaires:

Online surveys and questionnaires are a common and effective way to gather customer feedback. Use tools like SurveyMonkey, Google Forms, or Typeform to create surveys that ask specific questions about their experiences, preferences, and satisfaction levels. Keep surveys concise and focused to encourage higher response rates.

Customer Interviews:

Conduct one-on-one interviews with customers to gain deeper insights into their experiences and opinions. These interviews can be conducted in person, over the phone, or via video calls. Prepare open-ended questions that encourage detailed responses and explore their feedback in depth.

Focus Groups:

Organize focus groups with a diverse group of customers to discuss their experiences and gather collective feedback. Focus groups provide an opportunity for interactive discussions, allowing you to explore different perspectives and ideas.

Feedback Forms:

Include feedback forms on your website, mobile app, or physical locations to make it easy for customers to share their thoughts. Ensure that feedback forms are user-friendly and accessible.

Social Media and Online Reviews:

Monitor social media platforms and online review sites like Yelp, Google Reviews, and TripAdvisor to gather feedback from customers. Engage with customers who leave reviews, responding to their comments and addressing any concerns.

Employee Feedback

Employees are a valuable source of feedback, providing insights into the internal workings of your business and how you can improve the work environment. Here are some ways to collect employee feedback:

Employee Surveys:

Conduct regular employee surveys to assess their satisfaction, engagement, and overall experience. Use tools like SurveyMonkey, Officevibe, or Qualtrics to create anonymous surveys that encourage honest feedback. Include questions about their job satisfaction, work-life balance, leadership, and opportunities for growth.

One-on-One Meetings:

Schedule regular one-on-one meetings with employees to discuss their experiences, concerns, and suggestions. These meetings provide a safe space for employees to share their feedback and for managers to provide support and guidance.

Focus Groups:

Organize focus groups with employees to discuss specific topics or issues. Focus groups encourage open dialogue and collaboration, allowing you to gather diverse perspectives and ideas.

Suggestion Boxes:

Implement suggestion boxes, either physical or digital, where employees can anonymously submit their feedback and ideas. Regularly review and act on the suggestions to demonstrate that their input is valued.

Exit Interviews:

Conduct exit interviews with employees who are leaving the company to gather insights into their reasons for leaving and any areas for improvement. Use this feedback to identify trends and address underlying issues.

Stakeholder Feedback

Stakeholders, including investors, suppliers, and community members, provide valuable feedback that can influence your business strategy and operations. Here are some ways to collect stakeholder feedback:

Stakeholder Surveys:

Conduct surveys with your stakeholders to gather their feedback on your business performance, communication, and overall relationship. Use tools like SurveyMonkey or Google Forms to create surveys that address their specific needs and concerns.

Stakeholder Meetings:

Schedule regular meetings with key stakeholders to discuss their feedback and expectations. These meetings provide an opportunity for open dialogue and collaboration, helping you build stronger relationships.

Advisory Boards:

Establish advisory boards composed of key stakeholders who can provide ongoing feedback and guidance. Advisory boards offer a structured forum for stakeholders to share their insights and contribute to your business strategy.

Community Engagement:

Engage with the local community through events, forums, and town hall meetings to gather feedback and understand their needs and concerns. Demonstrating a commitment to the community can enhance your reputation and build trust.

Utilizing Feedback Effectively

Collecting feedback is only the first step; the true value lies in how you utilize the feedback to drive improvements and achieve your business goals. Here are some strategies for effectively utilizing feedback:

Analyze and Interpret Feedback

Once you have collected feedback, analyze and interpret the data to identify key themes, trends, and insights. Use data analytics tools to categorize and quantify the feedback, making it easier to identify patterns and prioritize areas for improvement. Look for common issues or suggestions that appear across different feedback sources, as these may indicate critical areas that need attention.

Develop Action Plans

Based on the insights gained from the feedback, develop actionable plans to address the identified issues and opportunities. Set clear, specific, and measurable goals that align with your overall business objectives. Assign responsibilities and establish timelines to ensure accountability and progress. Involve relevant teams and stakeholders in the planning process to ensure that the action plans are comprehensive and achievable.

Communicate Changes and Improvements

Keep your customers, employees, and stakeholders informed about the changes and improvements you are making based on their feedback. Transparency is key to building trust and demonstrating that you value their input. Use various communication channels, such as newsletters, social media, meetings, and reports, to share updates and progress. Highlight specific actions taken in response to their feedback and the expected impact.

Monitor and Measure Results

Implementing changes is not enough; you need to monitor and measure the results to ensure that they are effective. Establish key performance indicators (KPIs) and metrics to track the impact of your actions. Regularly review and assess the outcomes, comparing them against your goals and objectives. This ongoing evaluation will help you determine whether the changes are delivering the desired results and identify any further adjustments needed.

Foster a Culture of Continuous Improvement

Feedback should be an integral part of your business culture, where continuous improvement is embraced by everyone. Encourage a mindset of learning and growth, where feedback is seen as an opportunity rather than a criticism. Recognize and reward employees who contribute valuable feedback and innovative ideas. Create an environment where open communication and collaboration are encouraged, and everyone feels empowered to share their insights.

Close the Feedback Loop

Closing the feedback loop involves following up with the individuals who provided feedback to let them know how their input has been used. This step is crucial for building trust and demonstrating that you value their opinions. Thank them for their feedback, share the actions taken, and explain the impact of those actions. This communication reinforces their importance to your business and encourages ongoing feedback.

Continuously Solicit Feedback

Feedback collection should not be a one-time activity but an ongoing process. Regularly solicit feedback from your customers, employees, and stakeholders to stay informed about their evolving needs and expectations. Use a variety of methods and channels to ensure that you reach a broad and diverse audience. By continuously seeking feedback, you can stay agile and responsive, adapting to changes and driving sustained success.

Practical Examples and Case Studies

To illustrate the importance and effectiveness of feedback, let's explore some practical examples and case studies from various industries.

Customer Feedback in Retail

A retail company regularly conducts customer satisfaction surveys and collects feedback through its online store and physical locations. Based on the feedback, the company identifies that customers are dissatisfied with the checkout process, citing long wait times and a lack of available staff. In response, the company implements a self-checkout system and increases staffing during peak hours. These changes result in shorter wait times, improved customer satisfaction, and an increase in sales.

Employee Feedback in Technology

A technology company conducts quarterly employee engagement surveys to assess job satisfaction and identify areas for improvement. The surveys reveal that employees feel disconnected from senior leadership and lack opportunities for professional development. To address these concerns, the company implements regular town hall meetings where leadership shares updates and engages with employees. Additionally, the company introduces a mentorship program and provides funding for external training courses. These initiatives lead to higher employee engagement, reduced turnover, and a more positive work environment.

Stakeholder Feedback in Healthcare

A healthcare provider gathers feedback from patients, staff, and community members through surveys, focus groups, and town hall meetings. The feedback indicates a need for better communication and more personalized care. In response, the provider implements a patient portal that allows patients to access their medical records, schedule appointments, and communicate with healthcare professionals online. The provider also invests in training staff on effective communication and patient-centered care. These changes result in improved patient satisfaction, better health outcomes, and stronger community relationships.

Supplier Feedback in Manufacturing

A manufacturing company regularly seeks feedback from its suppliers to understand their challenges and improve collaboration. The feedback reveals that suppliers face difficulties with inconsistent order volumes and unclear communication about production schedules. To address these issues, the company implements a more transparent and consistent ordering process and establishes regular communication channels with suppliers. This leads to stronger supplier relationships, more reliable supply chains, and improved production efficiency.

Gathering feedback from customers, employees, and stakeholders is a critical component of any successful business strategy. Feedback provides valuable insights that can drive continuous improvement, enhance customer satisfaction, improve employee engagement, and build stronger stakeholder relationships. By adopting a strategic approach to collecting and utilizing feedback, you can make informed decisions that support your business goals and ensure long-term success.

To effectively gather feedback, it is essential to use a variety of methods and channels that reach a broad and diverse audience. Regularly analyze and interpret the feedback to identify key themes, trends, and insights. Develop actionable plans to address the identified issues and opportunities, and communicate the changes and improvements to your stakeholders. Monitor and measure the results to ensure that your actions are delivering the desired outcomes, and foster a culture of continuous improvement where feedback is valued and acted upon.

By continuously seeking and utilizing feedback, you can stay agile and responsive, adapting to changes and driving sustained success.

Embrace feedback as a powerful tool for learning, growth, and innovation, and leverage it to create a positive and thriving business environment.

Adapt Your Strategies and Plans as Needed to Achieve Success

Adaptability is a cornerstone of success in the dynamic world of business. The ability to adjust strategies and plans in response to changing conditions, unforeseen challenges, and new opportunities is what differentiates thriving businesses from those that falter. Understanding the importance of adaptability and learning how to effectively pivot your strategies are crucial for long-term success. This section will explore why adaptability is essential and provide practical tips for adjusting your strategies and plans to ensure your business remains resilient and competitive.

The Importance of Adaptability in Business

In today's fast-paced and ever-changing business environment, static strategies can quickly become obsolete. Adaptability allows businesses to remain relevant and competitive by responding to external and internal shifts. Here are several reasons why adaptability is crucial for business success:

Responding to Market Changes

Markets are constantly evolving due to technological advancements, changing consumer preferences, and economic fluctuations. Businesses that can quickly adapt to these changes can capture new opportunities, while those that cannot may struggle to survive. Adaptable businesses can reorient their strategies to align with current market conditions, ensuring they continue to meet customer needs and remain competitive.

Embracing Innovation

Innovation is a driving force behind business growth and success. Companies that are adaptable are more likely to embrace new technologies, processes, and ideas. This openness to innovation can lead to the development of new products, services, and business models that provide a competitive edge.

Mitigating Risks

The ability to adapt allows businesses to anticipate and respond to potential risks more effectively. By being proactive and flexible, businesses can implement contingency plans and make necessary adjustments to mitigate the impact of disruptions, such as economic downturns, regulatory changes, or supply chain issues.

Enhancing Customer Satisfaction

Customer preferences and expectations are continually evolving. Adaptable businesses can quickly adjust their offerings and customer service practices to meet these changing demands, leading to higher customer satisfaction and loyalty. By staying attuned to customer feedback and market trends, businesses can ensure they consistently deliver value.

Fostering a Resilient Workforce

Adaptability is not only important at the organizational level but also within the workforce. Encouraging adaptability among employees fosters a culture of resilience and continuous improvement. Employees who are adaptable are better equipped to handle change, solve problems, and contribute to the overall success of the business.

Tips for Adjusting Your Strategies and Plans

Adapting your business strategies and plans requires a proactive and systematic approach. The following tips will help you effectively adjust your strategies to ensure long-term success:

Stay Informed and Anticipate Change

To adapt effectively, you must stay informed about industry trends, market conditions, and emerging technologies. Regularly conduct market research, monitor competitor activities, and stay updated on regulatory changes. By anticipating change, you can prepare for potential disruptions and identify new opportunities early on.

Set Flexible Goals and Objectives

While setting clear goals and objectives is important, it's equally crucial to maintain flexibility. Establish goals that are adaptable and can be adjusted as needed based on new information or changing circumstances. Regularly review and update your goals to ensure they remain relevant and achievable.

Encourage a Culture of Agility

Foster a culture of agility within your organization by encouraging open communication, collaboration, and continuous learning. Empower employees to take initiative, share ideas, and contribute to decision-making processes. A culture of agility promotes innovation and enables your team to respond quickly to changes.

Implement Continuous Improvement Processes

Adopt continuous improvement methodologies, such as Lean or Six Sigma, to identify areas for enhancement and streamline processes. By continually assessing and improving your operations, you can maintain efficiency, reduce waste, and stay competitive.

Develop Contingency Plans

Prepare for potential disruptions by developing contingency plans. Identify possible scenarios that could impact your business and outline strategies for addressing them. Contingency plans provide a roadmap for navigating challenges and minimizing their impact on your operations.

Utilize Data and Analytics

Leverage data and analytics to make informed decisions and identify trends. Use key performance indicators (KPIs) and other metrics to measure the effectiveness of your strategies and track progress. Data-driven insights enable you to make adjustments based on real-time information and ensure your strategies are aligned with your goals.

Engage With Stakeholders

Regularly engage with customers, employees, suppliers, and other stakeholders to gather feedback and understand their needs and expectations. Stakeholder input provides valuable insights that can inform your strategies and help you identify areas for improvement. Actively listen to feedback and incorporate it into your planning processes.

Monitor and Review Performance

Continuously monitor and review your business performance to ensure your strategies are delivering the desired results. Conduct regular performance assessments, analyze outcomes, and identify areas for adjustment. A systematic review process allows you to stay on track and make necessary changes to achieve your objectives.

Invest in Training and Development

Invest in the training and development of your employees to equip them with the skills and knowledge needed to adapt to change. Provide opportunities for continuous learning, professional development, and cross-functional training. A well-trained and adaptable workforce is essential for implementing new strategies and driving innovation.

Maintain a Long-Term Perspective

While it's important to be responsive to immediate challenges, maintaining a long-term perspective is equally crucial. Balance short-term adjustments with long-term planning to ensure your business remains sustainable and resilient. Regularly revisit your long-term goals and strategies to ensure they align with your vision and market realities.

Case Studies and Practical Examples

To illustrate the importance of adaptability and how businesses can successfully adjust their strategies, let's explore some real-world examples from various industries.

Netflix: Adapting to Technological Change

Netflix is a prime example of a company that has successfully adapted its strategies to stay ahead of the curve. Originally a DVD rental service, Netflix recognized the potential of streaming technology early on. In 2007, the company shifted its focus to online streaming, investing heavily in digital infrastructure and content acquisition. This strategic pivot allowed Netflix to capitalize on the growing demand for on-demand content and positioned it as a leader in the entertainment industry. By continuously adapting its business model and embracing new technologies, Netflix has maintained its competitive edge and achieved sustained growth.

Procter & Gamble: Responding to Consumer Preferences

Procter & Gamble (P&G) is a global consumer goods company that has demonstrated adaptability by responding to changing consumer preferences. In recent years, P&G noticed a growing demand for environmentally friendly and sustainable products. In response, the company developed and launched a range of eco-friendly products across its brands, such as Tide, Pampers, and Gillette. P&G also committed to reducing its environmental footprint through sustainable sourcing, packaging, and manufacturing practices. By aligning its strategies with consumer values and market trends, P&G has strengthened its brand reputation and continued to drive sales.

Toyota: Continuous Improvement and Lean Manufacturing

Toyota is renowned for its commitment to continuous improvement and lean manufacturing principles. The Toyota Production System (TPS) emphasizes efficiency, quality, and adaptability. By continuously assessing and refining its processes, Toyota has maintained its position as a leader in the automotive industry. For example, Toyota's ability to adapt quickly to changes in demand and market conditions allowed it to recover swiftly from the disruptions caused by the COVID-19 pandemic. The company's agile supply chain management and production flexibility enabled it to meet changing consumer needs and maintain operational efficiency.

Airbnb: Pivoting in Response to Market Disruption

Airbnb, the online marketplace for lodging and travel experiences, faced significant challenges during the COVID-19 pandemic as global travel came to a halt. To adapt, Airbnb shifted its focus from traditional travel accommodations to long-term stays and local experiences. The company introduced new features, such as enhanced cleaning protocols and flexible cancellation policies, to address safety concerns and changing consumer preferences. Additionally, Airbnb promoted local travel and remote work opportunities, tapping into emerging trends. These strategic adjustments allowed Airbnb to weather the crisis and position itself for recovery and growth.

Practical Steps for Adapting Strategies

Adapting your business strategies and plans requires a systematic approach that involves assessment, planning, implementation, and continuous evaluation. Here are practical steps to guide you through the process:

1. Conduct a Comprehensive Assessment

Begin by conducting a comprehensive assessment of your current strategies, performance, and market conditions. Analyze internal and external factors that could impact your business, such as economic trends, competitive landscape, technological advancements, and regulatory changes. Identify strengths, weaknesses, opportunities, and threats (SWOT analysis) to gain a holistic understanding of your business environment.

2. Set Clear and Flexible Objectives

Based on your assessment, set clear and flexible objectives that align with your long-term vision and goals. Ensure that your objectives are specific, measurable, achievable, relevant, and time-bound (SMART goals). Flexibility is key, so be prepared to adjust your objectives as needed based on changing circumstances.

3. Develop a Strategic Plan

Create a strategic plan that outlines the actions and initiatives required to achieve your objectives. Define key milestones, responsibilities, and timelines to ensure accountability and progress. Consider multiple scenarios and develop contingency plans to address potential risks and uncertainties.

4. Engage Stakeholders in the Planning Process

Involve key stakeholders, including employees, customers, suppliers, and investors, in the planning process. Gather their input and feedback to ensure that your strategies are well-informed and aligned with their expectations. Engaging stakeholders fosters buy-in and support, which is crucial for successful implementation.

5. Implement the Plan

Execute your strategic plan with a focus on effective communication, collaboration, and resource allocation. Ensure that all team members understand their roles and responsibilities and have the necessary resources to achieve their objectives. Monitor progress regularly and address any challenges or obstacles that arise.

6. Monitor Performance and Gather Feedback

Continuously monitor your performance using key performance indicators (KPIs) and other metrics. Gather feedback from customers, employees, and stakeholders to assess the effectiveness of your strategies and identify areas for improvement. Regular performance reviews and feedback loops are essential for staying on track and making timely adjustments.

7. Make Data-Driven Adjustments

Use data and analytics to make informed decisions and adjustments to your strategies. Analyze performance data, market trends, and feedback to identify patterns and insights. Based on this analysis, make data-driven adjustments to optimize your strategies and improve outcomes.

8. Foster a Culture of Continuous Improvement

Encourage a culture of continuous improvement within your organization by promoting innovation, learning, and adaptability. Provide opportunities for professional development, cross-functional training, and knowledge sharing. Recognize and reward employees who contribute to improvements and innovative solutions.

9. Review and Update the Strategic Plan Regularly

Regularly review and update your strategic plan to ensure it remains relevant and aligned with your long-term goals. Conduct periodic assessments and adjust your plan based on new information, changing market conditions, and performance outcomes. A dynamic and iterative approach to planning ensures that your strategies evolve with your business environment.

10. Communicate Changes and Celebrate Successes

Communicate any changes to your strategies and plans to your team and stakeholders to ensure transparency and alignment. Celebrate successes and milestones achieved along the way to boost morale and maintain momentum. Effective communication and recognition foster a positive and motivated work environment.

Conclusion

Adaptability is a fundamental attribute for achieving long-term success in business. The ability to adjust strategies and plans in response to changing conditions, unforeseen challenges, and new opportunities is essential for remaining competitive and resilient. By staying informed, setting flexible goals, fostering a culture of agility, and continuously monitoring performance, businesses can effectively navigate the complexities of the modern business landscape.

Practical steps for adapting strategies include conducting comprehensive assessments, setting clear and flexible objectives, developing strategic plans, engaging stakeholders, implementing plans, monitoring performance, making data-driven adjustments, fostering continuous improvement, and regularly reviewing and updating plans. These steps ensure that your business remains agile, responsive, and well-positioned for sustained growth and success.

Real-world examples from companies like Netflix, Procter & Gamble, Toyota, and Airbnb highlight the importance of adaptability and demonstrate how businesses can successfully pivot their strategies to achieve positive outcomes. By embracing adaptability and following a systematic approach to adjusting strategies, you can ensure your business remains resilient, innovative, and capable of achieving long-term success.

Afterword

As we reach the conclusion of this guide, it's essential to recap the key points and action items that have been covered. This book has aimed to provide you with a comprehensive roadmap to launching and managing your Limited Liability Company (LLC) successfully. Whether you are at the beginning of your entrepreneurial journey or looking to refine and grow an existing business, the strategies and insights provided here are designed to equip you with the knowledge and confidence needed to navigate the complexities of running an LLC.

Recap of the Step-by-Step Guide and Key Action Points

Starting from the very basics, this guide has taken you through each critical phase of establishing and managing an LLC. Let's summarize the major steps and key actions you should take:

Understanding the Basics of an LLC

Understanding what an LLC is and its benefits over other business structures sets the foundation for your journey. Recognizing the legal protections, tax advantages, and flexibility offered by an LLC is crucial.

Planning and Setting Up Your LLC

Detailed planning is essential before you take any concrete steps. This includes conducting market research, creating a business plan, and determining your LLC's name. Ensuring your name is unique and compliant with state regulations is a fundamental step.

Filing the Necessary Documents

Filing the Articles of Organization and creating an Operating Agreement are pivotal. These documents formalize your business, outline ownership, and define operational procedures.

Complying with Legal Requirements

Ensuring compliance with all legal requirements, including obtaining the necessary licenses and permits, registering for state and federal taxes, and adhering to labor laws, is non-negotiable. These steps help avoid legal pitfalls and establish a solid legal foundation for your LLC.

Establishing Financial Systems

Setting up a robust financial system involves opening a business bank account, implementing accounting software, and developing a budget. This will help you manage finances efficiently and make informed financial decisions.

Building and Leading Your Team

Hiring the right talent and creating a positive work culture are crucial for your LLC's success. Leadership skills, employee engagement, and professional development opportunities are key elements that contribute to a motivated and high-performing team.

Marketing and Sales Strategies

Developing effective marketing and sales strategies to reach your target audience is essential. Leveraging digital marketing, social media, and traditional advertising methods can drive customer acquisition and retention.

Community Engagement and Corporate Social Responsibility

Engaging with your local community and demonstrating corporate social responsibility can enhance your brand's reputation. Building strong relationships with local stakeholders and contributing to community initiatives create goodwill and long-term loyalty.

Personal Development and Growth

Setting personal and professional goals, practicing self-care, and seeking mentorship are critical for your growth as a business leader. Continuous learning and professional development keep you adaptable and resilient.

Global Expansion and Future Planning

If you aim to expand internationally, researching markets, understanding legal requirements, and developing a long-term growth strategy are necessary. Global expansion requires meticulous planning and adaptability to new markets.

Review and Adaptation

Regularly reviewing your LLC's performance, gathering feedback, and adapting your strategies ensure continuous improvement and long-term success. Flexibility and responsiveness to change are vital traits of successful businesses.

Encouragement for Readers to Take Action and Implement Learnings

Now that you have a comprehensive understanding of the steps involved in launching and managing an LLC, it's time to take action. The knowledge and insights gained from this guide will only be valuable if you apply them in your entrepreneurial endeavors. Here are a few reasons why taking immediate action is crucial:

Turning Ideas into Reality

You may have brilliant business ideas, but without action, they remain mere concepts. Taking the first step, no matter how small, sets the wheels in motion and turns your ideas into tangible outcomes.

Building Momentum

Once you start implementing the strategies outlined in this guide, you'll build momentum. Each completed task, no matter how minor, contributes to your progress and keeps you moving forward.

Learning Through Experience

While this guide provides a wealth of knowledge, real learning happens through experience. Implementing these strategies will allow you to understand the nuances of running an LLC and adapt them to your unique circumstances.

Overcoming Fear and Uncertainty

Taking action helps you overcome the fear and uncertainty that often accompany entrepreneurship. By stepping out of your comfort zone and tackling challenges head-on, you build confidence and resilience.

Achieving Your Goals

Ultimately, the goal of this guide is to help you achieve your entrepreneurial aspirations. Whether you aim to create a successful local business or expand globally, taking action is the only way to reach your goals.

Wishes for Success on Their Entrepreneurial Journey

As you embark on or continue your entrepreneurial journey, I extend my best wishes for your success. The path of an entrepreneur is filled with challenges, but it is also incredibly rewarding. The insights and strategies provided in this guide are designed to equip you with the tools needed to navigate these challenges and seize opportunities.

Believe in Yourself

Confidence in your abilities and vision is crucial. Believe that you have what it takes to overcome obstacles and achieve your goals. Your belief in yourself will inspire confidence in others, including your team, customers, and stakeholders.

Stay Resilient

Entrepreneurship is not a linear journey. There will be highs and lows, successes and setbacks. Stay resilient in the face of challenges, learn from your experiences, and keep pushing forward. Resilience is the key to long-term success.

Keep Learning

The business landscape is constantly evolving. Stay curious and committed to continuous learning. Whether through formal education, mentorship, or self-study, ongoing learning keeps you adaptable and innovative.

Build Strong Relationships

Success in business often depends on the relationships you build. Foster strong connections with your customers, employees, partners, and community. These relationships provide support, insights, and opportunities for collaboration.

Celebrate Your Achievements

Take the time to celebrate your achievements, no matter how small. Recognizing your progress and milestones boosts morale and motivates you to keep striving for excellence.

In conclusion, launching and managing an LLC is a multifaceted endeavor that requires careful planning, strategic thinking, and continuous adaptation. This guide has provided you with a comprehensive roadmap, covering everything from the basics of LLC formation to advanced strategies for growth and adaptability. By following these steps and taking decisive action, you can build a successful and sustainable business.

Remember, the journey of entrepreneurship is uniquely yours. While this guide offers valuable insights and strategies, your passion, dedication, and creativity will ultimately drive your success. Embrace the challenges, learn from your experiences, and remain steadfast in your pursuit of your entrepreneurial dreams. With determination and the right tools, there is no limit to what you can achieve. Best of luck on your entrepreneurial journey, and may your LLC thrive and prosper.

Thank You for Reading!

I hope this book helped lay out a clear path forward in starting and growing your business. Now it's time for me to ask for a little help from you. Your feedback is incredibly valuable to me and helps other readers discover this book.

If you could take a moment to leave a review on your favorite book platform, it would mean a lot.

Thank you for your support!

Best regards,

David Whitehead

www.ingramcontent.com/pod-product-compliance
Lightning Source LLC
Chambersburg PA
CBHW030449210326
41597CB00013B/601